A COMPANION
— *to the* —

BOOK OF
ENOCH

A READER'S COMMENTARY, VOL. I
The Book of the Watchers (1 Enoch 1–36)

DR. MICHAEL S. HEISER

DEFENDER

CRANE, MO

A Companion to the Book of Enoch: A Reader's Commentary, Volume I: The Book of the Watchers (1 Enoch 1–36)
by Michael S. Heiser
© Copyright 2019 Defender Publishing.

Unless otherwise noted, Scripture quotations are from The Holy Bible, English Standard Version, copyright © 2001 by Good News Publishers. Used by permission. All rights reserved.

As noted in the work, unless otherwise indicated in the footnotes, the translation of 1 Enoch is that of R. H. Charles, which is in the public domain.

Cover design by Jeffrey Mardis.

ISBN: 9781948014304

Dedication

To all enthusiasts of the Book of Enoch and
those merely curious as to why anyone would care about it.
I hope this helps a bit.

Contents

A Reader's Commentary on 1 Enoch 1–36
(The Book of the Watchers)

Abbreviations of Ancient Sources

Abbreviations used in this book follow those recommended by *The SBL Handbook of Style*, Second Edition (Atlanta, GA: SBL Press, 2014), 125–134.

Deuterocanonical (Apocryphal) Works and Septuagint

Tob	Tobit
Jdt	Judith
Add Esth	Additions to Esther
Wis	Wisdom of Solomon
Sir	Sirach/Ecclesiasticus
Bar	Baruch
Ep Jer	Epistle of Jeremiah
Add Dan	Additions to Daniel
Pr Azar	Prayer of Azariah
Sg Three	Song of the Three Young Men
Sus	Susanna
Bel	Bel and the Dragon
1–2 Macc	1–2 Maccabees
1 Esd	1 Esdras
Pr Man	Prayer of Manasseh
Ps 151	Psalm 151
3 Macc	3 Maccabees
2 Esd	2 Esdras
4 Macc	4 Maccabees

Old Testament Pseudepigrapha

Ahiqar	Ahiqar
Ant. bib.	Use LAB
Apoc. Ab.	Apocalypse of Abraham
Apoc. Adam	Apocalypse of Adam
Apoc. Dan.	Apocalypse of Daniel
Apoc. El. (C)	Coptic Apocalypse of Elijah
Apoc. El. (H)	Hebrew Apocalypse of Elijah
Apoc. Ezek.	Use Apocr. Ezek.
Apoc. Mos.	Apocalypse of Moses
Apoc. Sedr.	Apocalypse of Sedrach
Apoc. Zeph.	Apocalypse of Zephaniah
Apoc. Zos.	Use Hist. Rech.
Apocr. Ezek.	Apocryphon of Ezekiel
Aris. Ex.	Aristeas the Exegete
Aristob.	Aristobulus
Artap.	Artapanus
As. Mos.	Assumption of Moses
Ascen. Isa.	Mart. Ascen. Isa. 6–11
2 Bar.	2 Baruch (Syriac Apocalypse)
3 Bar.	3 Baruch (Greek Apocalypse)
4 Bar.	4 Baruch (Paraleipomena Jeremiou)
Bib. Ant.	Use LAB
Bk. Noah	Book of Noah
Cav. Tr.	Cave of Treasures
Cl. Mal.	Cleodemus Malchus
Dem.	Demetrius (the Chronographer)
El. Mod.	Eldad and Modad
1 En.	1 Enoch (Ethiopic Apocalypse)
2 En.	2 Enoch (Slavonic Apocalypse)
3 En.	3 Enoch (Hebrew Apocalypse)

Eup.	Eupolemus
Ezek. Trag.	Ezekiel the Tragedian
4 Ezra	4 Ezra
5 Apoc. Syr. Pss.	Five Apocryphal Syriac Psalms
Gk. Apoc. Ezra	Greek Apocalypse of Ezra
Hec. Ab.	Hecataeus of Abdera
Hel. Syn. Pr.	Hellenistic Synagogal Prayers
Hist. Jos.	History of Joseph
Hist. Rech.	History of the Rechabites
Jan. Jam.	Jannes and Jambres
Jos. Asen.	Joseph and Aseneth
Jub.	Jubilees
LAB	Liber antiquitatum biblicarum (Pseudo-Philo)
LAE	Life of Adam and Eve
Lad. Jac.	Ladder of Jacob
Let. Aris.	Letter of Aristeas
Liv. Pro.	Lives of the Prophets
Lost Tr.	The Lost Tribes
3 Macc.	3 Maccabees
4 Macc.	4 Maccabees
5 Macc.	5 Maccabees (Arabic)
Mart. Ascen. Isa.	Martyrdom and Ascension of Isaiah
Mart. Isa.	Mart. Ascen. Isa. 1–5
Odes Sol.	Odes of Solomon
PJ	Use 4 Bar.
Ph. E. Poet	Philo the Epic Poet
Pr. Jac.	Prayer of Jacob
Pr. Jos.	Prayer of Joseph
Pr. Man.	Prayer of Manasseh
Pr. Mos.	Prayer of Moses
Ps.-Eup.	Pseudo-Eupolemus

Ps.-Hec.	Pseudo-Hecataeus
Ps.-Orph.	Pseudo-Orpheus
Ps.-Philo	Use LAB
Ps.-Phoc.	Pseudo-Phocylides
Pss. Sol.	Psalms of Solomon
Ques. Ezra	Questions of Ezra
Rev. Ezra	Revelation of Ezra
Sib. Or.	Sibylline Oracles
Syr. Men.	Sentences of the Syriac Menander
T. 12 Patr.	Testaments of the Twelve Patriarchs
T. Ash.	Testament of Asher
T. Benj.	Testament of Benjamin
T. Dan	Testament of Dan
T. Gad	Testament of Gad
T. Iss.	Testament of Issachar
T. Jos.	Testament of Joseph
T. Jud.	Testament of Judah
T. Levi	Testament of Levi
T. Naph.	Testament of Naphtali
T. Reu.	Testament of Reuben
T. Sim.	Testament of Simeon
T. Zeb.	Testament of Zebulun
T. 3 Patr.	Testaments of the Three Patriarchs
T. Ab.	Testament of Abraham
T. Isaac	Testament of Isaac
T. Jac.	Testament of Jacob
T. Adam	Testament of Adam
T. Hez.	Testament of Hezekiah (Mart. Ascen. Isa. 3:13–4:22)
T. Job	Testament of Job

T. Mos.	Testament of Moses
T. Sol.	Testament of Solomon
Theod.	Theodotus, *On the Jews*
Treat. Shem	Treatise of Shem
Vis. Ezra	Vision of Ezra
Vis. Isa.	Use Ascen. Isa.

Dead Sea Scrolls and Related Texts

Q	Qumran
Hev	Nahal Hever
Hev/Se	Used for documents earlier attributed to Seiyal
Mas	Masada
Mird	Khirbet Mird
Mur	Murabbaʿat

Note (*SBL Handoook*, 127): The different caves at each site are denoted with sequential numbers—for example, 1Q, 2Q, and so on. Different copies of the same composition from the same cave are indicated by the use of raised lowercase letters—for example, 1QIsa^a, 1QIsa^b.

The first seven scrolls from Cave 1 are commonly given these abbreviations:

1QapGen ar	Genesis Apocryphon
1QH^a	Hodayot^a or Thanksgiving Hymns^a
1QIsa^a	Isaiah^a
1QIsa^b	Isaiah^b
1QM	Milhamah *or* War Scroll
1QpHab	Pesher Habakkuk
1QS	Serek Hayahad *or* Rule of the Community
CD	Cairo Genizah copy of the Damascus Document

Philo

Abr.	*De Abrahamo*
Abraham	*On the Life of Abraham*
Aet.	*De aeternitate mundi*
Eternity	*On the Eternity of the World*
Agr.	*De agricultura*
Agriculture	*On Agriculture*
Anim.	*De animalibus*
Animals	*Whether Animals Have Reason (= Alexander)*
Cher.	*De cherubim*
Cherubim	*On the Cherubim*
Conf.	*De confusione linguarum*
Confusion	*On the Confusion of Tongues*
Congr.	*De congressu eruditionis gratia*
Prelim. Studies	*On the Preliminary Studies*
Contempl.	*De vita contemplativa*
Contempl. Life	*On the Contemplative Life*
Decal.	*De decalogo*
Decalogue	*On the Decalogue*
Deo	*De Deo*
God	*On God*
Det.	*Quod deterius potiori insidari soleat*
Worse	*That the Worse Attacks the Better*
Deus	*Quod Deus sit immutabilis*
Unchangeable	*That God Is Unchangeable*
Ebr.	*De ebrietate*
Drunkenness	*On Drunkenness*
Exsecr.	*De exsecrationibus*
Curses	*On Curses (= Rewards 127–172)*
Flacc.	*In Flaccum*

QE 1, 2	*Quaestiones et solutiones in Exodum I, II*
QE 1, 2	*Questions and Answers on Exodus 1, 2*
QG 1, 2, 3, 4	*Quaestiones et solutiones in Genesin I, II, III, IV*
QG 1, 2, 3, 4	*Questions and Answers on Genesis 1, 2, 3, 4*
Sacr.	*De sacrificiis Abelis et Caini*
Sacrifices	*On the Sacrifices of Cain and Abel*
Sobr.	*De sobrietate*
Spec. 1, 2, 3, 4	*De specialibus legibus I, II, III, IV*
Sobriety	*On Sobriety*
Spec. Laws 1, 2, 3, 4	*On the Special Laws 1, 2, 3, 4*
Somn. 1, 2	*De somniis I, II*
Virt.	*De virtutibus*
Dreams 1, 2	*On Dreams 1, 2*
Virtues	*On the Virtues*
Josephus	
Vita	*Vita*
A.J.	*Antiquitates judaicae*
Life	*The Life*
Ant.	*Jewish Antiquities*
C. Ap.	*Contra Apionem*
B.J.	*Bellum judaicum*
Ag. Ap.	*Against Apion*
J.W.	*Jewish War*
Apostolic Fathers	
Barn.	Barnabas
1–2 Clem.	1–2 Clement
Did.	Didache

Diogn.	Diognetus
Herm. Mand.	Shepherd of Hermas, Mandate(s)
Herm. Sim.	Shepherd of Hermas, Similitude(s)
Herm. Vis.	Shepherd of Hermas, Vision(s)
Ign. Eph.	Ignatius, To the Ephesians
Ign. Magn.	Ignatius, To the Magnesians
Ign. Phld.	Ignatius, To the Philadelphians
Ign. Pol.	Ignatius, To Polycarp
Ign. Rom.	Ignatius, To the Romans
Ign. Smyrn.	Ignatius, To the Smyrnaeans
Ign. Trall.	Ignatius, To the Trallians
Mart. Pol.	Martyrdom of Polycarp
Pol. Phil.	Polycarp, To the Philippians

What's a "Reader's Commentary"?

The book you hold in your hands is a commentary on the Book of Enoch, more properly known as 1 Enoch. Most readers will be familiar with books called "commentaries" due to the proliferation of Bible commentaries. A Bible commentary is just what it sounds like: a book that provides comments on the Bible. This is commentary on 1 Enoch, so at least the general approach should be familiar. But there are many kinds of commentaries, and all are not created equal. Consequently, the most straightforward way to explain the concept of a reader's commentary is to first distinguish it from other commentaries.

One thing that sets commentaries apart from each other is their scope. Bible commentaries range from a single book about the entire Bible to a multivolume series about each book of the Bible. As you might guess, there's a great deal more detail in an entire book written about one biblical book (e.g., Esther) than the dozen or so pages devoted to talking about Esther in a one-volume commentary that covers the entire Bible. As a result, the level of detail also differentiates one type of commentary from another.

Aside from something as obvious as page count, there are many other differences between commentaries. They may be popular or devotional (written for the layperson and aimed at applying what a given English translation of the Bible says), expositional (a verse-by-verse examination of the Bible using a particular English translation as its base), or scholarly (a verse-by-verse and even word-by-word analysis of the original language text that produces a new translation with attention to grammar and literary technique).

Obviously, readers who don't know the original languages of the biblical books are best served by the first two types of commentaries. However, you shouldn't conclude that scholarly commentaries would be impenetrable. While it's true you'd see a lot of Greek and Hebrew on the pages of such commentaries, there is also a lot of discussion that would benefit anyone with a deep interest in understanding the biblical text.

In general terms, the purpose of a reader's commentary is to help readers of 1 Enoch comprehend what they're reading with greater insight and clarity of understanding. That's my goal. This *Reader's Commentary on 1 Enoch* therefore is not written for scholars. Rather, it's written for anyone who has decided to devote the time to reading 1 Enoch, perhaps for the first time.

Toward helping readers of 1 Enoch get more out of their reading experience, this is something of a hybrid work. In a certain respect, it falls in between the expositional and scholarly commentary categories described earlier. This requires some brief explanation.

First, this *Reader's Commentary* is based on the translation of 1 Enoch by R. H. Charles.[1] The rationale for doing so is twofold: (1) The Charles translation is in the public domain; and (2) I presume a readership of nonspecialists who do not know Hebrew, Aramaic, Greek, or Ethiopic. Nothing from the 1917 edition of Charles' translation is changed, save for stylistic issues (e.g., converting capital letters of the initial words in lines presented in stanzas to lowercase). The Charles translation informs readers of the meaning of the following symbols, which are retained in the presentation of the translation in this commentary:[2]

---

1. Specifically, I use the edition that includes an introduction by W. O. E. Oesterley: Charles, R. H., and W. O. E. Oesterley, *The Book of Enoch* (London: Society for Promoting Christian Knowledge, 1917).
2. Charles and Oesterley, *The Book of Enoch*, xxvii.

⌐¬   The use of these brackets means that the words so enclosed are found in G⁸ but not in E.

⌐¬¹   The use of these brackets means that the words so enclosed are found in E but not in G⁸ or G^s. [3]

⟨ ⟩   The use of these brackets means that the words so enclosed are restored.

[ ]   The use of these brackets means that the words so enclosed are interpolations.

( )   The use of these brackets means that the words so enclosed are supplied by the editor.

The use of **thick type (boldfacing)** denotes that the words so printed are emended. (Chapter numbers are also shown in bold type.)

† . . . † The use of this type of ellipses indicates corruption in the text.

. . .   The use of this type of ellipses indicates that some words have been lost.

---

3.   G⁸ = "the large fragment of the Greek Version discovered at Akhmîm, and deposited in the Gizeh Museum, Cairo"; G^s = the fragments of the Greek Version preserved in Syncellus." (Charles and Oesterley, *The Book of Enoch*, xxvii). I will rarely distinguish between these manuscripts in commentary. Rather, when a reading is found in Greek (vs. Ethiopic or Aramaic), I will merely note the reading is found in "the Greek (Grk) material."

In addition, the formatting of the Charles translation has been pre-served (e.g., compare 1 Enoch 1 and 5; the latter has the verses broken out into separate lines).

Second, this *Reader's Commentary* spends little to no time chasing scholarly rabbit trails about subjects like the textual (manuscript) trans-mission of 1 Enoch, the compositional and editorial history of its sec-tions, and comparative literary analysis of its content. While scholars are absorbed by such minutiae, these sorts of discussions are distractions to the general reader.

Third, this *Reader's Commentary* is neither a verse-by-verse nor a word-by-word treatment of 1 Enoch. Instead, the focus is on terms and phrases that are of the most consequence in understanding what is being read. The discussion in this regard is academic, as attention is paid to how more recent scholarly translations (Black, Nickelsburg, Charlesworth) dif-fer from the public-domain Charles translation. Nevertheless, the litmus test for comparing translations and discussing original-language vocabu-lary is whether doing so illumines the content in some significant way.[4] No effort is made to explain or comment upon every difference between these translations. This work focuses only upon items that this author believes might interest the reader or that help the reader comprehend or interpret important items of content in 1 Enoch.

Translation Abbreviations

In the interest of readability, I have adopted a few conventions and abbreviations.

When comparing the Charles translation to other, more recent, trans-lations, I avoid footnotes and instead reference the other translations with the following abbreviations:

---

4.   Readers must remember that R. H. Charles and James H. Charlesworth are
      not the same writer!

- B—Matthew Black's translation and textual analysis[5]
- N—Nickelsburg's translation and commentary[6]
- CW—Ephraim Isaac's translation of 1 Enoch within Charlesworth's *Old Testament Pseudepigrapha*, vol 1[7]

When referring to original languages, the following abbreviations apply:

- Heb—Hebrew
- Aram—Aramaic
- Grk—Greek
- Eth—Ethiopic

---

5.   Matthew Black, *The Book of Enoch or 1 Enoch: A New English Edition with Commentary and Textual Notes in Consultation with James C. VanderKam* (SVTP 7; Leiden: Brill, 1985).

6.   George W. E. Nickelsburg, *1 Enoch: A Commentary on the Book of 1 Enoch* (*Hermeneia—a Critical and Historical Commentary on the Bible*; ed. Klaus Baltzer; Minneapolis, MN: Fortress, 2001). The translation in this commentary covers 1 Enoch 1–36, 81–108. Since this is the first in a series of intended volumes and covers 1 Enoch 1–36, my translation interests involve only Nickelsburg's first volume. The translation found in Nickelsburg's first commentary volume is the same (for those chapters) as the separately published translation: George W. E. Nickelsburg and James C. VanderKam, *1 Enoch: A New Translation; Based on the Hermeneia Commentary* (Fortress Press, 2004). VanderKam's name appears on this published translation because he assisted Nickelsburg on the second volume of his scholarly commentary on 1 Enoch: George W. E. Nickelsburg and James C. VanderKam, *1 Enoch 2: A Commentary on the Book of 1 Enoch, Chapters 37–82* (*Hermeneia—a Critical and Historical Commentary on the Bible*; ed. Klaus Baltzer; Minneapolis, MN: Fortress, 2012).

7.   Ephraim Isaac, "1 (Ethiopic Apocalypse of) Enoch," in *Old Testament Pseudepigrapha*, vol. 1 (ed. James H. Charlesworth; Garden City, NY: Doubleday, 1983–85), 5–89.

Original-language words will appear in transliteration (English keyboard characters). These characters will be familiar to those who have had a year of Hebrew and Greek;[8] *otherwise they can be ignored.*

Format of Presentation

Readers should take note of the format adopted for this *Reader's Commentary*:

Section

The Book of the Watchers (1 Enoch 1–36) can be divided into thematic sections:
>   1 Enoch 1–5
>   1 Enoch 6–11
>   1 Enoch 12–16
>   1 Enoch 17–19
>   1 Enoch 20–36

Section Summary

Each of the above sections will commence with a brief summary of the content of the section.

Translation

Each chapter within a section will be *individually* presented in translation.

---

8.   As a Semitic language, Ethiopic mostly follows the same transliteration scheme. However, it has a few more consonantal characters than Hebrew or Greek.

Commentary

Comments will focus on one chapter at a time, in succession. Words drawn from the translation for comment are placed in *italics*.

Introduction to the Book of Enoch
(1 Enoch)[9]

I. Why 1 Enoch?

The book known popularly as the Book of Enoch is properly called 1 Enoch. This is no mere academic convention. The name is essential for distinguishing it from other books of Enoch (2 Enoch, 3 Enoch). The content, date, and original language of 2 Enoch and 3 Enoch differ from 1 Enoch in certain ways. Second Enoch "is an amplification of Genesis 5:21–32; that is, it covers events from the life of Enoch to the onset of the Flood."[10] It survives only in Old Slavonic and dates to the late first century AD. Third Enoch is even later. As Alexander notes, the book "purports to be an account by R. Ishmael of how he journeyed into heaven, saw God's throne and chariot, received revelations from the archangel Meṭaṭron, and viewed the wonders of the upper world."[11] The book was written in Hebrew and, if the attribution to Rabbi Ishmael is

---

9. Some of the material in this introduction appears in the appendixes to the author's earlier work, *Reversing Hermon: Enoch, the Watchers, and the Forgotten Mission of Jesus Christ* (Defender, 2017).

10. F. I. Andersen, "A New Translation and Introduction," in *The Old Testament Pseudepigrapha* (vol. 1; New York; London: Yale University Press, 1983), 191.

11. P. Alexander, "A New Translation and Introduction," in *The Old Testament Pseudepigrapha* (vol. 1; New York; London: Yale University Press, 1983), 1223.

accepted, must therefore date to the second century AD. (Rabbi Ishmael died shortly before the Bar Kokhba War in AD 132).[12]

II. Authorship and Date

First Enoch as we know it today is actually a composite literary work with parts dated to different periods. As Isaac notes, "1 Enoch is clearly composite, representing numerous periods and writers."[13] This determination is based on several considerations: (a) internal evidence (e.g., historical reference points in 1 Enoch); (b) paleography (scribal handwriting style); and (c) grammatical-linguistic features. As the subject of date pertains to 1 Enoch 1–36 (the Book of the Watchers), the portion of the book covered in this commentary, Archie Wright summarizes the current scholarly assessment:

> A scholarly consensus for the date of the Book of Watchers places the extant Aramaic form sometime in the third century BCE based on the paleography of the Qumran fragments; some suggest pushing the date farther back into an earlier Hellenistic period or perhaps the Persian period.[14]

12. Alexander, 1225–226.

13. E. Isaac, "1 Enoch: A New Translation and Introduction," in *The Old Testament Pseudepigrapha* (vol. 1; New York; London: Yale University Press, 1983), 16.

14. Archie T. Wright, "Introduction to the Book of Watchers," in *Early Jewish Literature: An Anthology* (ed. Brad Embry, Ronald Herms, and Archie T. Wright; vol. 2; Grand Rapids, MI: William B. Eerdmans Publishing Company, 2018), 193. In regard to this assessment, Wright refers his readers to Devorah Dimant, "1 Enoch 6–11: A Methodological Perspective," in *Society of Biblical Literature Seminar Papers* 1978 (Missoula: Scholars, 1978), 323–39.

The composite nature of the book (Section III) and the fragmentary *early* manuscript evidence (Aramaic, Greek; Section IV) for the book as we know it make more precise dating impossible.

III. The Books That Make Up 1 Enoch

As Wright notes, "One of the difficulties in dealing with 1 Enoch is that it is not a single work of one author, but rather a collection of at least seven (possibly eight) pieces of work."[15] The composite whole of 1 Enoch includes 108 chapters, most of them very short. Specialists in 1 Enoch outline the book as follows:[16]

Chapters 1–36: Book of Watchers

This portion of 1 Enoch is classified in the Second Temple genre of "Rewritten Bible" in that it expands upon Genesis 6:1–5 and the Flood story. The section deals with the primeval rebellion of members of God's heavenly host, their role in the proliferation of depravity on earth, and the expectation of their eschatological judgment. Enoch is commissioned as a prophet for this purpose and foresees the immediate and prospective judgment of the Watchers when he is brought into the heavenly realms for that commissioning.

Chapters 37–71: Similitudes of Enoch (Book of Parables)

This is the longest section of 1 Enoch, dominated by three extended parables that deal with (and slightly alter) the account of Enoch's visions during his heavenly journey.

---

15. Wright, "First Enoch," vol. 2, 178.
16. Ibid., vol. 2, 178.

Chapters 72–82: Book of the Luminaries (Astronomical Book)

This portion of 1 Enoch deals extensively with astronomical observations and sacred calendar. More specifically, "the text as it presently stands is a narrative in which Enoch recounts to Methuselah (76:14; 79:1) his journey through the heavens and over the earth, during which Uriel, the angel in charge of the luminaries, interpreted what Enoch saw."[17]

Chapters 83–90: Book of Dreams (Chapters 85–90: Animal Apocalypse)

These chapters have Enoch recounting two dream visions to Methuselah: a vision of the Flood (chapters 83–84) and an extended allegory that tells the story of human history from Adam to the end of days wherein the people of God and the nations are portrayed as animals (chapters 85–90).

Chapters 93:1–10 and 91:11–17: Apocalypse of Weeks

Akin to the Animal Apocalypse, "this work presents itself as a selective review of the history of the world from antediluvian times until the eschatological future when the purposes of the God of Israel will ultimately be realized."[18]

---

17. George W. E. Nickelsburg, "Enoch, First Book of," *The Anchor Yale Bible Dictionary* (ed. David Noel Freedman; New York: Doubleday, 1992), 509.

18. Loren T. Stuckenbruck, "Introduction to the Apocalypse of Weeks," in *Early Jewish Literature: An Anthology* (ed. Brad Embry, Ronald Herms, and Archie T. Wright; vol. 2; Grand Rapids, MI: William B. Eerdmans Publishing Company, 2018), 245.

Chapters 91:1–19; 92:1–5; 93:11–105:2: Exhortation and Epistle of Enoch

This section is in and of itself a patchwork composite whose points of focus include the state of human wickedness (in conjunction with the sin of the Watchers and the Flood), idolatry, and an apocalyptic vision of the end. Readers are exhorted to be ready.

Chapters 106–7: Book of Noah

These two brief chapters deal with the unusual circumstances of Noah's birth.

Chapter 108: Another Book of Enoch

This chapter is thought to have been added to the preceding chapters "as a final word of exhortation to the righteous of the end time....[in that] it presents a brief vision of the place of punishment as evidence of the coming judgment and calls on the suffering righteous to endure in anticipation of their glorification."[19]

The composite nature of the book means that we cannot assume its various components were written in the order of the chapter sequence that is familiar to us. The order of the chapters conforms to the latest manuscript evidence (Ethiopic) for the book as an assembled whole. This also means that we cannot assume a common provenance and setting for the sections. Wright once again summarizes the current consensus in this regard:

A general setting is the period of the early Hellenization of Palestine and Judaism. Alexander the Great had conquered the land in

---

19. Nickelsburg, "Enoch, First Book of," *The Anchor Yale Bible Dictionary*, 512.

approximately 332 BCE, which began the process of bringing the Greek world into the religious life of the Jews of Palestine. Not long after his victory, Alexander died an early death (at the age of thirty-three) in 323 BCE while conquering Persia. Shortly after his death, a power struggle among his generals began for control of the conquered world. This struggle, known as the "Wars of the Diadochi" (successors), lasted about forty years. As the land bridge between the Egyptian Empire and the rest of Alexander's world, Palestine became a point of contention between two of the warring generals—Ptolemy and Seleucus; it would also become the location of the conflict between the God-fearing Jews and those who chose to become more adapted to the Hellenism that was now permeating their land. It has been argued that much of the Jewish literature that came out of this period was a direct result of this conflict…. It appears that the authors of 1 Enoch were speaking out of this cultural demise (in their eyes) when they wrote the material. In addition, despite the authors' awareness of the Israelite religion and culture, it is clear that Greek and Mesopotamian sources have influenced their cosmology. It seems though that the authors were reacting in a polemical fashion against much of this outside influence.[20]

IV. Original Language and Manuscript Sources for 1 Enoch

The entirety of 1 Enoch is known only from Ethiopic translations of the book. The manuscripts for Ethiopic 1 Enoch are quite late, the earliest being from the fifteenth century AD. Earlier portions of 1 Enoch exist in Greek manuscripts and Aramaic fragments, with the latter being the most ancient. Consequently, the scholarly consensus is that 1 Enoch (probably

---

20. Wright, "First Enoch," vol. 2, 179–180.

in all its parts) was originally written in Aramaic.[21] The Aramaic material was unknown until the twentieth century:

> Modern research on the Book of Watchers had its beginning in 1773 with the discovery of the whole of 1 Enoch in three Ethiopic manuscripts, which were translated into English, German, and French in the nineteenth century. In the late 1800s, the discovery of the Greek fragments of the Akhmim manuscript of chapters 1–32 (fifth or sixth century CE) advanced the research of the Book of Watchers in the Greek tradition; in addition, the Greek manuscript of George Syncellus (ninth century CE) offers some significant translations of the Book of Watchers. R. H. Charles furthered the research work with his translation and commentary in 1912. The most significant advance came with the initial publication by Milik of the Aramaic fragments from Qumran in the 1950s. This was followed in 1978 with a text-critical two-volume work by Michael Knibb that incorporated the Ethiopic, Greek, and Qumran material into the discussion.[22]

---

21. George W. E. Nickelsburg, *1 Enoch: A Commentary on the Book of 1 Enoch* (ed. Klaus Baltzer; *Hermeneia—a Critical and Historical Commentary on the Bible*; Minneapolis, MN: Fortress, 2001), 9. Some scholars still speculate that some of the authors of portions of 1 Enoch may have written in Hebrew. Nickelsburg's footnote at the end of this selection reads (in part) as follows: "Throughout his edition, Milik assumes that Aramaic was the original language (J. T. Milik, *The Books of Enoch: Aramaic Fragments of Qumran Cave 4* [Oxford: Clarendon, 1976]…Michael A. Knibb (*The Ethiopic Book of Enoch: A New Edition in the Light of the Aramaic Dead Sea Fragments*, vol. 2:6–7) also considers an Aramaic original 'most probable.'"

22. Wright, "Introduction to the Book of Watchers," in *Early Jewish Literature: An Anthology*, vol. 2, 194.

Since modern scholars believe parts of 1 Enoch were written at different times, this presumed division of sources affects the language composition issue. As Esler explains, 1 Enoch "was written mostly in Aramaic in stages from the third century BCE to the first century CE, translated into Greek around the turn of the first millennium and then from Greek into Ge'ez in the fifth and sixth centuries CE in Ethiopia."[23] In regard to the Ge'ez (Ethiopic) translation, Ephraim Isaac includes the following manuscripts (in all the languages) in his introduction to 1 Enoch:[24]

1. *Aramaic*: Aramaic fragments of 1 Enoch were found at Qumran and have been recently published, together with a major study of the text and history of 1 Enoch.

2. *Ethiopic*: As has been indicated above, the complete version of 1 Enoch is preserved only in Ethiopic. Below is a list of five major and important manuscripts, one of which (A) has been utilized as the base text of the present English translation and another of which (C) has been used extensively in the same work:

    a. Kebrān 9/II (Hammerschmidt—*Ṭānāsee* 9/II); fifteenth century.

    b. Princeton Ethiopic 3 (Garrett collection—Isaac 3); eighteenth or nineteenth century.

    c. EMML 2080; fifteenth (possibly fourteenth) century.

    d. Abbadianus 55; possibly fifteenth century.

    e. British Museum Orient 485 (Wright 6); first half of the sixteenth century.

3. *Greek:* The Greek fragments are found principally in the following:

    a. Codex Panopolitanus (two eighth-century or later manuscripts, found in 1886–87 in a Christian grave in Akhmim, Egypt), containing 1 Enoch 1:1–32:6 (designated G^a in this work).

---

23. Philip F. Esler, *God's Court and Courtiers in the Book of the Watchers: Re-interpreting Heaven in 1 Enoch 1–36* (Wipf and Stock Publishers, 2017), 7.

24. E. Isaac, "1 Enoch," 16. Isaac also includes mention of one Latin fragment (1 Enoch 106:1–18) that dates to the eighth century AD.

b. Chronographia of Georgius Syncellus (c. 800), containing 1 Enoch 6:1–10:14; 15:8–16:1 (designated G^s in this work).

c. Chester Beatty papyrus of 1 Enoch containing 97:6–104; 106f. (published by C. Bonner, *The Last Chapters of Enoch in Greek*) (designated G^p in this work).

d. Vatican Greek MS 1809, containing 1 Enoch 89:42–49.

The following Dead Sea Scrolls from Qumran are the heretofore noted Aramaic fragments of 1 Enoch:[25]

- *4QEn^a (4Q201); DSSC,* 80; Milik, *Enoch,* 140–63; Stuckenbruck, DJD 36:3–7
- *4QEn^b (4Q202); DSSC,* 80–81; Milik, *Enoch,* 164–78
- *4QEn^c (4Q204); DSSC,* 81; Milik, *Enoch,* 178–217
- *4QEn^d* (4Q205); DSSC, 81; Milik, *Enoch,* 217–25
- *4QEn^e* (4Q206); DSSC, 81; Milik, *Enoch,* 225–44
- *4QEn^f* (4Q207); DSSC, 81; Milik, *Enoch,* 244–45
- *4QEn^g* (4Q212); DSSC, 82; Milik, *Enoch,* 245–72
- *4QEnastr^a (4Q208); DSSC,* 81; Tigchelaar and García Martínez, DJD 36:104–31
- *4QEnastr^b (4Q209); DSSC,* 81–82; Milik, *Enoch,* 274, 287–89, 293–96; Tigchelaar and García Martínez, DJD 36:132–71

---

25. Nickelsburg, *1 Enoch,* 9–10. See this source for descriptions of the contents of these fragments. These fragments are *not* manuscripts of the Book of Giants. The abbreviated sources in Nickelsburg's listing are: *DSSC* = *The Dead Sea Scrolls Catalogue: Documents, Photographs and Museum Inventory Numbers* (Compiled by Stephen E. Reed. Revised and Edited by Marilyn J. Lundberg with the collaboration of Michael B. Phelps; SBLRBS 32; Atlanta: Scholars Press, 1994); *Milik* = J. T. Milik, *The Books of Enoch: Aramaic Fragments of Qumrân Cave 4* (Oxford: Clarendon, 1976); *DJD* = Discoveries in the Judaean Desert (Oxford: Oxford University Press, 1951–2011). *DJD* is the forty-volume *edition princeps* series of scholarly editions of Dead Sea Scrolls.

- *4QEnastr^c (4Q210); DSSC,* 82; Milik, *Enoch,* 287–88, 292
- *4QEnastr^d (4Q211); DSSC,* 82; Milik, *Enoch,* 296–97

V. Reception of 1 Enoch by Jews in the Second Temple Period

Elements of sectarian Judaism appear to have considered 1 Enoch to be sacred. This is in part indicated by the presence of 1 Enoch in Aramaic at Qumran, along with the fact that many Second Temple Period books drew on 1 Enoch's content. Stuckenbruck notes in this regard that "not only the Enochic manuscripts themselves, but also materials among the Dead Sea Scrolls that belong to other documents, attest to the influence of the Enochic tradition."[26] Nickelsburg elaborates on the scrolls that contain material known from 1 Enoch, especially the Book of the Watchers:

> The influence of the Enochic tradition at Qumran is evident also in the community's possession of (multiple copies of) texts that employ or quote from the Enochic texts. These include the *Book of Jubilees* (eight copies) and a related text (three copies), the Genesis Apocryphon (one copy), a fragmentary Hebrew text from Cave 1 that contained a form of the story of the watchers very close to 1 Enoch 6–11 (1Q19), a *pešer* [*pesher*] on the story of the watchers (4Q180–181), a commentary or expansion on the Apocalypse of Weeks (4Q247), and the Damascus Document (eight copies), which knows the story of the rebellion of the watchers and a tradition about the giants (CD 2:16–20; see comm. on 7:2) and also appeals to the authority of the *Book of Jubilees* (CD 16:2–4).[27]

---

26. Loren T. Stuckenbruck, "The Book of Enoch: Its Reception in Second Temple Jewish and Christian Tradition," *Early Christianity* 4 (2013): 7–40 (esp. p. 11).
27. Nickelsburg, *1 Enoch,* 77.

The term *pesher* means "interpretation," so *pesher* texts get their name from the fact that they are commentaries—interpretations of certain writings. *Pesher* texts known from Qumran are based on books in the Hebrew Bible. The fact that Jewish scribes at Qumran would produce a *pesher* text on the Book of the Watchers suggests that 1 Enoch was highly regarded, if not considered Scripture.

VI. Reception of 1 Enoch in the Early Church

It is well known that a handful of early Christian writers treated 1 Enoch as Scripture. Stuckenbruck notes, "The *Epistle of Barnabas,* composed during the late 130s CE, cites the patriarch Enoch as 'scripture' twice in 16.5 f when reviewing material from the Animal Apocalypse (1 En. 89.56, 60, and 66f) and the Apocalypse of Weeks (1 En. 91.13—which is taken as a prediction of an eschatological temple)."[28]

Tertullian (ca. AD 155–240) used the same vocabulary. In his *On the Apparel of Women,* Book I, Chapter III, he calls 1 Enoch "Scripture" and defends its status using 2 Timothy 3:16:

> I am aware that the Scripture of Enoch, which has assigned this order (of action) to angels, is not received by some, because it is not admitted into the Jewish canon either. I suppose they did not think that, having been published before the deluge, it could have safely survived that world-wide calamity, the abolisher of all things. If that is the reason (for rejecting it), let them recall to their memory that Noah, the survivor of the deluge, was the great-grandson of Enoch himself; and he, of course, had heard and remembered, from domestic renown and hereditary tradition, concerning his own great-grandfather's "grace in the sight of

28. Stuckenbruck, "The Book of Enoch: Its Reception in Second Temple Jewish and Christian Tradition," 17–18.

God," and concerning all his preachings; since Enoch had given no other charge to Methuselah than that he should hand on the knowledge of them to his posterity. Noah therefore, no doubt, might have succeeded in the trusteeship of (his) preaching; or, had the case been otherwise, he would not have been silent alike concerning the disposition (of things) made by God, his Preserver, and concerning the particular glory of his own house.

If (Noah) had not had this (conservative power) by so short a route, there would (still) be this (consideration) to warrant our assertion of (the genuineness of) this Scripture: he could equally have *renewed* it, under the Spirit's inspiration, after it *had* been destroyed by the violence of the deluge, as, after the destruction of Jerusalem by the Babylonian storming of it, every document of the Jewish literature is generally agreed to have been restored through Ezra.

But since Enoch in the same Scripture has preached likewise concerning the Lord, nothing at all must be rejected *by* us which pertains *to* us; and we read that "every Scripture suitable for edification is divinely inspired." By the *Jews* it may now seem to have been rejected for that (very) reason, just like all the other (portions) nearly which tell of Christ. Nor, of course, is this fact wonderful, that they did not receive some Scriptures which spake of Him whom even in person, speaking in their presence, they were not to receive. To these considerations is added the fact that Enoch possesses a testimony in the Apostle Jude.[29]

---

29. Tertullian, "On the Apparel of Women," in *Fathers of the Third Century: Tertullian, Part Fourth; Minucius Felix; Commodian; Origen, Parts First and Second* (ed. Alexander Roberts, James Donaldson, and A. Cleveland Coxe; trans. S. Thelwall; vol. 4; The Ante-Nicene Fathers; Buffalo, NY: Christian Literature Company, 1885), 415–16.

Irenaeus (ca. AD 130–200) knew 1 Enoch well and accepted the recounting of primeval history described in the Book of the Watchers. In the tenth chapter of his work, *Against Heresies* (section 1), he wrote:

The Church, though dispersed throughout the whole world, even to the ends of the earth, has received from the apostles and their disciples this faith: [She believes] in one God, the Father Almighty, Maker of heaven, and earth, and the sea, and all things that are in them; and in one Christ Jesus, the Son of God, who became incarnate for our salvation; and in <u>the Holy Spirit, who proclaimed through the prophets</u> the dispensations of God, and the advents, and the birth from a virgin, and the passion, and the resurrection from the dead, and the ascension into heaven in the flesh of the beloved Christ Jesus, our Lord, and His [future] manifestation from heaven in the glory of the Father "to gather all things in one," and to raise up anew all flesh of the whole human race, in order that to Christ Jesus, our Lord, and God, and Saviour, and King, according to the will of the invisible Father, "every knee should bow, of things in heaven, and things in earth, and things under the earth, and that every tongue should confess" to Him, and that He should execute just judgment towards all; that He may send "spiritual wickednesses," <u>and the angels who transgressed and became apostates, together with the ungodly, and unrighteous, and wicked, and profane among men, into everlasting fire</u>; but may, in the exercise of His grace, confer immortality on the righteous, and holy, and those who have kept His commandments, and have persevered in His love, some from the beginning [of their Christian course], and others from [the date of] their repentance, and may surround them with everlasting glory.[30]

---

30. Irenaeus of Lyons, "Irenaeus against Heresies," in *The Apostolic Fathers with Justin Martyr and Irenaeus* (ed. Alexander Roberts, James Donaldson, and A. Cleveland Coxe; vol. 1; The Ante-Nicene Fathers; Buffalo, NY: Christian Literature Company, 1885), 1330–331.

VanderKam comments as follows regarding this passage:

It is not impossible that Irenaeus, in the wording of his lines about the angels, is thinking of 2 Pet 2:4 and Jude 6, but the language he uses does not reproduce their vocabulary very closely. There is, however, some verbal similarity with 1 Enoch…. If Irenaeus is here reflecting the Watcher story, he is attributing it to the Holy Spirit's inspiration of the prophets and including it within a brief statement of the Christian faith shared throughout the scattered churches.[31]

VII. The Relationship of 1 Enoch to the Book of the Giants from Qumran

Though closely related in content, the Book of Giants is not synonymous with 1 Enoch. However, nine of the Qumran Aramaic fragments of 1 Enoch (found in caves 1, 2, 4, and 6) contain portions of the Book of Giants.[32] Wright summarizes the similarities of this book with 1 Enoch as well as some of the differences:

The fragments of the Book of Giants from Qumran describe the actions and fate of the progeny of the rebellious Watcher angels found in the Book of Watchers (*see* Book of Watchers [1 Enoch 1–36]) and other Second Temple period literature. Similar to

---

31. James C. VanderKam, "1 Enoch, Enochic Motifs, and Enoch in Early Christian Literature," *The Jewish Apocalyptic Heritage in Early Christianity* (ed. James C. VanderKam and William Adler; *Compendia rerum iudaicarum ad Novum Testamentum* 3/4; Minneapolis: Fortress Press, 1996), 43.

32. Wright, "First Enoch," in *Early Jewish Literature: An Anthology*, vol. 2, 182. See also Nickelsburg, *1 Enoch*, 9–11.

the Book of Watchers' focus on the antediluvian actions of the giants (7:2–5; 9:9), their postdiluvian existence (15:8–12; 16:1), and their final destruction in the judgment to come, the Book of Giants describes or alludes to the fall of the Watcher angels (4Q531 17) and their punishment (4Q203 7A, 8). In the same vein, the Book of Giants takes up 1 Enoch 12–16 and expands on the account of the punishment of the giant offspring of the Watchers and their future judgment.

Absent from the other versions of the giant tradition in Second Temple Period literature but included in the Book of Giants are the names of the progeny of the Watchers (e.g., Gilgamesh, Hahyah, Hobabish, Mahaway, and 'Ohyah). Similar to the Watchers in the Book of Watchers, the giants are assigned specific tasks within the storyline; however, contrary to Enoch telling the Watchers of their fate in the Book of Watchers, the giants learn of their own fate through dreams and visions (see 2Q26; 4Q530 2; 4Q531 17.11.11–12; 6Q8 2). The active role of Enoch as seen in the Book of Watchers is downplayed in the Book of Giants. His role as intercessor and deliverer of the message of the fate of the Watchers is taken over by the giant Mahaway to a certain degree. He receives the message from Enoch and proceeds to pass it on to the Watchers, who in turn tell the giants (4Q530 3). The account of the giants in the Book of Giants appears more detailed than the accounts found in other texts such as the Book of Watchers and Jubilees (*see* The Book of Jubilees).[33]

---

33. Wright, "Introduction to the Book of Giants," in *Early Jewish Literature: An Anthology* (ed. Brad Embry, Ronald Herms, and Archie T. Wright; vol. 2; Grand Rapids, MI: William B. Eerdmans Publishing Company, 2018), 212.

VIII. General Overview of 1 Enoch:
What's the Book About?

First Enoch is apocalyptic literature; that is, it is broadly about the end of days. John J. Collins defines apocalyptic literature this way:

> A genre of revelatory literature with a narrative framework, in which a revelation is mediated by an otherworldly being to a human recipient, disclosing a transcendent reality which is both temporal, insofar as it envisages eschatological salvation, and spatial insofar as it involves another, supernatural world.[34]

In regard to 1 Enoch, Susan Docherty explains:

> The expectation that God will soon come in judgement is expressed from the first chapter of *1 Enoch* to the last, although no one systematic picture is given of this event. This theme of judgement is presented as a positive rather than a fearful message, as it is intended to console those who may be enduring suffering and oppression with the belief that something better awaits them. The scriptural flood narrative is a paradigm for this future act of God, so the figure of Noah is prominent throughout *1 Enoch*, and pre-existing sources about him may have been incorporated (see e.g. 10.1–22; 54.7–55.2; 60.1–25; 65.1–67.3; 106.1–19).[35]

In addition, the figure of Moses and the importance of the Sinai covenant are downplayed in 1 Enoch in favor of the Enoch of Genesis 5:22–24. One reason for this is that the work is apocalyptic—concerned with what

---

34. John J. Collins, "Introduction: Towards the Morphology of a Genre," *Semeia 14: Apocalypse* (1979): 9.

35. Susan Docherty, *The Jewish Pseudepigrapha: An Introduction to the Literature of the Second Temple Period* (London: SPCK, 2014), 130.

God is up to in the heavenly realms as the end of days unfolds on earth. It is Enoch, naturally, who would be privy to this information—not Moses, whose revelation from God has already played out.

Because 1 Enoch is apocalyptic in nature and tone, the *reason* for the final judgment is part of the work. Docherty again explains:

> The reason for the presence of evil in the world is also a major theme [in 1 Enoch 1–16], and the origins of sin are not attributed, as in some traditions, to the disobedience of Adam (Gen. 3:1–24; cf. *4 Ezra* 3:20–6; 4:30; 7:118; *2 Bar.* 23.4; 48.42–3; 54.15; 56.5–8), but to an angelic rebellion against God. The story of the coming to earth of heavenly beings who mate with human women, known also from Genesis 6:1–4, is therefore told here in a much more elaborate form (6.1–10.22). It is these fallen angels who are said to have led human beings astray, by teaching them all kinds of things which God did not intend them to know, such as how to make weapons of war, and how to ornament themselves with make-up and jewellery (*sic*; 8.1–2).... This narrative assumes a very significant place within the Enochic tradition (see also e.g. 64.1–2; 69.1–15; 86.1–6), and it affirms the supernatural rather than human origins of sin, although individual responsibility for sin is affirmed elsewhere in the text (e.g. 98.4).[36]

First Enoch continues on (chapters 17–36) to provide readers with a heavenly tour. This is no mere entertainment escapade. Rather, the tour is designed to convey the authoritative, heavenly nature of the revelation given to Enoch and relayed in the book that bears his name. To this end, Enoch is allowed access to God's throne in divine council scenes much like those of the biblical prophets (e.g., 1 Kings 22:19; Isaiah 6:1–4; Ezekiel 1:3–28; Daniel 7:9–14).[37]

---

36. Ibid., 131.
37. Ibid., 132.

Chapters 37–71 (known as the "Similitudes of Enoch" to scholars) present an apocalyptic vision of wisdom—that is, like biblical wisdom literature, this passage's main purpose is to encourage right (wise) living, since God will vindicate the righteous and punish the wicked in the end, which is soon approaching.

The rest of 1 Enoch reinforces these themes. Enoch, as a heavenly scribe, understands the passage of time and history. Hence the Book of the Luminaries (stars; chapters 72–82) is "a kind of compendium of ancient knowledge about astronomy and cosmology, which serves to illustrate the association of apocalyptic literature with learned circles."[38] The remainder of the book constitutes more review of history and impending apocalypse in the form of allegory, in particular, the Animal Apocalypse of chapters 85–90 and some of the circumstances of Noah's birth, the central figure in the Flood.

IX. Modern Scholarly Interpretations of 1 Enoch

Modern scholars of 1 Enoch of course assign no validity to its events, particularly the sin of the Watchers in 1 Enoch 6–11. As such, they look for the meaning of the events described elsewhere, either in terms of theology, abstract allegory, or satire of historical events and persons.

For example, some scholars take the rebellion as a contrived theological explanation for the origin of evil on the earth.[39] This may strike readers as odd, given the rebellion in Eden and the serpent (nachash). Scholars often exclude Genesis 3 from a discussion of the origins of evil because

---

38. Ibid., 135.

39. Representative of this view is Paul D. Hanson, "Rebellion in Heaven, Azazel, and Euhemeristic Heroes in 1 Enoch 6–22," *Journal of Biblical Literature* 96 (1977): 195–223.

they feel the fact that the serpent is never called "Satan" in the Old Testament eliminates that chapter from a theological consideration for evil.[40]

The most common explanation for the rebellion of the Watchers is that the content of 1 Enoch 6–11 is a veiled retelling of the apostasy of the Jerusalem priesthood. That is, 1 Enoch must be read as "actually" telling readers how the Jerusalem priesthood became impure. This approach takes several nuanced forms.

The work of David Suter has been quite influential among scholars of 1 Enoch. Esler summarizes:

> David Suter has argued that the explanation of 1 Enoch 6–16 lies in an issue of purity among priests serving the temple of Jerusalem during the third and second centuries BCE: they needed to be careful that they married appropriate wives.... In 1979 [he] argued that the marriages of the Watchers to human women in 1 Enoch "seem to reflect a concern with illegitimate marriages on the part of the priests." At this time there was a view among some priests at least that priests should only marry the virgin daughters of other priests, meaning that priestly marriages were to occur

---

40. The logic of this position leaves much to be desired. The events of Genesis 3 are the first of three supernatural rebellions that explain evil in God's good world. Rebellion against God in any sense in the supernatural sphere is, by definition, supernatural evil. See Michael S. Heiser, *Demons: What the Bible Really Says About the Powers of Darkness* (forthcoming, Lexham Press, 2020). Nevertheless, it is true that, in 1 Enoch 1–36, it is Cain's murder of Abel— not the deception of the serpent or the deeds of the Watchers—"that signals the arrival of evil among human beings, even though the activities of the Watchers, the Giants, and, above all, of the evil spirits of the Giants who will roam the earth until the final judgment dramatically increase the sway of evil on the earth" (Esler, *God's Court*, 10).

within a small and closed circle. Suter proposed that the Enochic author supported this view and critiqued those who failed to
adhere to it under the guise of a narrative attacking the Watchers
for similar behavior.[41]

A second view that filters the content of 1 Enoch 1–36 through the
lens of the Jerusalem priesthood is that of George Nickelsburg, who saw
the Watchers as priests who had deserted the Jerusalem sanctuary, thus
defiling themselves.[42] Esler again provides a coherent summary:

> [Nickelsburg] suggested that 1 Enoch 12–16 present God as liv-
> ing in a heavenly temple. He likened 1 Enoch 14–16 to a "throne
> vision." He regarded 1 Enoch as similar to Ezekiel 40–48 and as
> describing Enoch's "ascent to the heavenly temple...." Nickels-
> burg proposed that God is attended by angels "who are sometimes
> described as if they were priests," for which view he cited the word
> "approach" used of "the holy ones of the Watchers" coming near
> to God in 1 Enoch 14:23 on the basis that it had "technical cul-
> tic associations" and the fact of the angels being there night and
> day.... [For Nickelsburg] the text represents an attempt by the
> Enochic tradition, which associated itself with Mount Hermon
> in the north, to criticize the Jerusalem priesthood as impure and
> defiled.[43]

---

41. Esler, *God's Court*, 10, 81. The Suter quotations comes from: David W. Suter,
    "Fallen Angel, Fallen Priest: The Problem of Family Purity in 1 Enoch 6–16,"
    Hebrew Union College Annual 50 (1979): 115–135.

42. George W. E. Nickelsburg, "Enoch, Levi, and Peter: Recipients of Revelation
    in Upper Galilee," *Journal of Biblical Literature* 100 (1981): 575–600.

43. Esler, *God's Court*, 82–83, citing Nickelsburg's article identified above. As with
    Suter, Esler refutes Nickelsburg's thesis in his book.

The third variation of the Jerusalem Temple cipher for 1 Enoch is that of Martha Himmelfarb, who believes that the problem 1 Enoch 6–16 is hinting at was not priests marrying the wrong sort of Jewish women, but marrying *foreign* women (an idea she claims Nickelsburg's position suggests as well). Esler devotes an entire chapter to dissecting her view before dismissing it.[44] Esler's work (*God's Court*) is essentially a book-length critique of the perspective that the Book of the Watchers is "really" about the Jerusalem priesthood. Esler, correctly in the mind of this author, sees the setting for 1 Enoch as the divine court (God's council and its bureaucracy) and divine rebellion within that court.

---

44. Ibid., 85–87, 109–135.

A Reader's Commentary on
1 Enoch 1–5

Section Summary

First Enoch 1–5 is an introduction to the rest of the Book of the Watchers. The content of these first five chapters breaks down as follows:

- Superscription (1:1)
- Introduction to a theophany scene, wherein Enoch is introduced as "a righteous man who saw heavenly visions that were interpreted by angels"[45] (1:2–3b)
- Description of the theophany (1:3c–9)
- Indictment of those who do not follow "the Great and Holy One" (God, who was described in the theophany scene; 2:1–5:4)
- The destiny of the righteous and the wicked—i.e., those who have and have not aligned themselves with God (5:5–9)

These introductory chapters therefore present the Book of the Watchers as a prophetic oracle that is ultimately not about the past, but about impending judgment. This is one of many reasons 1 Enoch is classified by scholars in the apocalyptic genre.

---

45. Nickelsburg, "Enoch, First Book of," *The Anchor Yale Bible Dictionary*, 509.

Translation: Chapter 1

1¹The words of the blessing of Enoch, wherewith he blessed the elect «and» righteous, who will be living in the day of tribulation, when all the wicked «and godless» are to be removed. ²And he took up his parable and said—Enoch a righteous man, whose eyes were opened by God, saw the vision of the Holy One in the heavens, ‹which› the angels showed me, and from them I heard everything, and from them I understood as I saw, but not for this generation, but for a remote one which is for to come. ³Concerning the elect I said, and took up ‹my› parable concerning them:

The Holy Great One will come forth from His dwelling,
⁴And the eternal God will tread upon the earth, (even) on
    Mount Sinai,
[And appear from His camp]
and appear in the strength of His might from the heaven ‹of
    heavens›.
⁵And all shall be smitten with fear,
And the Watchers shall quake,
And great fear and trembling shall seize them unto the ends of
    the earth.
⁶And the high mountains shall be shaken,
And the high hills shall be made low,
And shall melt like wax before the flame.
⁷And the earth shall be ‹wholly› rent in sunder,
And all that is upon the earth shall perish,
And there shall be a judgement upon all (men).
⁸But with the righteous He will make peace,
And will protect the elect,
And mercy shall be upon them.
And they shall all belong to God,
And they shall be prospered,

And they shall ⟨all⟩ be blessed.
⟨And He will help them all⟩,
And light shall appear unto them,
⟨And He will make peace with them⟩.
⁹And behold! He cometh with ten thousands of ⟨His⟩ holy ones
To execute judgement upon all,
And to destroy ⟨all⟩ the ungodly:
And to convict all flesh
Of all the works ⟨of their ungodliness⟩ which they have ungodly
    committed,
⟨And of all the hard things which⟩ ungodly sinners ⟨have spoken⟩
    against Him.

Commentary

1:1

The words of the blessing of Enoch—This opening line is similar to Deuteronomy 33:1 ("This is the blessing with which Moses the man of God blessed the people of Israel before his death"), prompting some scholars to suggest a deliberate imitation. The writer's motive would be to make 1 Enoch read as Scripture. This suspicion is likely confirmed once we note that "the words of," while not appearing in Deuteronomy 33:1, appear in the first verse of other canonical books of the Hebrew Bible (Nehemiah 1:1; Ecclesiastes 1:1; Jeremiah 1:1; Amos 1:1). The content of the book is characterized as a blessing, because it will describe the glorious fate of the righteous and the terrible fate of the wicked.

the elect «and» righteous—other translations read "righteous chosen" (N) and "righteous elect" (B). This is no surprise, given the double brackets around "and," indicating that the conjunction isn't in all manuscripts. Consequently, it is certain that two separate groups are *not* in view. Charles' own commentary on 1 Enoch notes that the phrase is found elsewhere in

1 Enoch (38:2, 3, 4; 39:6, 7; 48:1; 58:1, 2; 60:13; 63:12, 13, 15; 70:3).[46] Since 1 Enoch is a Second Temple Jewish text, the "elect" has Old Testament Israel as a reference point. The elect are righteous (faithful) Jews.

in the day of tribulation—A time of great judgment. The referent is clarified by the ensuing "when all the wicked «and godless» are to be removed." This tribulation, then, is not a general time of judgment on Jews. Rather, those judged are the enemies of the righteous and God, regardless of ethnicity.[47] As 1 Enoch precedes the advent of Christianity, there is no sense of Christians escaping judgment at the expense of Jews. The passage is therefore no support for a particular view of Christian eschatology. Rather than a tribulation period of popular eschatology, the ensuing description of the tribulation (verses 4–9) bears close resemblance to the Old Testament Day of the Lord.

Nickelsburg adds "and the righteous will be saved" to the end of 1:1 after "when all the wicked «and godless» are to be removed." While the phrase is not found in Ethiopic here, it is found in the parallel verse of 1 Enoch 10:17.

1:2

his parable—(see also verse 3). N has "his discourse," perhaps to avoid a connotation of allegory. The Greek reads *parabolē*, which can be reconciled

---

46. Robert Henry Charles, ed., *Commentary on the Pseudepigrapha of the Old Testament* (vol. 2; Oxford: Clarendon Press, 1913), 188.

47. A survey of the judgment phrases in 1 Enoch informs us that "day of judgment" is more common than "day of tribulation." See Daniel Assefa, "Matthew's Day of Judgment in the Light of 1 Enoch," in *Enoch and the Synoptic Gospels: Reminiscences, Allusions, Intertextuality* (ed. Loren T. Stuckenbruck and Gabriele Boccaccini; *Early Judaism and Its Literature* 44; SBL Press, 2016), 199–213 (esp. 204).

with the Aramaic fragment of the verse (4QEn[a] 1 1:2) where the noun is *matlâh*. This Aramaic noun is cognate to Hebrew *mashal*, which is to be understood as a wise proverbial saying, not an allegory. In the Septuagint, *parabolē* is the predominant translation of *mashal*. Silva writes that *mashal* "simply denotes a proverb, which may often contain a comparison (1 Samuel 10:12; 24:13; Ezekiel 18:2); if the saying or comparison makes fun of or disparages a person as a bad example, the term takes on the sense "taunt" (Isaiah 14:4; Habakkuk 2:6)."[48] Parables are fundamentally about comparison. The means of the comparison (allegory or not) can vary.

Enoch—Enoch is here referred to in the third person, making it clear that the biblical Enoch of Genesis 5:21–24 is *not* cast as the author of 1 Enoch. Rather, an unknown writer purports to quote the biblical Enoch, so 1 Enoch is about Enoch, not authored by Enoch.

in the heavens—This reflects the Greek material. Ethiopic has "who is in heaven." Since "Holy One" is the referent, there is no discernible distinction in meaning.

‹which› *the angels showed me*—This reading follows the Ethiopic text. Greek reads "which he showed me." The "angels" reading makes good sense of the plural pronouns that follow ("from them I heard everything… from them I understood").

from them I heard everything, and from them I understood as I saw—This translation reflects the Greek material. Nickelsburg reconstructs the text from Ethiopic as: "From the words of the watchers and holy ones I heard everything; and as I heard everything from them, I also understood what I

---

48. Moisés Silva, ed., *New International Dictionary of New Testament Theology and Exegesis* (Grand Rapids, MI: Zondervan, 2014), 609.

saw." Black (B) does the same: "words of the [watchers and] holy ones."[49]
Nickelsburg (N) makes several other detailed observations:

> In the parallel passage at 93:2, Ethiopic "and from the word of the
> holy angels" has as its Aramaic prototype "…from the word of the
> watchers and holy ones." This double designation—well known
> from (Aramaic) Dan 4:10, 14, 20 (Engl.: 13, 17, 23)—appears
> in Aramaic of 1 Enoch also at 22:6, where Greek and Ethiopic
> read "angel." "Watcher" alone appears to be indicated also at
> 33:3, where Ethiopic reads "holy angel." The double designation
> is suggested by the word pair "watchers"/ "holy ones" at 12:2,
> where there is no extant Aramaic…. The Greek word ἐγρήγοροι
> (egrēgoroi), "watchers," is used throughout 1 Enoch 6–16 as the
> special designation for the rebel angels: "the watchers" unquali-
> fied, 1:5; 10:7, 9, 15; 16:2; "the watchers, the sons of heaven,"
> 6:2; 14:3; "the watchers of heaven," 12:4; 13:10; 15:2; "the holy
> watchers," 15:9…. Elsewhere in 1 Enoch 1–36 and 83–108, the
> normal designation of the heavenly beings is "angels" (Gk. ἄγγελοι
> (angeloi) Ethiopic malāʾekt), and sometimes "angels of (or 'in')
> heaven," which formulation parallels "watchers of heaven."
>
> A pattern seems to emerge from this evidence: (a) Nowhere
> do the Qumran fragments of 1 Enoch attest the Aram. אכאלמ
> (malʾakaʾ; "angel") even where the Greek and Ethiopic have
> ἄγγελος (angelos) and malʾak; (b) with the exception of 12:3, the
> Greek and Ethiopic reserve "watcher" as a designation for the rebel
> angels, with the qualifier "holy" being used only at 15:9 (cf. 5:4);

---

49. Black, *The Book of Enoch*, 121. Black further points out that in 1 Enoch
    6:2; 13:8; 14:3 they are called "sons of heaven" akin to the "sons of God"
    of Genesis 6:2. Citing Fitzmyer for agreement, Black believes that "sons of
    heaven" is synonymous with "sons of God" (see Joseph A. Fitzmyer, *The
    Genesis Apocryphon of Qumran Cave 1 (1Q20): A Commentary* (Third Edition;
    Roma: Pontificio Istituto Biblico, 2004), 84.

(c) with a few isolated exceptions (19:1, 2; the doublet at 21:10; and 106:5–6, 12, where the counterparts in 1QapGen 2:1, 16 read "watchers, holy ones, watchers, sons of heaven") the Greek and Ethiopic never use "angel" to designate the rebel heavenly beings. This pattern suggests that the Greek translator(s) adopted "watchers" as the designation for the rebels and thus distinguished them from the others, who were almost uniformly known as "angels." Only in isolated contexts (chaps. 12, 19, 21, 106) is this pattern broken. While we cannot be certain, because the Aramaic evidence is fragmentary, it is possible, and perhaps likely, that the original Aramaic uniformly designated the heavenly ones as וְירִיע ("watchers"), reserved וְשִידקוּ וְירִיע ("watchers and holy ones") for the unfallen heavenly beings, and used אִימֹשׁ יד וְירִיע ("watchers of heaven") as a neutral term that designated both the good and evil beings as entities of heavenly provenance or as those who belonged to God, who is referred to by the circumlocution "heaven."[50]

In this initial scene, the Watchers are unfallen beings. However, "since two hundred of them descended from heaven to earth and seduced the daughters of men, the term has come also to refer to these fallen watchers."[51] As in Daniel, they are called "holy ones," a description that does *not* describe a different class of being, but is appositional to "Watchers."[52] In

---

50. Nickelsburg, *1 Enoch*, vol. 1, 140.

51. Ibid., 121.

52. The term occurs three times in the Old Testament (Daniel 4:13, 17, 23) in translation of Aramaic *'îr* (cf. the Aramaic versification of Daniel 4:10, 14, 20). The etymology of the Aramaic term is the subject of debate. See Michael S. Heiser, *Angels: What the Bible Really Says About God's Heavenly Host* (Lexham Press, 2018), 20–21, and J. J. Collins, "Watcher," *Dictionary of Deities and Demons in the Bible* (Edited by Karel van der Toorn, Bob Becking, and Pieter W. van der Horst; Leiden; Boston; Köln; Grand Rapids, MI; Cambridge: Brill; Eerdmans, 1999).

Daniel 4:13 the Aramaic phrasing עִיר וְקַדִּישׁ (*'îr wᵉqaddîsh*) is to be translated "a watcher, a holy one" instead of the more common "a watcher and a holy one," which suggests two entities, perhaps of different class. The *waw* conjunction between the two nouns should be understood as creating apposition between them. This is certain from the context—only *one* heavenly being speaks with Daniel in the passage. In addition, the singular participles that follow that are used for the heavenly figure's proclamation in Daniel 4:14 point to one entity. First Enoch is imitating Daniel's wording and style.

Further, "from I heard everything, and from them I understood" informs us that these holy watchers will be interpreting for Enoch. The "interpreting angel" idea is quite common in both the Bible and Second Temple literature.[53] It is rare for God or a figure who is identified with/as God to explain revelation.

1:3

The Holy Great One will come forth from his dwelling—A number of scholars take this language as indicating a theophany. In simplest terms, a theophany is an appearance of God. VanderKam is one who reads 1 Enoch 1:3–7, 9 as a theophany. Citing the work of J. Jeremiahs, he explains: "I use theophany as Jeremias has defined it. According to him a theophany contains two essential elements: a description of God's advent and the upheaval in nature which ensues."[54] Given this definition (which is certainly coherent against

---

53. See David P. Melvin, "In Heaven as It Is on Earth: The Development of the Interpreting Angel Motif in Biblical Literature of the Neo-Babylonian, Persian, and Early Hellenistic Periods," PhD Dissertation, Baylor University, 2012; Karin Schöpflin, "God's Interpreter: The Interpreting Angel in Post-Exilic Prophetic Visions of the Old Testament," in *Angels: The Concept of Celestial Beings—Origins, Development and Reception* (Berlin: DeGruyter, 2007), 189–203.

54. James VanderKam, "The Theophany of 1 Enoch 1:3b–7, 9," *Vetus Testamentum* 23:2 (1973):129–150 (esp. 131).

the Old Testament backdrop), 1 Enoch 1 contains the stock elements. A number of Old Testament passages describing Yahweh's "march from the South" find their way into 1 Enoch 1 (cp. Habakkuk 3:3–7; Judges 5:4–5; Deuteronomy 33:1–2; see "Sinai" in 1 Enoch 1:4). A few notes of elaboration from VanderKam's essays are worth noting here:

> The first essential element of a theophany receives relatively extended treatment in vv. 3b, 4. The verbs used in these verses stem from similar passages in the Old Testament.... It should be noted, however, that En. i 3b–4 speaks of God's theophany, not from Sinai, but to Sinai from his heavenly home. This thought puts it in line with those Old Testament theophanies, usually later in date, which represent God as dwelling in heaven and as descending from there to a mountain.[55]

The apocalyptic judgment language of Isaiah 26:21 in particular strikes a chord with the context of 1 Enoch 1: "For behold, the LORD is coming out from his place to punish the inhabitants of the earth for their iniquity, and the earth will disclose the blood shed on it, and will no more cover its slain."

1:4

tread upon the earth, (even) on Mount Sinai—See the preceding comments on theophany. The wording here alludes to several Old Testament passages where Yahweh/the Holy One "comes from" Sinai (or its environs), his dwelling place, as a divine warrior (Deuteronomy 33:2; Habakkuk 3:3; Psalm 68:7–8; Judges 5:4–5; cp. Micah 1:3; Isaiah 26:21; Jeremiah 25:30). The author is drawing on this "warrior from Sinai" tradition to convey the idea that God is going to descend from heaven to return to

---

55. Ibid., 132–133.

earth "on" Mount Sinai to exact punishment on the wicked. The wording evokes the divine warrior motif.[56]

appear in the strength of His might—This follows the Greek material.

the heaven ‹of heavens›—The phrase denotes "the highest heaven," and is not an allusion to a specific number of heavens (Deuteronomy 10:14; 1 Kings 8:27; 1 Enoch 60:1; 71:5).[57] Nevertheless, "levels" of heavens were part of ancient Jewish cosmology. Lunde notes:

> Subsequent Jewish literature draws heavily on these diverse portrayals of heaven, developing them far beyond the detail found in the OT. Frequently, the physical aspects of heaven are discussed, as the human author is given a cosmic tour to observe its secrets (e.g., *T. Levi* 2:6–3:8; *1 Enoch* 17:2–18:14; 43:1–4; 72:1–80:8). At the end of the age these will be involved in the catastrophic and apocalyptic events that transpire (e.g., 4 Ezra 5:4–5; *T. Levi* 4:1; *1 Enoch* 1:4; 80:2–7; *Sib. Or.* 3:75–90).
>
> Under the influence of such OT phrases as "heaven of heavens" and "heaven and heaven of heavens" (Deut 10:14; 1 Kings 8:27; 2 Chron 2:6 [MT 2:5]; 6:18), the belief in multiple layers of heaven developed (e.g., *T. Levi* 2:6–3:8; *b. Roš Haš.* 24b; *b. Sanh.*

---

56. See Patrick D. Miller, *The Divine Warrior in Early Israel* (Harvard Semitic Monographs; Cambridge: Harvard University Press, 1973); idem, "God the Warrior: A Problem in Biblical Interpretation and Apologetics," in *Israelite Religion and Biblical Theology: Collected Essays* (ed. Patrick D. Miller; *Journal for the Study of the Old Testament Supplement Series 267*; Sheffield: Sheffield Academic Press, 2000).

57. Nickelsburg (pp. 145–146) draws attention to 1 Enoch 14:8–23, "where the landmarks of Enoch's journey are not a series of heavens, but the walls and buildings in the heavenly temple complex."

110a). At the uppermost height is God's throne (*T. Levi* 3:4; 5:1), surrounded by angels (*T. Levi* 3:1–8; *1 Enoch* 51:4; 61:10–11). *Paradise,* usually identified as the Garden of Eden, was believed to be preserved with God in heaven. It would ultimately be opened to the righteous in the next age so that they might eat of the Tree of Life (*T. Levi* 18:10–11; cf. also *2 Apoc. Bar.* 4:3–7). In 4 Ezra 7:36–38 the author presents "paradise" as a place of "delight and rest" opposite the pit of "hell." This may provide evidence of a tradition similar to which Jesus draws upon in Luke 16:19–31.[58]

1:5

The Watchers shall quake—It is unclear whether these are holy (unfallen) watchers, but the context suggests it. Since there is no reason for holy, loyal watchers in heaven to fear the judgment that is coming to earth, this is likely a reference to the fear of the fallen watchers, imprisoned until just this time, the final days of judgment (1 Enoch 10:8–16).

1:6–7

And the high mountains shall be shaken, and the high hills shall be made low, and shall melt like wax before the flame. And the earth shall be ‹wholly› rent in sunder, and all that is upon the earth shall perish, and there shall be a judgement upon all (men).—These are stock elements in biblical theophanies. God's appearance to judge is regularly accompanied by descriptions of cosmic upheaval. As Nickelsburg puts it, "The text describes the mightiest structures on earth—the everlasting mountains and hills—disintegrating helplessly before the presence of "the Great Holy One."[59]

---

58. J. Lunde, "Heaven and Hell," *Dictionary of Jesus and the Gospels* (ed. Joel B. Green and Scot McKnight; Downers Grove, IL: InterVarsity Press, 1992), 307.

59. Nickelsburg, *1 Enoch: A Commentary on the Book of 1 Enoch*, vol. 1, 146.

Since God's "coming down" is described in the Old Testament with the same terminology as we find here—which did not result in the physical destruction of the earth (many times over for each appearance)—it is best to see these descriptions not as literal cataclysmic events (Judges 5:4–5; 2 Samuel 22:7–11; Psalm 68:7–8; Jeremiah 25:30–31; Micah 1:3–4). Rather, the point is poetic: The earth itself reacts to God's anger; it recoils from His fearsome judgment. As prophets were rendered completely helpless in God's presence (Isaiah 6:5; Daniel 10:10), so will the earth be on the Day of Judgment. One scholar summarizes the imagery:

> Some references to earthquakes appear to be bald statements of historic fact and seem to have little, if any, symbolic value (Amos 1:1, cf. Zech 14:5; Acts 16:26). Most references, however, particularly in the poetic parts of the Bible, accord a high degree of symbolism to earthquakes. Earthquakes in Scripture are often seen as manifestations of the direct action of God's power. The example that is probably alluded to most is the earthquake at the giving of the law at Sinai (Ex 19:18). In their poetic reviews of the Exodus, later writers seem to have emphasized this element (Ps 68:8; 77:18; 114:4–7) and broadened its scope to cover the whole exodus event. Matthew's linkage of the earthquake at Jesus' crucifixion with the rending of the temple veil (Mt 27:54) is thus far more than a statement of physical cause and effect: it is profoundly symbolic. The covenant inaugurated at Sinai is now ended. In Revelation at least some of the earthquake imagery relates back to Sinai.
>
> From this association of earthquakes with God's revealing himself comes the substantial presence of this imagery in apocalyptic literature…. Earthquakes reminded men and women then as well as now that the only fixed ground is God himself. Not even the earth is ultimately stable. They also point to the fact that one

day God will shake down all human kingdoms with the appearing of Christ in Glory (Zech 14:4–5).[60]

1:8

and light shall appear unto them—Charles notes that this line is restored from the Greek material.[61] Black comments: "'Light' is the lot of the righteous, 'darkness' the destiny of the wicked (1 Enoch 10:5; 92:5; 94:9; 103:8). The "light" is likely a reference to the glory of God or the presence of God (Job 29:3; Psalm 118:27; Habakkuk 3:4). In the New Testament, the believer's destiny is described the same way: "But you are a chosen race, a royal priesthood, a holy nation, a people for his own possession, that you may proclaim the excellencies of him who called you out of darkness into his marvelous light" (1 Peter 2:9).

He will make peace.... And they shall all belong to God, and they shall be prospered, and they shall ‹all› be blessed.—Because of the context of Mount Sinai (1:4) and the fact that the Greek text aligns well with LXX of the Aaronic benediction of Numbers 6:24–26, scholars have taken this as covenantal language. Nickelsburg observes:

> The verse is an elaboration of the key motifs in the Aaronic benediction (Num 6:24–26), placed here in a different order.... In 1 Enoch 1:8 the ancient priestly blessing of the nation is interpreted as the eschatological blessing to a part of that nation, the *true* Israel, here called "righteous and chosen." "Righteous" is the most frequent designator of God's people in 1 Enoch and refers to

---

60. Leland Ryken et al., *Dictionary of Biblical Imagery* (Downers Grove, IL: InterVarsity Press, 2000), 225.
61. Robert Henry Charles, ed., *Commentary on the Pseudepigrapha of the Old Testament* (vol. 2; Oxford: Clarendon Press, 1913), 189.

their faithful obedience to God's will, "the way of righteousness" spelled out in the divine law.[62]

1:9

This verse is quoted in Jude 14–15, almost in its entirety, as a prophecy from "the seventh from Adam" (Enoch).[63] Though the Enochic source of the statement is clear from observing the Greek of Jude and 1 Enoch 1:9, the Enochic writer may have also been influenced by two other Old Testament passages.

Jeremiah 25:30–31:

The LORD will roar from on high,
and from his holy habitation utter his voice;
he will roar mightily against his fold,
and shout, like those who tread grapes,
against all the inhabitants of the earth.
The clamor will resound to the ends of the earth,
for the LORD has an indictment against the nations;
he is entering into judgment with all flesh,

---

62. Nickelsburg, *1 Enoch*, vol. 1, 147.

63. Ibid., 149. Nickelsburg notes that Jude "quotes all but line c." Bauckham adds that "the seventh from Adam" is "a traditional description of Enoch (*1 Enoch* 60:8; 93:3 = 4QEn[g] 1:3:23–24; *Jub.* 7:39; *Lev. Rab.* 29:11), arrived at by reckoning the generations inclusively (Gen. 5:3–19)." Richard J. Bauckham, *2 Peter, Jude* (vol. 50; *Word Biblical Commentary*; Dallas: Word, Incorporated, 1998), 96. The reader will note from Bauckham's citation that we have Aramaic evidence for this quotation. Bauckham (p. 94) raises the obvious questions: "Has Jude followed the Greek version (C) or made his own translation from the Aramaic?... Has Jude adapted the text to meet his own requirements?" See the discussion on pages 94–95 of Bauckham's commentary.

and the wicked he will put to the sword,
declares the LORD.

Isaiah 66:15–16:

For behold, the LORD will come in fire,
and his chariots like the whirlwind,
to render his anger in fury,
and his rebuke with flames of fire.
For by fire will the LORD enter into judgment,
and by his sword, with all flesh;
and those slain by the LORD shall be many.

ten thousands of ⟨His⟩ holy ones…to execute judgement—The descriptive phrase "holy ones" is "a common Enochic term for heavenly beings, which appears in the absolute form and in combination with 'watchers'."[64] The statement brings to mind passages like Deuteronomy 33:1–2 and Daniel 7:10 (cp. Daniel 7:18, 22, 25) and 1 Enoch 14:22–23, where multitudes of holy ones are present with God to dispense the law (Deuteronomy 33:1–2) or render judgment.[65]

Translation: Chapter 2

2[1] Observe ye everything that takes place in the heaven, how they do not change their orbits, ⟨and⟩ the luminaries which are in the heaven, how they all rise and set in order each in its season, and transgress not against

---

64. Ibid., 149. Examples listed by Nickelsburg include: 9:3 (Eth); 14:23, 25; 47:2, 4; 57:2; 60:4; 61:10, 12; 69:13; 71:4; 81:5; 93:11.

65. For Old Testament examples of the heavenly host coming with or at the behest of Yahweh for judgment, see Heiser, *Angels*, 52–54. For New Testament examples, see the same resource at pp. 136–138.

their appointed order. ²Behold ye the earth, and give heed to the things which take place upon it from first to last, ⟨how **steadfast** they are⟩, how ⟨none of the things upon earth⟩ change, ⟨but⟩ all the works of God appear ⟨to you⟩. ³Behold the summer and the winter, «how the whole earth is filled with water, and clouds and dew and rain lie upon it.»

Commentary

2:1

Scholars note that 2:1 begins a new thematic section within the book. Nickelsburg explains:

> A new section of text is indicated at 2:1 by an abrupt shift in form, style, and content. The parallel poetry of 1:3–9 gives way to a run of prose (albeit "a rhythmical or poetic prose") that extends from 2:1 to 5:3…. The new section of text is delimited by 5:4, which is in part a doublet of 1:9 that forms a closing bracket for the section….
>
> The section is addressed in the second person plural to the sinners whose condemnation in the coming judgment has been announced in 1:9. "All the deeds of their wickedness that they have done" and the arrogant words that they have spoken (1:9) are juxtaposed to "all the works" that are "done" in heaven and earth by the obedient elements of God's nonhuman creation. The sinners are told to observe and contemplate this unchanging faithful obedience to God's commands, which stands in striking contrast to the sinners' perverse transgression of God's word…. The final line of 5:4 announces the consequences of this conduct. In contrast to the righteous and chosen, who have been promised "peace" (1:8), the sinners are told: "You will have no peace." This contrast will be elaborated in 5:5–8, in a series of predictions of blessings and curses.[66]

66. Nickelsburg, *1 Enoch*, vol. 1, 151–152.

luminaries which are in the heaven—The reference is obviously celestial objects in light of the context of verse 3, which deals with natural processes. The language is similar to Psalm 8:4.

2:2

‹*how* **steadfast** *they are*›, *how* ‹*none of the things upon earth*› *change*— These lines point us to the theme of the entire section, which juxtaposes the theme of creation with God's goodness to humankind: "In [1 Enoch] 2–5:3 the order of nature is contrasted with the disorder of man's world."[67] As Nickelsburg notes, this has ramifications for material later in the book:

> The major point in 2:1 is clear. The heavenly bodies move with a regularity that accords with the divinely ordained structures of creation. God has set their paths through the heavens and has fixed the timing of their movement along these paths; as obedient creatures, they do not change God's order and thus transgress God's commands. This assertion is demonstrated at great length in the astronomical and calendrical treatise(s) now summarized in chaps. 72–82.[68]

Translation: Chapter 3

3[1]Observe and see how (in the winter) all the trees seem as though they had withered and shed all their leaves, except fourteen trees, which do not lose their foliage but retain the old foliage from two to three years till the new comes.

---

67. Charles, *Commentary on the Pseudepigrapha of the Old Testament*, vol. 2, 189.
68. Nickelsburg, *1 Enoch*, vol. 1, 155.

Commentary

3:1

fourteen trees—The number and purpose of the trees is enigmatic. Charles, Charlesworth, Nickelsburg, and Milik all cite the same parallel text with little to no explanation: *Geoponica* 11.1.[69] The term "Geoponica" relates to literature about agriculture—in this case, a work compiled in the tenth century AD. Scholars have compared 1 Enoch 3:1 to known lists of trees in ancient contemporary documents, but there is no precise parallel.[70] The Aramaic Levi document and the Book of Jubilees both contain lists of trees. The trees in those texts appear to have something to do with the kinds of trees to be used (or not) for sacrificial fire. The fourteen trees mentioned here in 1 Enoch 3:1 do not have that association. The Bible itself gives no rule about the trees to be used for burning sacrifices. Leviticus 1:7 only comments about the placement of wood on the altar. Jubilees 21:12–15, on the other hand, does deal with the examination of wood for sacrifice (e.g., stipulations about aroma and burning time).

Translation: Chapter 4

4[1]And again, observe ye the days of summer how the sun is above the earth over against it. And you seek shade and shelter by reason of the heat of the sun, and the earth also burns with glowing heat, and so you cannot tread on the earth, or on a rock by reason of its heat.

---

69. The specific reference is to *Geoponica sive Cassiani Bassi scholastici de re rustica eclogue* (ed. H. Beckh; Leipzig, 1895), 326, lines 17–20.
70. See Jonas C. Greenfield, Michael Stone and Esther Eshel, *The Aramaic Levi Document: Edition, Translation, Commentary* (Studia in Veteris Testamenti Pseudepigrapha 19; Leiden: E. J. Brill, 2004), 164–170.

Commentary

4:1

the days of—The Aramaic (4QEn^a 1 2:6) has "signs of." Nothing eschatological or mystical is in view, merely the orderly cycle of nature (cp. 1 Enoch 2:3). Ethiopic supports "the days of." First Enoch 3 and 4, obviously quite short at one verse each, describe two of the four seasons. Milik notes this and believes, on the basis of material later in 1 Enoch (the Astronomical Book or Book of Luminaries, 1 Enoch 72–82), chapters 3 and 4 originally had something to say about all four seasons (cf. 1 Enoch 20:4; 82:15–20). Both of these portions of 1 Enoch associate the luminaries and celestial operation of the seasons with spiritual beings. As noted above, this section (2:1–5:3) intentionally contrasts orderly nature with disorderly (wicked) humanity. Nature obeys, humanity disobeys. But the author of 1 Enoch (whether an Essene member of the Qumran community that had 1 Enoch in Aramaic) believed that heavenly beings were responsible for the orderly maintenance of the celestial objects. For this reason, the Qumran priests believed that the natural astronomical calendar (364 days via naked-eye astronomy) was actually a corruption of an original, mathematically perfect, 360-day calendar that began at Creation (Day 4). The astronomer-priests at Qumran knew that the two calendars were not in sync. Something had happened. The astronomical book that comprises part of 1 Enoch makes it clear that they blamed the cosmic malfunction on the rebellion of the Watchers.[71]

---

71. See Roger T. Beckwith, *Calendar and Chronology, Jewish and Christian: Biblical, Intertestamental and Patristic Studies* (Leiden: E. J. Brill, 2001), 113–115.

Translation: Chapter 5

5[1]Observe ye how the trees cover themselves with green leaves and bear fruit: wherefore give ye heed ‹and know› with regard to all ‹His works›, and recognize how He that liveth for ever[72] hath made them so. [2]And ‹all› His works go on ‹thus› from year to year ‹for ever›, and all the tasks which they accomplish for Him, and ‹their tasks› change not, but according as God hath ordained so is it done. [3]And behold how the sea and the rivers in like manner accomplish and ‹change not› their tasks ‹from His commandments›.

> [4]But ye—ye have not been steadfast, nor done the commandments
>   of the Lord,
> But ye have turned away and spoken proud and hard words
> With your impure mouths against His greatness.
> Oh, ye hard-hearted, ye shall find no peace.
> [5]Therefore shall ye execrate your days,
> And the years of your life shall perish,
> And the ‹years of your destruction› shall be multiplied in eternal
>   execration,
> And ye shall find no mercy.
> [6a]In those days ye shall make your names an eternal execration
>   unto all the righteous,[73]
> [b]And by you shall ‹all› who curse, curse,
> ‹And all› the sinners ‹and godless› shall imprecate by you,
> [7c]And for you the godless there shall be a curse.

---

72. This is Charles' spelling instead of the modern "forever."

73. The Charles translation makes no comment about why some of the verses in the translation have superscripted letters. I have nevertheless preserved this formatting. It seems the superscripted letters are designed to inform readers of how Charles rearranged stanzas.

^{6d}‹And all the…shall rejoice,

^eAnd there shall be forgiveness of sins,

^fAnd every mercy and peace and forbearance:

^gThere shall be salvation unto them, a goodly light.

ⁱAnd for all of you sinners there shall be no salvation,

^j But on you all shall abide a curse›.

^{7a}But for the elect there shall be light and joy and peace,

^bAnd they shall inherit the earth.

⁸And then there shall be bestowed upon the elect wisdom,

And they shall all live and never again sin,

Either through ungodliness or through pride:

But they who are wise shall be humble.

⁹And they shall not again transgress,

Nor shall they sin all the days of their life,

Nor shall they die of (the divine) anger or wrath,

But they shall complete the number of the days of their life.

And their lives shall be increased in peace,

And the years of their joy shall be multiplied,

In eternal gladness and peace,

All the days of their life.

Commentary

5:1

Observe ye how the trees cover themselves with green leaves and bear fruit— Reflects the Greek material. Ethiopic adds (N): "and they cover the trees. And all their fruit is for glorious honor."

His works go on ‹thus› from year to year ‹for ever›—"Forever" is present in the Greek but absent in the Ethiopic.

And ‹all› His works go on ‹thus› from year to year ‹for ever›, and all the tasks which they accomplish for Him, and ‹their tasks› change not, but according as God hath ordained so is it done.—As noted above, this section (which began in 2:1) is about the orderliness of God's creation, which provides a contrasting foil to the disorderly and wicked behavior of the unrighteous. The divergence is driven home in 5:3–4, which ends the section.[74] Nickelsburg writes:

> The section is addressed in the second person plural to the sinners whose condemnation in the coming judgment has been announced in 1:9. "All the deeds of their wickedness that they have done" and the arrogant words that they have spoken (1:9) are juxtaposed to "all the works" that are "done" in heaven and earth by the obedient elements of God's nonhuman creation. The sinners are told to observe and contemplate this unchanging faithful obedience to God's commands, which stands in striking contrast to the sinners' perverse transgression of God's word. The largest part of the section focuses on the creation and its regularity (2:1–5:3) and thus establishes an unmistakable paradigm and foil for the human behavior that is then described in two lines (5:4ab). Thus the paradigm prepares for the nuance that 5:4 adds to the description of sin in 1:9: sinners have not stood firm and have veered from the straight path of God's law. The final line of 5:4 announces the consequences of this conduct.[75]

Nickelsburg goes on to make the following observation in an excursus:

---

74. Nickelsburg (p. 152) notes: "The new section of text is delimited by 5:4, which is in part a doublet of 1:9 that forms a closing bracket for the section. Although 5:4 retains the second person plural address of 2:1–5:3, and 5:4abα continues its subject matter, the verse as a whole is marked by poetic parallelism, and 5:4bβ recasts 1:9e–f."

75. Nickelsburg, *1 Enoch*, vol. 1, 151–152.

A number of Israelite texts contrast nature's steadfast obedience to God's commands with humanity's divergence from the divine statutes. The language personifies nature's activity in a way that remythologizes the material creation; the natural elements are given personalities reminiscent of the polytheistic worldview that placed gods and demi-gods in charge of the various parts of the cosmos. As a result, the human and nonhuman worlds are spoken of in the same terms.[76]

This worldview element needs more commentary than Nickelsburg provides. In my judgment, it also needs different framing. The Israelite take on this was not exactly that of the polytheists. As I have written elsewhere:[77]

Israelites were not unique among the peoples of antiquity, or now for that matter. Death was a fearful thing. While the righteous hoped to be released from Sheol to be with God and other loved ones who worshipped the true God, there is no indication in the Old Testament that Israelites presumed that would happen immediately at death. The hope of the righteous for deliverance from the realm of the dead is often (but not exclusively) found in passages dealing with eschatological judgment and vindication. In other words, the Old Testament theology of afterlife included hope but conveyed uncertainty about when the hoped-for release would occur.

As a result, for Israelites, anything that threatened death might be associated with the realm of the dead and the disembodied spirits therein. This presents interpretive and theological difficulties that require careful navigation.

---

76. Ibid., 153.
77. Heiser, *Demons,* chapter 1 (forthcoming work). The footnotes in the excerpt also come from this source.

Ancient Near Eastern texts make it quite clear that people living in biblical times parsed natural disasters mythically. Storms, earthquakes, diseases, famines and the like were outbursts of divine wrath from a range of deities. Calamity, illness, or death might occur either because some deity didn't like you or your people, or as a side effect of a conflict with another deity. The question of whether biblical writers thought this way is one that arises from the text.

The short answer is "yes and no." One the one hand, in biblical thought, everything that threatens life is the result of divine rebellion. Natural disaster, disease, and death extend from humanity's failure to fulfill the Edenic mandate, a failure provoked through the deception of a divine rebellion. The earth was under a curse. Eden was lost.... For Israel, raised up by divine intervention on the part of Yahweh after Babel's judgment, things like plague, infertility, sickness, natural disasters, and external threats of violence were only to be feared in the wake of apostasy (Exod 15:26; Lev 26:14–39; Deut 28:15–68).[78]

This broad-stroke worldview put supernatural causation of natural disaster, illness, and death "on the table" so to speak. But it would be an exaggeration to presume that all such things, or even most, would have been viewed as having divine causation. Ancient people, especially in complex societies, would have known that common sense and wisdom were behind undesirable circumstances as well. Their outlook was not wholly enchanted.[79]

---

78. For discussion on these and related matters, Michael L. Brown, *Israel's Divine Healer* (*Studies in Old Testament Biblical Theology*; Grand Rapids: Zondervan, 1995), 72–78, 99–104, 122–125, 133–148.

79. (From the forthcoming, Heiser, *Demons*, page 31, note 86): "Given our modern scientific knowledge of germs, viruses, bacteria, and genetics, we of course cast a much wider net when it comes to common sense (knowledge) and wisdom. But if we are not materialist atheists or deists, divine causation

The terms that follow, then, do not name demons, but reflect the biblical worldview that the threats of the natural world were somehow tied to a cosmic struggle involving the spiritual world.

5:5

Of the transition at this point to a new section, Nickelsburg writes: "The great judgment has been announced in 1:6, 9, and alluded to in 5:4. The present section concludes the introduction by explicating the consequences of the judgment in a series of alternating descriptions of the curses and blessings that will befall the sinners and the righteous."[80]

Therefore shall ye execrate your days—Ethiopic has (literally): "and the years of your life you will destroy." The Greek verb ("you will destroy") that would reflect this reading would be *apoleite*. The Greek text Charles used (G^a) read *apoleitai*. The difference is subtle, as the second-person form that reflects the Ethiopic in effect blames the unrighteous for their

---

and intervention is part of our worldview. For an ancient Israelite, if you didn't plant enough food or didn't keep animals away from crops, you were going to go hungry—not because of evil spirits, but because of stupidity. If you failed to build walls to protect your city, your poor thinking was the reason for your vulnerability. If you didn't nurse your child or if you abandoned it to the elements, you could expect it to die. The entire world wasn't enchanted, but if there was no *apparent* reason for tragedy, you would look to the supernatural for an explanation. Modern people who believe in God and the spiritual world do the same. We ask God to heal. We pray for a drought to end or for protection from the elements. We do not do so because we believe such things are in the job descriptions of particular entities. We do so to show dependence on God's sovereignty."

80. Nickelsburg, *1 Enoch*, vol. 1, 160.

own fate: *You* will destroy the years of your life (now and the years in the afterlife) by your own wickedness.

the ⟨years of your destruction⟩ shall be multiplied in eternal execration—N. translates this as: "the years of your destruction will increase in an eternal curse." The wording is supported by Aramaic 4QEnᵃ 1 2:15, which reveals the lemma for "eternal" to be עלם (*'lm*; "duration, eternity, world"). [81] While this lemma (in Aramaic, Hebrew, and other Semitic languages) can merely refer to a long time (i.e., something shy of eternity), the context here supports a semantic of eternality. Since the fate of the righteous is contrasted with that of the wicked, "shortening" the duration of the judgment of the wicked would require, for consistency, decreasing the blessings for the righteous (see verse 9). [82]

The intentional contrast brings to mind the blessings and curses of Deuteronomy 27–28. Nevertheless, an examination of "the specific elements and expressions in 5:5–9, as well as the alternating use of second and third person with reference to the wicked and the righteous, are most closely associated with the promises of a new heaven and new earth and a new Jerusalem in Isaiah 65–66." [83]

ye shall find no mercy—This follows the Ethiopic. The Greek material has "mercy or peace." The loss of "peace" is present in 5:4, so both are not

---

81. See Martin Abegg, *Glosses for the Qumran Sectarian Manuscripts* (Bellingham, WA: Logos Bible Software, 1999–2002); Ludwig Koehler, Walter Baumgartner, et al., *The Hebrew and Aramaic Lexicon of the Old Testament: Aramaic* (*The Hebrew and Aramaic Lexicon of the Old Testament; Leiden;* New York: E. J. Brill, 1994–2000), 1949.

82. This observation does not resolve, however, the debate over the biblical (and Second Temple Jewish) concept of hell. Both eternal damnation and annihilation are forever.

83. Nickelsburg, *1 Enoch*, vol. 1, 160.

necessary here to make the point (though the double referent is considered better by more recent scholars). The focus is of interest, because later (1 Enoch 12:6), the Watchers are denied "mercy and peace." Both the human wicked and the fallen Watchers share the same fate (cp. 1 Enoch 10:9–10, 17; Jubilees 23:25–28).

5:6

ye shall make your names an eternal execration—"Ye will make" is, more literally, "you will give" (Ethiopic). Greek actually reads "(your names) will be."[84]

And by you shall ⟨all⟩ who curse, curse, ⟨And all⟩ the sinners ⟨and godless⟩ shall imprecate by you—The language here (including the wording above) is close to Isaiah 65:16 ("You shall leave your name to my chosen for a curse, and the Lord GOD will put you to death"). Isaiah 65:11–16 contrasts two groups: those who follow Yahweh and those who do not. In Isaiah 65:16:

> The name of those who forsake God ("you" in v. 15a) will be used in an oath of cursing when "my chosen ones" (*běḥîray*) are casting a curse on some evil person. For example, in Jer 29:20–23 the prophet Jeremiah tells about the sins of Ahab, the son of Kolaiah, and Zedekiah, the son of Maaseiah, who prophesied deceptions, committed adultery, and did outrageous things. Because of these evil deeds God handed them over to Nebuchadnezzar, the Babylonian king so that he could put them to death. In 29:22 Jeremiah refers to a future curse in which people will say, "May the LORD treat you like Zedekiah and Ahab whom the king of Babylon burned in the fire." In Isaiah 65:15 the name of this group of people is not provided, but the destiny of that group and anyone

---

84. Ibid., 159, footnote b.

cursed using their name will be death.... This contrasts with the different name that God will give to his servants (65:15b). They will not have a name associated with a curse, for when God transforms a person's life and directs them on a new path, he often gives them a new name that points to their new destiny.[85]

‹And all the...shall rejoice—N, CW supply "chosen" or "elect" respectively, on analogy to the parallelism with verse 7 ("But for the elect").

a goodly light—Probably the glory of God (see note on 1:8).

on you all shall abide a curse.›—The "curse" refers to not inheriting the earth (cf. 5:7).

5:7

But for the elect there shall be light and joy and peace, And they shall inherit the earth.—N has "they shall inherit the earth" in the preceding verse as well to produce (in his thinking) an original doublet.[86] The phrase "inherit the earth" takes us back to the beatitude in Matthew 5:5 ("the meek shall inherit the earth"). There the "meek" are those humble enough to acknowledge their spiritual poverty and dependence upon the grace of God for salvation, and not their own merit. The righteous are in view here as well. Given the relationship of this section to Isaiah 65, it is possible that the language derives from Isaiah 65:9 ("I will bring forth offspring from Jacob, and from Judah possessors of my mountains; my chosen shall

---

85. Gary Smith, *Isaiah 40–66* (vol. 15B; *The New American Commentary*; Nashville, TN: Broadman & Holman Publishers, 2009), 714.

86. Nickelsburg (p. 159) explains: "This distich closely parallels the beginning of v 7ab and may be a doublet, intended as a foil to the following distich regarding the sinners."

possess it, and my servants shall dwell there"). The motif of inheriting the land can also be found in Psalms 37:9, 11, 22, and 29. The idea is quite in concert with the displacement of the ruling supernatural sons of God (the "Deuteronomy 32 worldview" about which I have written extensively) in the eschaton. It is believers who will judge these supernatural rebels (1 Corinthians 6:3) by replacing them as rulers over the nations, co-sovereigns with Jesus.[87] Black notes that the concept is ultimately about inheriting eternal life. This makes good sense, as reclaiming the nations from supernatural fallen sons of God is fulfilled in the global Eden, the new earth.

5:9

And they shall not again transgress, Nor shall they sin all the days of their life, Nor shall they die of (the divine) anger or wrath—Note the conceptual connection between sin and death (cf. Romans 5:12; 6:23).

---

87. See Michael S. Heiser, *The Unseen Realm: Recovering the Supernatural Worldview of the Bible* (Lexham Press, 2015), 110–122, 257–258, 311, 375. More specifically, or Deuteronomy 32:8 and the worldview that derives from it, see pp. 112–115. The Deuteronomy 32 worldview involves God's decision at the Babel episode (Genesis 11:1–9) to divorce the nations and allot them to lesser "sons of God" (Deuteronomy 32:8; cp. Deuteronomy 4:19–20; 17:1–3; 29:23–26; 32:17). The reading in Deuteronomy 32:8 "sons of God" is from the Dead Sea Scrolls. For a detailed discussion of that verse and the Hebrew data, see Michael S. Heiser, "Deuteronomy 32:8 and the Sons of God," *Bibliotheca Sacra* 158 (January–March 2001): 52–74.

A Reader's Commentary on
1 Enoch 6–11

Section Summary

First Enoch 6–11 narrates the rebellion of the Watchers. The book as a whole from this point forward will see in this revolt the primary explanation for human depravity and chaos on earth. As Wright summarizes, the Watchers "are guilty of breaching the cosmos, crossing into the realm of physical contact with humanity, having sexual relations with human females, and producing offspring of their own (6:1–2). This act defiled the angels' own heavenly nature. Following this deed, the author portrays the effect of this relationship on the Watchers, humanity, and the rest of creation."[88] In the course of presenting this account, the writer repurposes the biblical Flood story, "interpret[ing] the events of Genesis as a prototype of eschatological violence, judgment, and restoration in which evil that originated in demonic rebellion would find its cure in divine intervention."[89]

---

88. Wright, "Introduction to the Book of Watchers," in *Early Jewish Literature: An Anthology*, vol. 2, 191.

89. Nickelsburg, "Enoch, First Book of," *The Anchor Yale Bible Dictionary*, 510. On the use of the Flood story, see J. H. Le Roux, "The Use of Scripture in 1 Enoch 6–11," *Neotestamentica* 17 (1983) [Studies in 1 Enoch and the New Testament. Ed. P.G.R. de Villiers]. 28–37.

Many scholars of 1 Enoch believe that the book itself conflates two distinct traditions about this uprising. The two traditions can be discerned by noting that there are two leaders of the transgression (and hence two rebellion stories) within the book. Wright explains:

> Scholars have argued that at least two distinct versions of the events are depicted in chapters 6–16: the Shemiazaz[90] and Asa'el[91] (instruction) traditions. Each of these strands of tradition assigns some of the blame for the coming judgment of the cosmos to the angels. The Shemiazaz strand details how two hundred Watchers take women to sire offspring who appear as giants at their birth. The consequence of this endeavor is the flood depicted in Genesis 6–9. The second Watcher strand begins in chapter 8 and describes the instruction motif in which the angels, led by Asa'el, taught humanity how to construct tools of war and metalworking, the art of making jewelry, and the adorning of women with cosmetics. Each of the two hundred angels is identified with a specific form of instruction such as giving signs of the earth or the

---

90. Readers will also find this name spelled Semihazah or Semiḥazah (see commentary at 6:3, 7). Presenting and evaluating the assertion that 1 Enoch conflates two rebellion traditions is beyond the scope of a reader's commentary. Those interested in serious academic treatments of the subject are invited to read the following: Nickelsburge, *1 Enoch*, vol. 1, 191–193; C. Molenberg, "A Study of the Roles of Shemihaza and Asael in Enoch 6–11," *Journal of Jewish Studies* 35 (1984):136–146; R. T. Helm, "The Development of the Azazel Tradition," PhD Dissertation, Southern Baptist Theological Seminary, 1992; A. H. Jones, III, "Enoch and the Fall of the Watchers: 1 Enoch 1–36," PhD Dissertation, Vanderbilt, 1989; Carol A. Newsom, "The Development of I Enoch 6–11: Cosmology and Judgment," *Catholic Biblical Quarterly* 42 (1980): 310–329.

91. Also spelled Azazel by some scholars.

art of astrology. The improper use of this knowledge by humans resulted in their own corruption and contributed, in part, to the punishment of the Watchers.[92]

Translation: Chapter 6

6[1] And it came to pass when the children of men had multiplied that in those days were born unto them beautiful and comely daughters. [2] And the angels, the children of the heaven, saw and lusted after them, and said to one another: "Come, let us choose us wives from among the children of men and beget us children." [3] And Semjâzâ, who was their leader, said unto them: "I fear ye will not indeed agree to do this deed, and I alone shall have to pay the penalty of a great sin." [4] And they all answered him and said: "Let us all swear an oath, and all bind ourselves by mutual imprecations not to abandon this plan but to do this thing." [5] Then sware they all together and bound themselves by mutual imprecations upon it. [6] And they were in all two hundred; who descended ‹in the days› of **Jared** on the summit of Mount Hermon, and they called it Mount Hermon, because they had sworn and bound themselves by mutual imprecations upon it. [7] And these are the names of their leaders: Samîazâz, their leader, Arâkîba, Râmêêl, Kôkabîêl, Tâmîêl, Râmîêl, Dânêl, Êzêqêêl, Barâqîjal, Asâêl, Armârôs, Batârêl, Anânêl, Zaqîêl, Samsâpêêl, Satarêl, Tûrêl, Jômjâêl, Sariêl. [8] These are their chiefs of tens.

Commentary

6:1

beautiful and comely—Black observes: "The two terms are synonymous, but the repetition is not tautologous; the expression means 'very or surpassingly beautiful.'"[93] This is an embellishment of the Genesis 6 description.

---

92. Archie T. Wright, "Introduction to the Book of Watchers," in *Early Jewish Literature: An Anthology*, vol. 2, 191–192.

93. Black, *The Book of Enoch or 1 Enoch*, 116.

6:2

the angels, the children of the heaven—Other translations (N, B) read "the watchers" in place of "the angels" (see notes under 1:2). In this instance, Charles' "the angels" has the support of Eth and G^a, while "the watchers" is supported by G^s and Syriac material. The verse obviously follows Genesis 6:1 very closely. Nickelsburg comments:

> For "sons of God" (Gen 6:2) 1 Enoch 6:2a reads "sons of heaven" (cf. also 13:8; 14:3), a typical circumlocution. Cf. 1QS 4:22; 11:7–8; 1QH 11(3):22 and frg. 2:10. To this title is prefaced "the watchers" (so also 14:3).... Here and elsewhere in these chapters (cf. 10:7, 15), the additional substantive "and holy one(s)" is dropped with reference to the rebel watchers (cf. also 12:4; 13:10; 14:1, 3; 16:2, but note 15:4 and 15:9). Whatever may have been the later Jewish and Christian interpretations of "sons of God" in Genesis 6, here, and most explicitly in chaps. 12–16, they are identified as heavenly beings.[94]
>
> The most significant addition to Gen 6:2 in 1 Enoch 6:2a is the clause "and they desired them." The verb [*epithymein*] seems to have the pejorative meaning "to lust after." Since this desire and its fulfillment are outlawed, as the context will indicate, the use of this verb introduces the motif of sin.[95]

---

94. In his commentary on the Pseudepigrapha, Charles gives a short list of other texts that "harmonize" with Enoch's take on Genesis 6:1–4: cf. Jub. 4:15, 5:1 seqq.; Test. Reub. 5:6, 7, Test. Naph. 3:5, 2 En. 7, 18, Jude 6, 2 Pet. 2:4; Joseph; Ant. 1. 3. 1; Philo, *de Gigantibus*; Justin Martyr, *Apol.* 1. 5; Ps. Clement, *Hom.* 8. 13; Clem. Alex. *Strom.* 5. 1. 10; Tert. *de Virg. Veland.* 7; *Adv. Marcion.* 5. 18; *De Idol.* 9; Lact. *Instit.* 2. 15; Commodian, *Instruct.* 1. 3. In the *De Civ. Dei* 15. 23.
95. Nickelsburg, *1 Enoch*, 175–176.

6:3

Semjâzâ—Other spellings in translations are: *Shemihazah* (N), *Semyaz* (CW), and *Semhazah* (B). See verse 7 for explanation.

their chief—The descriptive title is supported by Eth, G^s. It is omitted by G^a. Nickelsburg observes: "Here and in 6:7; 8:3; 9:7; 10:11; and 4QGiants^a 8:5, Shemihazah is depicted as the chieftain of the watchers."[96]

a great sin—It is obvious from this wording that not only their leader, but the entire band of Watchers, knows that what they decide to do is sin.

6:5

upon it—Scholars are agreed that this refers to Mount Hermon (i.e., "upon the mountain"), but also that it is a scribal error (dittography: a mistaken replication) from the last line of verse 6 (the mountain is only mentioned in verse 6, not here in verse 5). G^a and Eth preserve the errors.

6:6

descended—This word in combination with the following "Jared" led some early (pre-Qumran) scholars to the impression that 1 Enoch had originally been composed in Hebrew. The reason is that "Jared" has the Hebrew consonants *y-r-d*, the same ones in the verb "to descend, go down" (*yarad*), whereas the verb "to descend" in Aramaic (the oldest texts of 1 Enoch known) is entirely different (*n-ḥ-t*). In other words, the word-play only works in Hebrew (for a possibly similar situation, see "Hermon" below). The consensus of more recent scholarship, however, is opposed to

---

96. Ibid., 175.

positing a Hebrew original, judging it more coherent to have an Aramaic original that occasionally borrowed Hebrew words for specific reasons of wordplay (as in the present instance). In any event, there is no extant ancient Hebrew material for 1 Enoch.

‹in the days› of Jared—Jubilees 4:15 has the same chronological note. Some comments on the chronology of 1 Enoch are in order. Esler's study on the defeat of evil in the Book of the Watchers pays close attention to such matters. He writes:

> To appreciate the nature of evil in the Book of the Watchers in a manner that is sensitive to the structure of the work, it is useful to draw a distinction between "dramatic time" and "narrative time." Here "dramatic time" refers to the time during which the plot of the work, involving the secession of the Watchers from heaven and the description of Enoch's activities, takes place. "Narrative time," on the other hand, means the (much larger) sweep of time that embraces all of the events referred to in the drama of the Watchers and Enoch, which actually extend from the creation to the period of the final judgment (and beyond)....
>
> It should be noted that the text does not always describe events in strictly chronological order, thus the Watchers descend to earth in 1 Enoch 6 (loosely based on Gen 6:1–4), whereas it is not until 1 Enoch 12 that we hear that "before these things" Enoch was taken (i.e. to heaven) which relates to the earlier period of Gen 5:24). This is one of several signs in the text that the author well understands the broad chronological course of universal and Israelite history, even though he is capable of jumping from one time to another. A second indication of this comes later in the text, in 1 Enoch 26, where the angel accompanying him shows Enoch the site of Jerusalem long before a city had been dwelt there, as

was appropriate, given Enoch's position in the remote past as the seventh patriarch.[97]

Esler adds a specific comment about "the days of Jared" later in a note:

Note that analysis of the genealogies in Genesis 5 and the further dates given in Gen 9:28–29 shows that Noah was some 370 years old when Jared, his great, great grandfather, died. About 130 years later Noah began to have his sons (Shem, Ham, and Japhet) and the flood occurred some 200 years after Jared's death. Bringing the material in 1 Enoch together with the dates in Genesis means that the events of Gen 6:1–4 must, in the mind of the Enochic author, have begun at least a hundred years before the birth of Noah's first son (to have occurred in the days of Jared).[98]

Mount Hermon—The identity of the mountain is secure, as "Hermon" is witnessed in "4QEn[a] in the first six words, which are corrupt in E[thiopic]."[99] Some see a Hebrew wordplay in this name, arguing that "Hermon" is based on the Hebrew root *ḥ-r-m*, and the same consonants comprise the verb meaning "devote to destruction."[100] The idea would be irony—that

---

97. Philip F. Esler, "Deus Victor: The Nature and Defeat of Evil in the Book of the Watchers (1 Enoch 1-36)," in *The Blessing of Enoch: 1 Enoch and Contemporary Theology* (ed. Philip F. Esler; Eugene, OR: Wipf & Stock, 2017), 166–190 (esp. p. 4).

98. Ibid., 6, note 13.

99. Nickelsburg, *1 Enoch*, vol. 1, 174, note c in verse 6.

100. See the notes on the name *ḥermānî* in the list of Watchers' names at 1 Enoch 6:7.

the Watchers who descend to the mountain would ultimately be "devoted to destruction" by God in judgment. Other scholars think it more likely to consider the noun to be wordplay in Aramaic, as the verb *ḥ-r-m* in Aramaic in the causative *Afel* stem means "to swear an oath," which is clearly part of the context. If the author knew Hebrew (and apparently he knew it well enough to bring in Hebrew terms when useful), perhaps both wordplay scenarios are in view.[101]

6:7

their leaders—The account of the rebellion of the two hundred Watchers (verse 6) ends with a list of its ringleaders (under the higher authority or influence of Shemihazah, "their leader"). There are twenty "heads of tens" (for the two hundred total) in all—though the Charles translation actually only lists nineteen (see below on the twentieth name). The present list appears again in 69:1–3, where it is followed in 69:4–13 by another list that corresponds to 1 Enoch 8, where the knowledge domain of certain heavenly beings is noted.[102] This other list, manuscript spelling differences for the names, and textual errors in some manuscripts account for the

---

101. For research on Mount Hermon, see Dennis Baly, "To the God Who Is in Dan," in *Temples and High Places in Biblical Times* (ed. Avraham Biran; Jerusalem: Hebrew Union College–Jewish Institute of Religion, 1981) 142–51; Edward Lipiński, "El's Abode: Mythological Traditions Related to Mount Hermon and to the Mountains of Armenia," *Orientalia Lovaniensia Periodica* 2 (1971) 13–69; Vassilias Tzaferis, "The 'God Who Is in Dan' and the Cult of Pan at Banias in the Hellenistic and Roman Periods," *Eretz Israel* 23 (1992) 128–35.

102. Nickelsburg, *1 Enoch*, vol. 1, 178. The names in CW for chapter 8 have several differences. Hence the correlations noted here will at times not align with that version of 1 Enoch.

variety of English transliteration for the names the reader will encounter in various translations and studies of 1 Enoch.[103]

Black, Nickelsburg, and Knibb offer detailed analyses of the name spellings, the nature of their morphology (grammatical elements) in all the witnessed languages, their possible etymologies, and their consequent meanings.[104] Those with some facility in Hebrew, Greek, and Aramaic will find his discussions of interest.

As we begin examining the names, Nickelsburg's initial observations are worth consideration:

> Of the nineteen names that are preserved or can be reconstructed with some certainty, sixteen are compounds with אֵל ('ēl, "God"): nos. 3, 4, 6, 7, 8, 9, 10, 12, 13, 14, 15, 16, 17, 18, 19, 20. The three remaining names (1, 2, 11) can perhaps be explained in the context of the story, as the others can be.
>
> Of the sixteen compounds with אֵל, two indicate functions of God: judge and creator (7, 10). Thirteen of the remaining fourteen 'ēl compounds are linked in their first element with astronomical, meteorological, and geographical phenomena. The names are of obvious relevance in the Enochic tradition with its interest in cosmology and astronomy and its frequent association of the elements and the angels in charge of them.[105]

---

103. See the table of transliterations in Black, *The Book of Enoch or 1 Enoch*, 118–119. Black goes into detailed philological and morphological analysis of the various spellings in the manuscripts on pages 119–123. Those with some facility in Hebrew, Greek, and Aramaic will find his discussions of interest.

104. See Black, *The Book of Enoch or 1 Enoch*, 119-123; Nickelsburg, 1 Enoch, vol. 1, 178–181; Michael A. Knibb, *The Ethiopic Book of Enoch: A New Edition in the Light of the Aramaic Dead Sea Fragments* (2 vols.; Oxford: Clarendon, 1978).

105. Nickelsburg, *1 Enoch*, vol. 1, 178.

One example of how morphology affects meaning with respect to the names is illustrated from Knibb's work (cited by Nickelsburg). The name לאישמש (*sh-m-sh-y-'- l*) is ostensibly composed of two nouns: *sh-m-sh* ("sun") and *'el* ("God"). The *y* between the two is an issue. The *y* (reading the Hebrew characters right to left) may be a first-person suffixed pronoun ("my"), in which case the name would mean "God is my sun." However, the *y* may be an example of the Hebrew morphological phenomenon called the *yod compaginis*, an archaic case-ending consonant that denoted a genitival relationship (i.e., that binds the first noun to the second in an "X of Y" relationship).[106] If this is the correct understanding, the name would mean "sun of God."

What follows here is a simplified approach for English readers. The names of the rebellious Watchers are numbered sequentially.[107]

1. *Samîazâz*—E. Isaac reads *šemîḥăzāh*, which is best understood as "my name has seen." Charlesworth has *Semyaz*, which is an abbreviated form of the same name.[108] The phrase "my name" refers to God (hence, "my God"). This hearkens back to Old Testament Name theology, where

---

106. See Friedrich Wilhelm Gesenius, *Gesenius' Hebrew Grammar* (Edited by E. Kautzsch and Sir Arthur Ernest Cowley; 2nd English ed. Oxford: Clarendon Press, 1910), 252 (par. 90k). Gesenius writes: "There is nothing impossible in the view formerly taken here that the *litterae compaginis*ʾ and ר are obsolete (and hence no longer understood) case-endings."

107. Nickelsburg's notes referenced in this section of the commentary are from Nickelsburg, *1 Enoch*, vol. 1, 179–181. The order of the names varies in the Greek and Ethiopic material. See Knibb, *The Ethiopic Book of Enoch*, 70, for comparative sequencing.

108. Isaac is the translator of 1 Enoch in Charlesworth's *Old Testament Pseudepigrapha* edition of 1 Enoch. For Isaac's transliterations of the names, see Ephraim Isaac, "1 (Ethiopic Apocalypse of) Enoch," in *Old Testament Pseudepigrapha*, vol. 1, 15.

"the Name" is another way of referring to God.[109] Nickelsburg observes, "The angelic name may be an ironic anticipation of the motif of God's seeing the sins committed on earth (9:1, 5, 11), a motif picked up from Gen 6:5, 12. In the very name that the angelic chieftain bears is the recognition that his sin will be found out."[110]

2. *Arâkîba*—Isaac again has an abbreviated form (*Arakeb*). This transliteration by Charles should be corrected to 'Ar'tĕqoph (following G[s] and 1 Enoch 69:2). Milik translated this name as "the earth is power."[111] If this is the case, the idea being communicated is far from clear. For that reason, on the basis of other contextual meanings of Aramaic *tĕqoph*, Nickelsburg proposes "earth is a stronghold" and notes, "This would offer an interesting foil to the previous name: Heaven may see what we do, but Earth will provide a defensible fortress against Heaven's wrath." The meaning "earth is a stronghold" may be supported by 1 Enoch 8:3, where this particular Watcher teaches "signs of the earth," perhaps suggesting that this Watcher has expertise in "earth functions" that might be used in opposition to God.

3. *Râmêêl*—This reading is considered a corruption, even by Charles. Two other spellings have been proposed based on possible readings of the Aramaic material (one of the consonants is not clear): *Ramṭ'el* and *Remaš'ēl*. The former may mean "burning ashes of God," a possible reference to volcanic activity caused by cataclysmic upheavals. The latter

---

109. See Heiser, *The Unseen Realm*, 141–148. Some scholars, including some evangelicals, are reticent about the name theology of the Old Testament. For a recent defense of the idea (and rebuttal of recent criticisms), see Michael B. Hundley, "To Be or Not to Be: A Reexamination of Name Language in Deuteronomy and the Deuteronomistic History," *Vetus Testamentum* 59 (2009): 533–55.

110. Nickelsburg, *1 Enoch*, vol. 1, 179.

111. Milik, *The Books of Enoch*, 155.

would be rendered "evening of God,"[112] but as Knibb notes, this transliteration "is reflected in none of the versions."[113] The former seems more
consistent with the theme of cosmic upheaval caused by the transgression
of the Watchers.

4. *Kôkabîêl*—Also spelled *kôkab'êl*. This name is straightforward: "star
of God." In 1 Enoch 8:3, this Watcher had knowledge of the constellations. Isaac omits this name in his CW translation.

5. *Tâmîêl*—The name means "perfection of God," but scholars writing after Charles admit this name is the most difficult, as this spelling is
not present in several manuscripts. Charles is following one Greek manuscript (apparently G^a), but G^s and Ethiopic material (including the name's
occurrence in 1 Enoch 69:2) are quite different. Black reconstructs the
name as *'Ur'el* ("light of God"), but admits it's nothing more than speculation and may seem contradictory to the Uriel of later chapters.[114] Other
conjectures, trying to discern the readings found in manuscripts, include
(*'orām'ēl*, "God is their light") and (*'armmāh 'ēl*, "God is prudence").[115]
None of these options is certain.

6. *Râmîêl*—An alternate spelling is very close: *ra'm'ēl*. The latter
option means "thunder of God," which is likely correct, since its counterpart ("lightning of God") will appear in the ninth name.

7. *Dânêl*—The name cannot mean (see the note on morphology
above) "judge of God," for that would be blasphemous. Rather, "God is
my judge" is correct. This name is very close to biblical Daniel (*dāniyy'el*)
and is an exact match for the wise *Dan'el* of Ugaritic literature. Many
scholars believe Ugaritic *Dan'el* is referred to in Ezekiel 14:14, 20 and
28:3. To muddle things even more, Jubilees 4:20 has Enoch marrying
the daughter of *Dan'el*. Whether this figure from Ugaritic literature is the
referent of these biblical verses (his character is nowhere near as pristine as

112. Black, *The Book of Enoch or 1 Enoch*, 119.

113. Knibb, *The Ethiopic Book of Enoch*, vol. 2, 72.

114. Ibid., 120.

115. Nickelsburg, *1 Enoch*, vol. 1, 180.

the biblical Daniel) or the Enoch tradition in Jubilees actually has Ugaritic Dan'el in Enoch's family is far from clear or coherent. As one scholar notes, "There may well be a kind of relationship between some of these figures, but none of these other texts throws direct light on our exilic hero [the biblical Daniel]."[116]

8. *Êzêqêêl*—Black and Nickelsburg both read *zîq 'ēl* ("shooting star of God").[117] Charles is again translating from a minority manuscript. It is unclear how his expertise ("the knowledge of the clouds") in 1 Enoch 8:3 is consistent with his name. However, if "shooting star" refers to lightning flashes or meteors, there may be some correlation (but see the next name).

9. *Barâqîjal*—Nickelsburg and Black spell the name *baraq 'el*. The meaning is the same no matter the spelling: "lightning of God." As noted earlier, this name is the bookend pair to name number six (*ra 'm 'ēl*). This Watcher's function is mastery of astrology (1 Enoch 8:3). Interestingly, Nickelsburg points out that, "according to 6Q8 1, a manuscript of the Book of Giants, *Baraq'el* is the father of the giant Mahawai."[118] The reference here is to column 1 of this Dead Sea Scroll. The actual relevant citation is 6Q8, column 1, line 4.[119] In his critical edition of the Book of Giants, Stuckenbruck summarizes the content of the discussion between the two giants, Ohyah and Mahaway, in this text:

---

116. Philip R. Davies, *Daniel* (*Old Testament Guides;* Sheffield: Society for Old Testament Study and Sheffield Academic Press, 1998), 41. On this subject, see John Day, "The Daniel of Ugarit and Ezekiel and the Hero of the Book of Daniel," *Vetus Testamentum* 30:2 (1980): 174–184; Harold P. Dressler, "The Identification of the Ugaritic Dnil with the Daniel of Ezekiel," *Vetus Testamentum* 29.2 (1979): 152–161.

117. Nickelsburg, *1 Enoch*, vol. 1, 180; Black, *The Book of Enoch or 1 Enoch*, 120.

118. Nickelsburg, *1 Enoch*, vol. 1, 180.

119. The *Book of Giants* material also clears up other textual oddities. Stuckenbruck writes: "Unless there has been an orthographic error, it is mistaken to read לאקרב as "Baraki'el" and thus to take this name as a reference to the father of Bitenos (*Jub.* 4:28). The Aramaic materials from

The conversation between 'Ohyah and Mahaway may be reconstructed on the basis of 6Q8 1 as follows: After Mahaway has delivered a message (a dream vision or dream interpretation?) to 'Ohyah (or before all the giants?), 'Ohyah responds by declaring rhetorically that the message leaves them no choice but to be afraid (l.3). 'Ohyah then challenges the authority of what Mahaway has said (l.3). In response, Mahaway appeals to the fact that his father Baraq'el was with him at the time (l.4). The text on l.5 takes the perspective of a narrator and assumes that Mahaway continues to communicate his message. 'Ohyah interrupts Mahaway (l.6) and expresses his own incredulity through a rhetorical question whose logic runs as follows: *If X were possible (but it is not!), then I would believe what you are saying (which I will not!).*[120]

10. *Asâêl*—Black and Nickelsburg transliterate this as *'āśa'ēl*. Again, the meaning is clear: "God has made." The name is found in the Hebrew Bible (2 Samuel 2:18–32; 3:27–30; 23:24; 2 Chronicles 17:8; 31:13; and Ezra 10:15; this last instance has full spelling of the final *heh* of the first element, which usually drops out). In 1 Enoch 8, Asa'el will be cast (in the view of many scholars) as the arch leader of the Watchers in place of Shemihazah. This seems to be the case in 1 Enoch after chapter 8, as it is Asa'el who is the first Watcher bound in 1 Enoch 10:4 and 13:1, but that is an inference, not an explicit detail of the text. Due to the close

---

Qumran are consistent in spelling the name of the ninth fallen angel as לאקרב (cf. l.4 with 4QEnoch*a* to *1 En.* 6:7 and 4QEnGiants*a* 1 l.2), while only in the Greek recension of Codex Panopolitanus is the name of this Watcher first attested with the pronunciation Βαρακιήλ (to *1 En.* 6:7)." See Loren T. Stuckenbruck, *The Book of Giants from Qumran: Texts, Translation, and Commentary* (ed. Martin Hengel and Peter Schäfer; vol. 63; Texte und Studien zum Antiken Judentum; Tübingen: Mohr Siebeck, 1997), 198.

120. Stuckenbruck, *The Book of Giants from Qumran*, 199.

resemblance of this name to Azazel, some manuscripts (and one followed by Charles in the present translation) read Azazel in place of Asa'el in 1 Enoch 8:1, 3. See that verse in the ensuing commentary.

11. *Armârôs*—Isaac and Knibb prefer this name, but once again, the names are widely variable in the manuscript data. Charles follows Ethiopic material here, but the Greek texts read *Pharmaros* (G^s) and *Arearôs* (G^g). Nevertheless, Black and Nickelsburg read *Hermānî* here, following the reconstruction of Sokoloff's study of the Aramaic Enoch fragments.[121] The name *Hermānî* means "the one of Hermon." Black's comments are of interest:

> The usual explanation that the angel derives his name from the mountain may not be the correct one, and the opposite might be true. חרמן (Hermon) occurs as a proper name at Elephantine (Cowley, *Aramaic Papyri*, 22.4) where the theophoric[122] element is the name of a subordinate deity of the Elephantine pantheon.... Hermon is the name of "the god of imprecations"...who punishes oath-breakers with his destroying curse. Mount Hermon could have been named after the deity, perhaps as a place with a cultic sanctuary where oaths were taken; it may also have been associated with practices related to ban-execration such as "spell-binding" or the practice of the black arts generally.... [In 1 Enoch 8:3] *Hermānî* (or *Armârôs* in Charles) taught wizardry, the loosing of spells, sorcery, and the art of divination.[123]

---

121. Michael Sokoloff, "Notes on the Aramaic Fragments of Enoch from Qumran Cave 4," *Maarav* 1 (1978–79) 197–224 (esp. p. 207).

122. This term means "divine" (a theophoric name is a name comprised in part of a deity name).

123. Black, *The Book of Enoch or 1 Enoch*, 122. See Lipinski's study referenced earlier.

The Elephantine papyri (Aramaic and Greek material) date to the fifth century BC and were first published in 1906. Elephantine is a site located in Upper Egypt, an island in the Nile opposite Aswan (ancient Syene).[124] As Weinstein summarizes:

> There was a late sixth and fifth-century B. C. military colony in the service of the Persians. The Elephantine Papyri, several groups of Aramaic documents found on the island, show that this colony included many Jews, who had their own temple to God, were permitted to celebrate the Passover festival, and lived both on the island and in Syene.[125]

The point of a Watcher bearing this name would again be irony, reveals the secondhand ("after the fact") nature of at least some of the names. For sure, this mountain had a long association with Sumerian-Mesopotamian deities,[126] but having a Watcher named for a place later associated with an Elephantine deity associated with spell-binding and oath-taking shows the content of 1 Enoch is considerably later than the historical time of Enoch, according to the biblical account.

12. Batârêl—Balck and Nickelsburg have *māṭār'ēl* ("rain of God"). The difference involves a scribe's confusion of Hebrew ב and מ, which is not uncommon, given the state of scribal handwriting. Since this name is followed by two that denote meteorological elements, *māṭār'ēl* ("rain of God") is likely correct. The point of the name is an ironic connection between the operation of the earth's natural processes and the upheaval brought on by cosmic rebellion.

---

124. Bezalel Porten, "Elephantine Papyri," *The Anchor Yale Bible Dictionary* (ed. David Noel Freedman; New York: Doubleday, 1992), 445.

125. J. M. Weinstein, "Elephantine," *Harper's Bible Dictionary* (ed. Paul J. Achtemeier; San Francisco: Harper & Row, 1985), 1003.

126. See Lipiński's work cited earlier: "El's Abode: Mythological Traditions Related to Mount Hermon and to the Mountains of Armenia."

13. *Anânêl*—This name has wide agreement (alternate spelling: *'Anan'el*) in the manuscript material and means "cloud of God." Both *'Anan'el* and *'Anî* are deity names in the Elephantine papyri.

14. *Zaqîêl*—Nearly every consonant of this name in the Aramaic material is in doubt (uncertain reading). This transliteration used by Charles is witnessed in some Ethiopic material. As Black's table of transliterations shows (p. 119), this is but one of four spellings known from other Ethiopic and Greek manuscripts. The textual data followed by more recent scholars has this as the eighth name (see above) and in place of *Zaqîêl* read *sĕtāw'ēl* (N) or *Sithwa'el* (B), both of which mean "winter of God." Neither of these conforms precisely to the existing manuscript spellings; they are theorized reconstructions that try to account for the diversity of those spellings.

15. *Samsâpêêl*—Charles himself correctly notes that this name is misspelled: "Gˢ in 8:3 assigns to the 7th [corresponding to this name in 6:7] *ta se'meia tou he'liou* ["the signs of the sun"]. So the name should be *Shamshiel* ("sun of God")."[127] Isaac has the lengthier *Sasomaspeᵂe'el*.

16. *Satarêl*—Black (*Sahre'el*) and Nickelsburg (*śahrî'ēl*) are essentially the same and are to be preferred, as their versions mean "moon of God," which is aptly juxtaposed to the preceding "sun of God." Knibb maintains that *Sahre'el* "is not quite certain" and suggests *Saḥre'el* (the *h* consonants in the two versions differ in Hebrew, *heh* vs. *ḥet*), which translates to "dawn of God."[128]

17. *Tûrêl*—Black notes that this name is unique in that all the manuscript material of all languages presents the same transliteration.[129] Neverthless, there is a sequencing issue. Knibb notes that the Ethiopic material "omits the seventeenth name, while the other versions offer three different

---

127. Charles, *Commentary on the Pseudepigrapha of the Old Testament*, vol. 2, 191. Recall that *sh-m-sh* = "sun" in Hebrew.

128. Knibb, *The Ethiopic Book of Enoch*, vol. 2, 74.

129. Black, *The Book of Enoch or 1 Enoch*, 122.

names."[130] *Tûrêl* therefore becomes the eighteenth name in Ethiopic and is so listed by Knibb. Nickelsburg also has *Tûrêl* (*tûrî'ēl*) in the eighteenth slot and fills in the missing seventeenth position with (*tummî'ēl*, "perfection of God"), which he speculates might refer to the original creation.[131] *Tûrêl* or *tûrî'ēl* mean "mountain of God."

18. *Jômjâêl*—Nickelsburg transliterates this name as "*yamî'ēl* or *yōmî'ēl*, 'sea of God' or 'day of God,'" depending on the vocalization.[132] Black is also undecided, while Knibb favors "day of God."[133]

19. *Sariêl*—This is the final name in Charles' translation, falling short of the needed twenty Watchers who each have authority over ten others for the required two hundred total. It is based on a Greek reading that is close to those favored by Knibb. The omission must be due in part to the sequential problem noted above where Ethiopic omits a name. Isaac has *Arazyal*. Knibb argues for either *Zaharî'el* or *Saharî'el*, both of which could mean either "light of God" or "moon of God."[134] First Enoch 8:3 assigns to this angel "signs of the moon(light)."

20. As noted earlier, Charles has no twentieth name. Nickelsburg has *yĕhaddî'ēl* ("God will guide") in this position.[135] Nickelsburg ends the list with some interesting observations:

> Two overall patterns are noteworthy among the angelic names. First, according to the interpretation above, several names emphasize God's judicial activity. The conspiracy is carried out in spite

---

130. Knibb, *The Ethiopic Book of Enoch*, vol. 2, 74.

131. Nickelsburg, *1 Enoch*, vol. 1, 181.

132. Ibid., 181.

133. Black, *The Book of Enoch or 1 Enoch*, 122; Knibb, *The Ethiopic Book of Enoch*, vol. 2, 74.

134. Knibb, *The Ethiopic Book of Enoch*, vol. 2, 75.

135. Nickelsburg, *1 Enoch*, vol. 1, 181.

of the awareness that God judges those who oppose him. It is an act of deliberate rebellion carried out with full knowledge of the consequences (cf. 6:2–4).

Second, the names help to identify the conspirators and give some sense of the authority and the scope of the conspiracy. The names suggest that the chiefs are high angels in charge of the orderly functioning of the heavenly and earthly phenomena: in heaven, not Uriel to be sure, but the angels over sun, moon, stars, shooting stars, thunder, and lightning; on earth, the angels in charge of sea and mountains, as well as the crucial rainy season and its clouds and rain. At the same time, the list lacks names associated with many other cosmic, meteorological, and geographic phenomena, and the total of two hundred angels is a small part of the thousands that a text such as 82:4–20 associates with the stars alone.

…The division of the two hundred watchers into groups of ten reflects Israelite practice from early biblical times to the Second Temple period…. Whether there are any military connotations in the arrangement here is uncertain, although the lack of reference to fifties and hundreds is noteworthy.[136]

Translation: Chapter 7

7[1]And all the others together with them took unto themselves wives, and each chose for himself one, and they began to go in unto them and to **defile** themselves with them, and they taught them charms and enchantments, and the cutting of roots, and made them acquainted with plants. [2]And they became pregnant, and they bare great giants, whose height was three thousand ells: [3]Who consumed all the acquisitions of men. [4]And when men could no longer sustain them, the giants turned against them

---

136. Ibid., 181.

and devoured mankind. ⁵And they began to sin against birds, and beasts, and reptiles, and fish, and to devour one another's flesh, and drink the blood. ⁶Then the earth laid accusation against the lawless ones.

Commentary

7:1

to go into—This is a normative biblical expression for sexual intercourse (e.g., Genesis 16:4; 30:4, 16; 38:2, 9). A later passage in Testament of Reuben 5:6–7 denies that there was actual intercourse between the Watchers and human women in an effort to explain the product being giants:

> ⁵Accordingly, my children, flee from sexual promiscuity, and order your wives and your daughters not to adorn their heads and their appearances so as to deceive men's sound minds. For every woman who schemes in these ways is destined for eternal punishment. ⁶For it was thus that they charmed the Watchers, who were before the Flood. As they continued looking at the women, they were filled with desire for them and perpetrated the act in their minds. Then they were transformed into human males, and while the women were cohabiting with their husbands they appeared to them. Since the women's minds were filled with lust for these apparitions, they gave birth to giants. For the Watchers were disclosed to them as being as high as the heavens.[137]

to defile themselves—Ethiopic material reads "to be promiscuous."[138] The defilement idea means that the Watchers became unclean by virtue of their actions. Nickelsburg writes:

---

137. Charlesworth, *The Old Testament Pseudepigrapha*, vol. 1 784.

138. Knibb, *The Ethiopic Book of Enoch*, vol. 2, 77.

Here and in 9:8, different from 10:11, the uncleanness is due simply to sexual contact and not contact with women's blood. Cf. 12:4 and 15:3 over against 15:4. While the author here does not spell out the implications of angelic defilement, as this is done in chap. 15, the inappropriateness of this state for the watchers is obvious and the motif underscores the sinful character of their deed.[139]

The notion of the Watchers' defilement operates behind the Second Temple Jewish belief about the origin of demons being the disembodied spirits of giants, the offspring of the Watchers (verse 2), a motif we will come to in 1 Enoch 9, 15.[140] Scholars such as Clinton Wahlen have established that the phrase "unclean spirits" used of demons in Second Temple Judaism and the New Testament originated in the perception that the transgression of the Watchers was an unnatural mixture (the contact of the spirits of dead giants with the corpses of their hosts was also a factor in determining this uncleanness). Wahlen writes:

> One of the more puzzling features of early Christian attitudes toward purity is the Gospels' frequent reference to spirits as impure. The absence of similar language in Graeco-Roman literature up through the second century C. E. is striking…. References to impure spirits in *4QIncantation* and to "unclean demons" in *Jubilees* are clearly based on the Watcher myth of *1 Enoch*, whereby evil spirits proceeded from dead bodies of the fallen giants, who were born as a result of the miscegenation of angels with women.

---

139. Nickelsburg, *1 Enoch*, vol. 1, 184.
140. See Archie T. Wright, *The Origin of Evil Spirits: The Reception of Genesis 6:1–4 in Early Jewish Literature* (Wissenschaftliche Untersuchungen zum Neuen Testament 198, second series; Tübingen: Mohr Siebeck, 2013).

These spirits are called unclean in analogy to the similar classifica-
tion of unclean animals: an unnatural combination of heavenly
and earthly beings, they represent an anomalous mixture of categories…. Evil spirits, in many Jewish sources, ultimately trace
their origins to the defiling union of these heavenly beings with
women. Like unclean animals, these "impure spirits" represent an
anomalous mixture of categories.[141]

*charms and enchantments, and the cutting of roots, and made them acquainted
with plants*—Charlesworth translates: "And they taught them magical
medicine, incantations, the cutting of roots, and taught them (about)
plants." The terms in Greek are *pharmakeia, epaoida, hrizotomias,* and
botanas. The first of these (*pharmakeia*) is found in Revelation 9:21. The
term can refer to drugs, poisons, magic potions, and medicines.[142] These
items could have varying levels of potency, from providing mild sedation
or a feeling of well-being to being mind-altering. Greek *epaoida* refers to a
charm potion created from plants.[143] *Hrizotomias* is a noun for "a cutter of
roots, herbalist, for purposes of medicine or witchcraft."[144] The final term,
botanas, is related to *botanē* (cf. botany) and refers to herbs or vegetation.[145]

141. Clinton Wahlen, *Jesus and the Impurity of Spirits in the Synoptic Gospels*
      (Wissenschaftliche Untersuchungen zum Neuen Testament 2. Reihe 185
      (Tübingen: Mohr Siebeck, 2004), 1, 66–67, 170.

142. William Arndt et al., *A Greek-English Lexicon of the New Testament and
      Other Early Christian Literature* (Chicago: University of Chicago Press,
      2000), 1050 (= *BDAG*); Henry George Liddell et al., *A Greek-English
      Lexicon* (Oxford: Clarendon Press, 1996), 1917.

143. Liddell-Scott, 610.

144. Liddell-Scott, 1570, cited in Black, *The Book of Enoch or 1 Enoch,* 125.

145. See *BDAG,* 181.

7:2

they bare great giants—On the basis of G^s, Nickelsburg expands this line: "And the giants begat Nephilim, and to the Nephilim were born Elioud. And they grew according to their greatness.'"[146] This in effect creates three generations of giants: the initial giants born to the Watchers and their wives, the Nephilim, and the Elioud. As Black notes, "this insertion is almost certainly a gloss" offered by Syncellus (G^s) to explain Genesis 6:2. If so, Syncellus is interpreting *gibborim* and *Nephilim* in Genesis 6:1–4 as two separate generations of giants. Elioud may, however, come from the Aramaic material (a Greek understanding of *yeludîn* ("were born to").[147] Consequently, Elioud would be a misreading on the part of Syncellus. Nickelsburg notes that "the parallel text in *Jub.* 7:22 reads *'ēlyo* in Ethiopic."[148] Interestingly, Charles observes that the words "and the giants begot the Naphilim and to the Naphilim were born the Eliud" have a corresponding passage in Jubilees: "*Jub.* 7:21–22 is based on this passage and enables us to correct 'begot' and 'were born' to 'slew.'"[149] This eliminates three distinct generations of giant offspring, but creates three subgroups (clans?) of the giants. Charles refers to them as "classes": "The three classes of giants go back to Gen. 6:4; cf., too, 1 En. 86:4, 88:2 and Jub. 7:21, 22 (Giants, Nâphîl, Eljô)."[150]

Whose height was three thousand ells—G^a and Ethiopic omit the extra generations inserted by Syncellus (above) and describe the giants' height in

---

146. Nickelsburg, *1 Enoch*, vol. 1, 182. The Eth. and the Giz. Gk. have lost this from the original. Jub. 7:21–22 is based on this passage and enables us to correct "begot" and "were born" to "slew."

147. Black, *The Book of Enoch or 1 Enoch*, 126.

148. Nickelsburg, *1 Enoch*, vol. 1, 185.

149. Charles, *Commentary on the Pseudepigrapha of the Old Testament*, vol. 2, 192.

150. Ibid., 192.

place of that material, respectively, as three thousand cubits (G^a) and three hundred cubits (Ethiopic). Syncellus omits the measurement. Charles' translation ("three thousand ells") follows G^a. The "ell" is a confusing unit of measurement to modern readers. It "was originally the same measure as a cubit, being derived from the *ulna*, a Latin name of a bone of the forearm."[151]

7:3

Who consumed all the acquisitions of men—See the next verse.

7:4

when men could no longer sustain them—On the basis of Ethiopic, Nickelsburg's translation adds this line ("and men were not able to supply them") to the end of verse 3, not here.[152]

devoured mankind—See verse 5.

7:5

This verse elaborates on the behavior of the giants. Nickelsburg writes:

> In Greek lore, too, giants are described as bellicose [see 10:9]....
> In the course of this exposition of Genesis 6, however, the author
> does make an important exegetical transformation. The giants are
> made the subject of the violence described in Gen 6:5–7, 11–12,
> and the human race and the animal world are its victims. More

151. *The Diagonal* (Yale University Press. 1920), 98. *The Diagonal* was an illustrated monthly magazine. Its issues are now in public domain.

152. Nickelsburg, *1 Enoch*, vol. 1, 182. See also Knibb, *The Ethiopic Book of Enoch*, vol. 2, 78.

important, however, is the brutality and savagery that characterizes this vignette. In effect, the giants are wild beasts rather than demi-gods. Throughout these verses, they are the subjects of a series of verbs denoting their lawless and unrestrained gluttony, as they seek to satisfy their ravenous and insatiable appetites. They are no mere warriors, plundering crops (cf. 103:11 for the idiom) and slaughtering, as armies are wont to do. They slaughter human beings in order to devour them in the place of the food they do not supply. Then they turn on the animal world, which was forbidden as food in the pre-diluvian world (Gen 1:29–30; 9:2–3). To the catalog of animals in Gen 6:7 are added the fish. The *whole* animal kingdom (cf. Gen 1:26) is the object of their violence. Then, as a logical and inevitable conclusion, they begin to cannibalize one another. As a climax to the description, the author adds "and they drank the blood"—in the eyes of a Jew, the ultimate abomination and violation of created life (Gen 9:5–6; cf. the exegetical expansion in *Jub.* 7:27–34 and 21:18–20; cf. also 1 Enoch 98:1.[153]

7:6

the lawless ones—The Greek lemma is *anomos* and denotes general wickedness and immorality.[154] It is found in the New Testament in several places, including in a description of the eschatological Antichrist figure (2 Thessalonians 2:8).

---

153. Nickelsburg, *1 Enoch*, vol. 1, 186. For a study of this passage and others, see Matthew Goff and Maxine L. Grossman, "Monstrous Appetites: Giants, Cannibalism, and Insatiable Eating in Enochic Literature," *Journal of Ancient Judaism* 1.1 (2010): 19–42; Matthew Goff, "Warriors, Cannibals and Teachers of Evil: The Sons of the Angels in Genesis 6, the Book of the Watchers and the Book of Jubilees," *Svensk Exegetisk Årsbok* 80 (2015): 79–97.
154. See *BDAG*, 85.

Translation: Chapter 8

8[1]And Azâzêl taught men to make swords, and knives, and shields, and breastplates, and made known to them **the metals** ⟨of the earth⟩ and the art of working them, and bracelets, and ornaments, and the use of antimony, and the beautifying of the eyelids, and all kinds of costly stones, and all colouring tinctures. [2]And there arose much godlessness, and they committed fornication, and they were led astray, and became corrupt in all their ways. [3]Semjâzâ taught enchantments, and root-cuttings, 'Armârôs the resolving of enchantments, Barâqîjâl (taught) astrology, Kôkabêl the constellations, **Êzêqêêl the knowledge of the clouds,** ⟨Araqiêl the signs of the earth, Shamsiêl the signs of the sun⟩, and Sariêl the course of the moon. [4]And as men perished, they cried, and their cry went up to heaven.

Commentary

On the meanings of the names in this chapter, see comments on 1 Enoch 6.

8:1

Azâzêl—Charles' translation follows Ethiopic, which CW adopts as well. G[a] reads "Asael" (which is followed by N, B), and G[s] has "First Azael, the tenth of the archons."[155]

Some scholars, noting the similarity between the names Asael and Azazel, believed that the rebellion of the Watchers tradition in 1 Enoch is either a borrowing from or an interpretation of the presence of Azazel in Leviticus 16 and the Day of Atonement ritual. For example, Hanson's study argues that the author of 1 Enoch repurposed Leviticus 16 because he believed that the Day of Atonement ritual was about making atone-

---

155. Nickelsburg, *1 Enoch*, vol. 1, 188.

ment for the earth since it was defiled by the Watchers.[156] Nickelsburg (along with other scholars) does not believe Hanson (or anyone else) has sufficiently "demonstrated the influence of Leviticus 16 on the Enochic Asael material."[157]

Basically, very little material in 1 Enoch's description of this rebellion is securely drawn from Leviticus 16 other than the name. Given this situation, it is difficult to establish that the writer of 1 Enoch was repurposing Leviticus 16. For this reason, Knibb believes the name Azazel in some manuscripts "would appear to be a corruption of Asael."[158] This seems to be most coherent conclusion. Knibb argues that corruption in Ethiopic 1 Enoch 8:1 (Azazel) is indicated by several inconsistencies.[159] For example, Ethiopic of 1 Enoch 6:7 reads Asael, not Azazel. The same consistency (reading either Asael or Azazel) shows up when other passages have the same figure in view (1 Enoch 10:4, 8; 13:1; 69:2). If the Watcher rebellion story linked into Leviticus 16 in substantive ways, one could arguably conclude the name should be Azazel, but it does not.

Nickelsburg, in agreement with Baumgarten, believes at least 1 Enoch 6–11 was produced (at least in part) "on the basis of Semitic culture hero traditions that underlay both the Greek Prometheus myth and other traditions attested in Berossus, Philo of Byblos, and others."[160] He further elaborates:

---

156. See Paul D. Hanson, "Rebellion in Heaven, Azazel, and Euhemeristic Heroes in 1 Enoch 6–11," *Journal of Biblical Literature* 96.2 (1977): 195–233.

157. Nickelsburg, *1 Enoch*, vol. 1, 192. For his specific criticisms, see George W. E. Nickelsburg, "Apocalyptic and Myth in 1 Enoch 6–11," *Journal of Biblical Literature* 96 (1977) 383–405.

158. Knibb, *The Ethiopic Book of Enoch*, vol. 2, 79.

159. Ibid., 73, 79.

160. Nickelsburg, *1 Enoch*, vol. 1, 192. Nickelsburg cites Albert L. Baumgarten, *The Phoenician History of Philo of Byblos: A Commentary* (Études préliminaires aux religions orientales dans l'empire romain 89; Leiden: Brill, 1981), 156–157.

The Asael material has significant points of similarity to the Prometheus myth, especially to Aeschylus's version of it. Asael, a
heavenly being, rebels against God by teaching humankind about
metallurgy, mining, and the making of dyes—for all of which fire
is essential. For this act of rebellion, Asael is bound hand and foot,
the earth is opened, and he is cast on a rocky bed in the wilderness, where he is entombed until a later time of punishment.[161]

This trajectory is hardly new, but other scholars point out that the
tales of Prometheus and other Greek writers (e.g., Hesiod), whose works
include stories about gods and Titans in association with the Great Flood,
have themselves refashioned much earlier ancient Near Eastern material.[162]
That the writer of 1 Enoch may have bypassed Hesiod or Prometheus and
created his own intentional version of events before and after the Flood
has been shown by other scholars, who trace the details of 1 Enoch more
directly to Mesopotamian texts that deal with the *apkallu*.[163]

---

161. Nickelsburg, *1 Enoch*, vol. 1, 193.

162. Studies in this regard include: Stephanie West, "Prometheus Orientalized,"
      Museum helveticum 51.3 (1994): 129–149; M. L. West, "The Prometheus
      Trilogy," *The Journal of Hellenic Studies* 99 (1979): 130–148; Ian
      Rutherford, "Hesiod and the Literary Traditions of the Near East," in *Brill's
      Companion to Hesiod* (Ledien: E. J. Brill, 2009): 9–35; Jan N. Bremmer,
      "Near Eastern and Native Traditions in Apollodorus' Account of the Flood,"
      Greek Religion and Culture, the Bible and the Ancient Near East (Leiden: E. J.
      Brill, 2008), 101–116.

163. For example, see Heiser, *Reversing Hermon*, chapter 3; Amar Annus, "On
      the Origin of the Watchers: A Comparative Study of the Antediluvian
      Wisdom in Mesopotamian and Jewish Traditions," *Journal for the Study of
      the Pseudepigrapha* 19.4 (2010): 277–320; David Melvin, "The Gilgamesh
      Traditions and the Pre-History of Genesis 6: 1–4," *Perspectives in Religious
      Studies* 38:1 (2011): 23–32; Ida Fröhlich, "Mesopotamian Elements and

*Asael taught men…and made known to them **the metals** of the earth and the art of working them*—A variant of the notion that the stories of Prometheus and Hesiod lay behind the condemnation of what the Watchers taught humanity is offered by Dimant. She believes the writer of 1 Enoch is simply elaborating on the characterization of Tubal-Cain in Genesis 4:22 ("he was the forger of all instruments of bronze and iron") under some influence of the Prometheus myth.[164] While it would be futile to deny the Greek and earlier Mesopotamian touchpoints with the Watcher rebellion story, the story of Cain and his genealogy does appear to play a role in the thought of 1 Enoch. By way of example, Esler has devoted attention to how the writer of 1 Enoch creates conceptual links between Cain and the Watchers:

> Cain must be understood, therefore, as the prototypical evil-doer on the earth, the first person to engage in what for the Enochic scribe is the worst kind of evil—acts of violence, in the case of Cain, and by necessary implication others after him, homicidal violence. Abel is the first, of many, to petition heaven on account of his murder…. The next evil in chronological order is that of the Watchers desiring women and wanting to beget children from them (6:2). Their leader recognizes this as a great sin (6:3).

the Watchers Traditions," in *The Watchers in Jewish and Christian Traditions* (ed. Angela Kim Hawkins, Kelley Coblentz Bautch, and John C. Endres, S. J.; Fortress Press, 2014), 11–24; Henryk Drawnel, "The Mesopotamian Background of the Enochic Giants and Evil Spirits," *Dead Sea Discoveries* 21:1 (2014): 14–38; Helge Kvanvig, *Primeval History: Babylonian, Biblical, and Enochic: An Intertextual Reading* (*Journal for the Study of Judaism Supplement* 149; Leiden: E. J. Brill, 2011).

164. Devorah Dimant, "1 Enoch 6–11: A Methodological Perspective," in *Society of Biblical Literature Seminar Papers* 18 (2 vols.; Missoula, Mont.: Scholars Press, 1978), vol. 1:323–339 (esp. 331).

When the Watchers do this, they are said to "defile" (*mainesthai*) themselves. The Watchers also impart knowledge to human beings…. But the true horror of the Watchers' secession from heaven emerges only in the actions of their progeny, the giants to which their wives give birth (1 En 7:4–5)…. The core of the evil they produce is violence, to the extent of killing and then eating human beings, the creatures of the earth and even themselves. Thus violence, initiated by Cain, reappears in a most extreme form with the giants.[165]

The point of these conceptual connections is that, for the writer of 1 Enoch, Cain is the prototypical murderer, the archetypal *human* agent of chaos after Adam and Eve were driven from Eden. Adam and Eve fell and sinned, but 1 Enoch and other Second Temple texts don't have them as the reason for depravity.[166] Instead, the proliferation of evil is attributed to

165. Philip Esler, "Deus Victor: The Nature and Defeat of Evil in the Book of the Watchers (1 Enoch 136)," In *The Blessing of Enoch: 1 Enoch and Contemporary Theology* (Eugene, Oregon: Wipf & Stock, 2017), 166–190 (esp. pp. 10–11, 13–14).

166. On the idea that the proliferation of evil and depravity are not attributed to Adam and Eve in Second Temple Jewish texts, see Miryam T. Brand, "'At the Entrance Sin is Crouching": The Source of Sin and Its Nature as Portrayed in Second Temple Literature," Ph.D. Dissertation, New York University, 2011, 33. Brand's dissertation was later published under the title, *Evil Within and Without: The Source of Sin and Its Nature as Portrayed in Second Temple Literature* (*Journal of Ancient Judaism Supplements* 9; Göttingen: Vandenhoeck & Rupprecht, 2013); Loren T. Stuckenbruck, Simon Gathercole, and Stuart Weeks, *Evil in Second Temple Judaism and Early Christianity* (Wissenschaftliche Untersuchungen Zum Neuen Testament 2. Reihe 417; Tübingen: Mohr Siebeck, 2016).

the Watchers. They are viewed as *supernatural* agents of chaos, guilty of priming the engine of human self-destruction. Cain therefore typifies the havoc the Watchers (and their spawn, the giants, from whom would come demons) would wreak on earth via their false teaching, which would spur idolatry and violence.

Human civilization in turn is viewed as a pitiful attempt to restore Eden, something only its original architect (God) could do. Human civilization and its "arts and sciences" are invariably less than Eden and could of course be anti-Eden. Humans cannot recreate utopia. They cannot restore what has been lost.

breastplates—The Greek lemma here is *thōraks/thōrax*. Nickelsburg notes that the Aramaic lemma is *siryōn*, which appears to indicate wordplay on one of the names for Mount Hermon (Deuteronomy 3:9; 4:48).[167]

use of antimony, and the beautifying of the eyelids, and all kinds of costly stones, and all colouring tinctures—Nickelsburg makes an interesting observation in regard to this list:

> According to the second part of this description, Asael also taught men how to obtain and work materials useful for the beautification of women: silver, gold, and precious stones for jewelry and ornaments; minerals for eye paint; dyes for colored garments. Although the Bible can mention fine clothing and ornaments for women without disparagement (cf. Ezek 16:10–14 of YHWH's bride), the classical reference to these things occurs in a scathing denunciation of the seductive conduct of the women of Jerusalem (Isa 3:16–24). As the end of the present verse indicates, these connotations are here also (cf. also [1 En] 98:1–3, of men adorning

---

167. Nickelsburg, *1 Enoch*, vol. 1, 193.

themselves like women). This is especially evident in his reference to the use of eye paint, which biblical authors mention only in connection with women of ill repute.[168]

they were led astray—The Greek form of the verb (aorist passive, third-person plural) is ambiguous; that is, it does not specify whether the women led the Watchers astray or the reverse. The writer of G[s] added an explanation: "And the sons of men made them for themselves and for their daughters, and they transgressed and led astray the holy ones." In this reading, it is obvious that the women were to blame for leading the Watchers astray. Since this wording is not present in G[a] and Ethiopic, it seems to be an intentional insertion. Nickelsburg admits that this explanatory reading, which he follows in his translation and commentary, "is not an accidental variant."[169] Nevertheless, he argues for its authenticity along two lines: the idea that the Watchers were the ones led astray is found in other Second Temple texts contemporaneous with 1 Enoch, and other passages in 1 Enoch are consistent with the reading:

> The text of v 1c is problematic. The text as printed is attested by G[s] and divides into two parts. The first clause summarizes v 1a and b: the sons of men made weapons for themselves and jewelry, ornaments, and cosmetics for their daughters. According to the second clause, these women then led the holy watchers astray…. Several pieces of external evidence indicate that this reading is ancient.[170]

The Second Temple texts marshaled by Nickelsburg are of unequal value. Several do not actually affirm the explanatory line. That is, they are ambiguous in their own right. First Enoch 86:1–4 (part of the Animal Apocalypse) has the stars (the Watchers) mating with the cows (the

168. Ibid., 194.
169. Ibid., 195.
170. Ibid., 195.

women), but no blame for seduction is offered. The Book of Jubilees famously portrays the Watchers as having been sent by God to teach humanity (Jubilees 4:15; 5:6), but does not say they were seduced. Rather, Jubilees 5:1–3 condemns the cohabitation that ensued because it led to the proliferation of evil on the earth. First Enoch 6 clearly has the Watchers vow to procure for themselves wives, knowing that it was evil. One Christian text (Justin Martyr's Second Apology 5:2) also blames the Watchers.

On the other hand, the added explanation is supported by the content of texts like Testament of Reuben 5.[171] In its infamous "women are evil" passage, we read:

> [5] Accordingly, my children, flee from sexual promiscuity, and order your wives and your daughters not to adorn their heads and their appearances so as to deceive men's sound minds. For every woman who schemes in these ways is destined for eternal punishment. [6] For it was thus that they charmed the Watchers, who were before the Flood. As they continued looking at the women, they were filled with desire for them and perpetrated the act in their minds. Then they were transformed into human males, and while the women were cohabiting with their husbands they appeared to them.[172]

While this pseudepigraphical work has the Watchers transforming into men, it is nevertheless apparent that the women are blamed. Targum Pseudo-Jonathan suggests the women are at fault as well:[173]

---

171. The later (third–fourth century AD) Christian text *Pseudo-Clementine Homilies* 8:11–15 (cited by Nickelsburg) reads very much like this excerpt from the Testament of Reuben.

172. Charlesworth, *The Old Testament Pseudepigrapha*, vol. 1, 784.

173. Kevin Cathcart, Michael Maher, and Martin McNamara (eds.), *The Aramaic Bible, Vol 1B: Targum Pseudo-Jonathan: Genesis* (trans. Michael Maher; vol. 1; Collegeville, MN: The Liturgical Press, 1992). The italics are original to the Targum resource.

The sons of *the great ones* saw that the daughters of men were beautiful, *that they painted their eyes and put on rouge, and walked about with naked flesh. They conceived lustful thoughts*, and they took wives to themselves from among all who pleased them. (Gen 6:2)

For our purposes, while Nickelsburg overstates the case for the added gloss that accuses the women, he does produce two references (Testament of Reuben 5; Targum Pseudo-Jonathan of Genesis 6:2) that support the content of the addition. It is dubious that these texts justify following the addition. First Enoch 8 is left ambiguous, given the vow of 1 Enoch 6 and how it portrays the Watchers as knowingly transgressing with their plan, then 1 Enoch 8:1c without the explanatory addition would suggest the Watchers were at guilty. This is in clear conflict with other depictions. There is no need to harmonize Jubilees and 1 Enoch. The point here is that Nickelsburg's support for the added explanatory gloss found in G^s is a good bit weaker than he indicates.

became corrupt in all their ways—This phrase suffers from the same ambiguity noted above, despite the fact that it likely refers to the women (cf. Genesis 6:5).

8:3

And as men perished, they cried, and their cry went up to heaven—The language (cf. earlier in 1 Enoch 7:6) is very close to Genesis 4:10, where God tells Cain, "The voice of your brother's blood is crying to me from the ground." The similarity is not accidental given the above comments in regard to the conceptual links between Cain and the Watchers.

Translation: Chapter 9

9^1And then Michael, Uriel, Raphael, and Gabriel looked down from heaven and saw much blood being shed upon the earth, and all lawless-ness being wrought upon the earth. [2]And they said one to another: "The earth made †without inhabitant cries the voice of their cryings† up to the gates of heaven. [3]«And now to you, the holy ones of heaven», the souls of men make their suit, saying, 'Bring our cause before the Most High.'" [4]And they said to the Lord **of the ages**: "Lord of lords, God of gods, King of kings, ⟨and God of the ages⟩, the throne of Thy glory (standeth) unto all the generations of the ages, and Thy name holy and glorious and blessed unto all the ages! [5]Thou hast made all things, and power over all things hast Thou: and all things are naked and open in Thy sight, and Thou seest all things, and nothing can hide itself from Thee. [6]Thou seest what Azâzêl hath done, who hath taught all unrighteousness on earth and revealed the eternal secrets which were (preserved) in heaven, which men were striving to **learn**: [7]And Semjâzâ, to whom Thou hast given authority to bear rule over his associates. [8]And they have gone to the daughters of men upon the earth, and have slept with the women, and have defiled themselves, and revealed to them all kinds of sins. [9]And the women have borne giants, and the whole earth has thereby been filled with blood and unrighteousness. [10]And now, behold, the souls of those who have died are crying and making their suit to the gates of heaven, and their lamentations have ascended: and cannot **cease** because of the lawless deeds which are wrought on the earth. [11]And Thou knowest all things before they come to pass, and Thou seest these things and Thou dost suffer them, and Thou dost not say to us what we are to do to them in regard to these."

Commentary

9:1

Michael, Uriel, Raphael, and Gabriel—Heavenly beings that bear names are, on the analogy that heaven is a council or royal court, likely denoting special status and proximity to the king.[174] The names in this verse

---

174. Esler, *God's Court*, 61.

and their order vary in the manuscript data. They are all present in the Aramaic material if two fragments are conflated (4QEn[a] 1 4:6 and 4QEn[b] 1 4:7).[175] Black notes that, "while G[[a]] and G[s] here agree with each other, no Eth. manuscript reproduces exactly the Greek list."[176] Note here that Charles' translation follows these Greek manuscripts, which read Uriel in the list. The name Raphel is omitted in most Ethiopic manuscripts, many of which (but not all) read Suriel (Suryal, Sariel) in place of Uriel.[177] Sariel also survives in Aramaic.[178] The names mean, respectively:

- Michael ("Who is like God?")[179]
- Uriel ("Light/light-bearer of God")
- Raphael ("Healer of God"; i.e., "God's healer"; or "God heals")
- Gabriel ("God is my Warrior")
- Sariel ("God is my prince"; i.e., leader, captain)

Looked down from heaven—The four named figures are heavenly beings ("holy ones" from verse 3). They are four of the archangels known from later Christian tradition (which numbers seven in other texts). Nickelsburg notes:

> A complement of four, and later seven, named archangels (here "holy ones") appears first in 1 Enoch 9–10 and then becomes something of a staple in Jewish and Christian literature…. They go forth from heaven, view the world, approach the divine throne with their petition in behalf of humanity, and are then dispatched to the world to act in God's behalf. Whether the unnamed and

175. See Knibb, *The Ethiopic Book of Enoch*, vol. 2, 84.

176. Black, *The Book of Enoch or 1 Enoch*, 129.

177. Ibid.

178. Ibid.

179. Michael appears in the Hebrew portions of the book of Daniel (Daniel 10:13, 21; 12:1) The "who" in this name is the interrogative particle (*mî*), so the name forms a question. This name element is *not* a relative pronoun.

unnumbered "holy ones" in the throne vision in 1 Enoch 14–16 are the same as these is uncertain. But the throne vision in the Book of Parables explicitly identifies the four figures on the four sides of God as Michael, Raphael, Gabriel, and Phanuel, the last of these replacing Sariel in chaps. 9–10…. The four angels are mentioned in the Qumran War Scroll, remarkably with the same names as here, in the order Michael, Gabriel, Sariel, and Raphael (1QM 9:15–16). Their association with the eschatological war is compatible with the activity of Raphael, Gabriel, and Michael in 1 Enoch 10…. In 1 Enoch 20–36 + 81 the number four is expanded to seven (adding Uriel, Reuel, and Remiel to Michael, Sariel, Raphael, and Gabriel) in order to provide a complement of angels who are associated with the places of Enoch's cosmic tour, rather than God's throne…. The NT Book of Revelation employs the traditions of both four and seven, describing both "the seven spirits who are before his throne" (1:4; 4:5) and the four living creatures that stand on the four sides of the throne (4:6–8).[180]

As to the duties of these holy ones, Nickelsburg adds:

Within the logic of the story, as narrated in 1 Enoch, the archangels serve not only as God's eyes on the world, but also as intercessors for the human race. The angels' prayer is an extension and explication of the cry of humanity…. The angels' function as "the eyes of God" is an integral part of their role as mediators and intercessors or advocates for humankind…. In almost all the strata of 1 Enoch, angels play a crucial role as intercessors for humanity. Essential in all cases is a judgment context and a concern that the righteous get their due (which is often not the case at the present time).[181]

---

180. Nickelsburg, *1 Enoch: A Commentary on the Book of 1 Enoch*, vol. 1, 207.
181. Ibid., 206–208.

Angelic "mediation" (i.e., taking the plight or case of humans before God) is a biblical idea. As I have written elsewhere:

> The verse of interest for our study is Job 33:23: "If there be for [a man] an angel, a mediator." The Hebrew term translated "mediator" is *mēlîṣ*. It occurs in the phrase *mal'āk mēlîṣ*, a grammatical construction that is *not* a construct phrase that would require a translation like "a messenger/angel of a mediator.... Job 33:23 puts forth the concept of angelic mediation for human beings....
>
> The notion that heavenly beings were presumed to function as mediators between the leadership of the divine council and mortal humans, in effect functioning as witnesses for humans to plead their case in the context of unjust suffering, is a very ancient one, perhaps going back to divine assemblies at Sumer.... [T]here is some indication that angelic mediation also involved record keeping. I refer here to the notion that either God or his heavenly agents keeps a record of human behavior (Isa 65:6–7; Dan 7:10; 10:21) or suffering (Ps 56:8), or of those who belong to God or not (Exod 32:32; Isa 69:28–29; Jer 17:13; Ps 87:5–7; Dan 12:1; Mal 3:16). While several of these passages have God keeping track of such things, the wider ancient Near Eastern context has such divine record keeping as a duty of the divine council. The metaphor conveys a simple but profound thought: God and his agents will not overlook evil, injustice, and faithfulness.[182]

---

182. Heiser, *Angels*, 24, 49, 51–52. In regard to Sumer and recordkeeping in the divine council, see Thorkild Jacobsen, "Primitive Democracy in Ancient Mesopotamia," *Journal of Near Eastern Studies* 2 (1943): 159–72; Samuel Noah Kramer, "Sumerian Theology and Ethics," *Harvard Theological Review* 49 (1956): 45–62 (59); Shalom Paul, "Heavenly Tablets and the Book of Life," in *Columbia University Ancient Near Eastern Studies* (New York: Columbia University, 1973), n.p.; Andrew R. George, "Sennacherib and the Tablet of Destinies," *Iraq* 48 (1986): 133–46.

9:2

made without inhabitant—Recall that the giants were devouring human beings. The hyperbole here is used to stress the dire nature of the situation.

to the gates of heaven—See verse 10. Since this is the destination of the petition, the expression refers to the judicial "chambers" of God; i.e., the meeting place of God and His council (cf. Daniel 7:9–10; 1 Kings 22:19–23 for God meeting with the members of His host to declare decrees). The phrase is part of the legal vocabulary that continues into verse 3. The term "gates" also gives the impression that heaven, God's abode, is a walled fortress. Ensuing descriptions of God's celestial residence will confirm this idea (1 Enoch 34–36).

9:3

make their suit...bring our cause—In other words, "plead our case." The "suit" in Charles' language refers to a lawsuit or legal case. The language is reminiscent of the "covenant lawsuit" genre known in the Old Testament, particularly the prophets, who were tasked with "charging" the people with not keeping God's covenant:

> God's intermediate and final judgments are depicted in terms of a courtroom scene. The OT prophets regard themselves as God's prosecutors in a covenant lawsuit against God's people (Jer 2:4–9; Hos 4; Mic 6:1–6; cf. Mt 21:33–46). In Isaiah 1:2 the heavens and earth are summoned as witnesses, harking back to Deuteronomy where these same natural elements bore witness to God's covenant with his people (Deut 4:26; 30:19; 31:28–29; 32:1). Now they bear testimony to the rightness of the impending judgment that Isaiah announces.
>
> In the case of the final judgment, God assumes the role of both prosecutor and judge of the wicked. The books bearing witness to

the resolute rebellion of the unrepentant are opened. They collapse under the weight of the damnation they have been laying up for themselves (Ps 1:5; 5:5). Their lack of any legitimate defense results in their being cast into the lake of fire (Rev 20:11–15).[183]

The above citation reveals why the covenant lawsuit is also referred to as the "prophetic lawsuit" genre. The motifs occur in many places in both the Old and New Testaments.[184]

before the Most High—In Second Temple Jewish literature, this description is reserved for the God of Israel:

> "Most High" (*hypsistos*) is the first of a number of divine appellatives in this context that stress the supremacy of God. In the Hellenistic period, the title is especially popular as a designation for the God of Israel. In 1 Enoch it occurs also in 10:1; 46:7; 60:1, 22; 62:7; 77:1; 94:8; 97:2; 98:7; 99:3 ("the Most High God," *tou hypsistou theou*); 99:10; 100:4; 101:1, 6. In the present section and in all of its occurrences in chaps. 92–101, except perhaps 99:10, God's activity as judge is in focus.[185]

---

183. Leland Ryken et al., *Dictionary of Biblical Imagery* (Downers Grove, IL: InterVarsity Press, 2000), 472.

184. See H. B. Huffmon, "The Covenant Lawsuit and the Prophets," *JBL* 78, 1959, pp. 286–295; Alan Bandy, *The Prophetic Lawsuit in the Book of Revelation* (New Testament Monographs 29; Sheffield: Sheffield Phoenix Press, 2010); K. Nielsen, *Yahweh as Prosecutor and Judge: An Investigation of the Prophetic Lawsuit (Rib-Pattern)* (JSOTSup 9; Sheffield: JSOT, 1978); Meira Kensky, *Trying Man, Trying God: The Divine Courtroom in Early Jewish and Christian Literature* (Wissenschaftliche Untersuchungen Zum Neuen Testament 2.Reihe 289; Tübingen: Mohr Siebeck, 2010)

185. Nickelsburg, *1 Enoch: A Commentary on the Book of 1 Enoch*, vol. 1, 208.

9:4

Lord of lords, God of gods, King of kings—"God of gods" of course makes the author's commitment to the ontological uniqueness of Israel's one God quite clear. "King of kings" and "Lord of lords" are royal titles known in the ancient Near East (e.g., Darius the Great of Persia and the Hellenistic pharaoh Sesoōsis).[186]

9:6

Thou seest what Azâzêl hath done—Here we see a direct articulation of Azazel's (Asael's[187]) crime. Specifically, the verse says he "taught all unrighteousness on earth and revealed the eternal secrets which were (preserved) in heaven, which men are striving to learn." In 1 Enoch 8:1, the content of his teaching was, specifically, "to make swords, and knives, and shields, and breastplates, and made known to them the metals of the earth and the art of working them, and bracelets, and ornaments, and the use of antimony, and the beautifying of the eyelids, and all kinds of costly stones, and all colouring tinctures." First Enoch 9:6 is therefore more of a summary statement. Nickelsburg observes that "verses 6–10 rehearse in prayer form what chaps. 6–8 have already presented in narrative form."[188]

Scholars regularly presume that the description is evidence of two disparate traditions, one with Asael and the leader of the rebellion, the other with Shemihazah as the leader. Again, this is an assumption based on what appears to be a single inference point: that it is Asa'el who is the first

---

186. Esler, *God's Court*, 54.
187. See the discussion under 8:1 for the relationship/confusion between the names.
188. Nickelsburg, *1 Enoch: A Commentary on the Book of 1 Enoch*, vol. 1, 212.

Watcher bound in 1 Enoch 10:4 and 13:1. Asael is never said to be the leader of the *group* of Watchers, whereas Shemihazah is given that label (1 Enoch 6:3, 7)—a label reiterated in the very next verse (9:7). In the latter reference, Shemihazah is called the leader of other leaders (the leaders of ten). The notion that condemning Asael (9:6) before Shemihazah (9:7) does not logically necessitate the conclusion that the latter is subordinate to the former. When it comes to specific statements of the texts, Shemihazah is consistently seen as the leader. It seems possible that Asael is the first one punished for another reason—namely, the proliferation of depravity and destruction of the image in the wake of his teaching. The point here is not to mislead the reader into thinking the interpretive issue is a simple one. Rather, it is to suggest that perhaps the presumed "two traditions" might be one, or at least less dissimilar than supposed. Nevertheless, readers should note that 1 Enoch 65:1–6 calls the Watchers the "armies of Azaz'el" and labels them as "satans," thus suggesting that Azazel was the "lead satan" (i.e., Satan himself). First Enoch 69:5–6 follows this same trajectory. First Enoch 54:4–6 explicitly labels Azazel as Satan. These make it clear that even if the relationship between Asael and Shemihazah might be cast as a rivalry and not as two separate competing traditions, Asael becomes identified with Satan.

9:7

Semjâzâ, to whom Thou hast given authority to bear rule over his associates— See the comments above regarding Asael and Shemihazah.

9:8–9

have gone to the daughters of men upon the earth, and have slept with the women, and have defiled themselves, and revealed to them all kinds of sins. And the women have borne giants—The wording here is a clear reference to Genesis 6:1–4. The "revealing to them all kinds of sins" refers to the forbidden teaching, itself part of the context for Genesis 6:1–4 (i.e., the Mesopotamian *apkallu* story).[189]

9:10

and making their suit to the gates of heaven—See the comments at 9:3.

9:11

Thou dost suffer them—The archangels are not charging God with apathy. Rather, they are observing that God knows what is going on and has not yet acted. They presume He intends to act, so they add the ensuing line.

Thou dost not say to us what we are to do to them in regard to these—The archangels want to know how God wants them to act to rectify the situation. What does God want them to do to the rebels ("to them") in regard to their crimes ("these")?

---

189. See Heiser, *Reversing Hermon*, chapter 3; Amar Annus, "On the Origin of the Watchers: A Comparative Study of the Antediluvian Wisdom in Mesopotamian and Jewish Traditions," *Journal for the Study of the Pseudepigrapha* 19.4 (2010): 277–320; David Melvin, "The Gilgamesh Traditions and the Pre-History of Genesis 6: 1–4," *Perspectives in Religious Studies* 38:1 (2011): 23–32; Ida Fröhlich, "Mesopotamian Elements and the Watchers Traditions," in *The Watchers in Jewish and Christian Traditions* (ed. Angela Kim Hawkins, Kelley Coblentz Bautch, and John C. Endres, S.J.; Fortress Press, 2014), 11–24; Henryk Drawnel, "The Mesopotamian Background of the Enochic Giants and Evil Spirits," *Dead Sea Discoveries* 21:1 (2014): 14–38; Helge Kvanvig, *Primeval History: Babylonian, Biblical, and Enochic: An Intertextual Reading* (*Journal for the Study of Judaism* Supplement 149; Leiden: E. J. Brill, 2011).

Translation: Chapter 10

10[1]Then said the Most High, the Holy and Great One spake, and sent **Uriel** to the son of Lamech, and said to him: [2]⟨"Go to Noah and⟩ tell him in my name "Hide thyself!" and reveal to him the end that is approaching: that the whole earth will be destroyed, and a deluge is about to come upon the whole earth, and will destroy all that is on it. [3]And now instruct him that he may escape and his seed may be preserved for all the generations of the world." [4]And again the Lord said to Raphael: "Bind Azâzêl hand and foot, and cast him into the darkness: and make an opening in the desert, which is in Dûdâêl, and cast him therein. [5]And place upon him rough and jagged rocks, and cover him with darkness, and let him abide there for ever, and cover his face that he may not see light. [6]And on the day of the great judgement he shall be cast into the fire. [7]And heal the earth which the angels have corrupted, and proclaim the healing of the earth, that they may heal the plague, and that all the children of men may not perish through all the secret things that the Watchers have **disclosed** and have taught their sons. [8]And the whole earth has been corrupted through the works that were taught by Azâzêl: to him ascribe all sin." [9]And to Gabriel said the Lord: "Proceed against the bastards and the reprobates, and against the children of fornication: and destroy [the children of fornication and] the children of the Watchers from amongst men: [and cause them to go forth]: send them one against the other that they may destroy each other in battle: for length of days shall they not have. [10]And no request that they (i.e. their fathers) make of thee shall be granted unto their fathers on their behalf; for they hope to live an eternal life, and that each one of them will live five hundred years." [11]And the Lord said unto Michael: "Go, **bind** Semjâzâ and his associates who have united themselves with women so as to have defiled themselves with them in all their uncleanness. [12]And when their sons have slain one another, and they have seen the destruction of their beloved ones, bind them fast for seventy generations in the **valleys** of the earth, till the day of their judgement and of their consummation, till the judgement that is for ever and ever is consummated. [13]In those days they shall be led off to the abyss of fire: ⟨and⟩ to the torment and the prison in which they shall be confined for ever. [14]And whosoever shall be **condemned** and destroyed will from thenceforth be bound together with them to the end of all generations. [15]And destroy all the spirits of the reprobate and the children of the Watchers, because they have wronged mankind. [16]Destroy all wrong from the face of the earth and let every evil work come to an end: and let the plant of righteousness and truth appear: ⟨and it shall prove a blessing; the works of righteousness and truth⟩ shall be planted in truth and joy for evermore.

[17]And then shall all the righteous escape,
And shall live till they beget thousands of children,
And all the days of their youth and their **old age**
Shall they complete in peace.

[18]And then shall the whole earth be tilled in righteousness, and shall all be planted with trees and be full of blessing. [19]And all desirable trees shall be planted on it, and they shall plant vines on it: and the vine which they plant thereon shall yield wine in abundance, and as for all the seed which is sown thereon each measure (of it) shall bear a thousand, and each measure of olives shall yield ten presses of oil. [20]And cleanse thou the earth from all oppression, and from all unrighteousness, and from all sin, and from all godlessness: and all the uncleanness that is wrought upon the earth destroy from off the earth. [21]⟨And all the children of men shall become righteous⟩, and all nations shall offer adoration and shall praise Me, and all shall worship Me. [22]And the earth shall be cleansed from all defilement, and from all sin, and from all punishment, and from all torment, and I will never again send (them) upon it from generation to generation and for ever."

Commentary

10:1

Sent Uriel to the son of Lamech—Instead of speaking directly to Noah (the son of Lamech; cf. Genesis 5:28–29) as in the biblical account (Genesis 6:8–9, 13ff.), God sends the archangel Uriel. This chapter has God acting through the agency of archangels in all the particulars of His response to the aftermath of the Watchers' rebellion and the mayhem caused by their offspring, the giants (1 Enoch 10:4, 9, 11). Nickelsburg and Black read Sariel in place of Uriel (see comments at 1 Enoch 9:1).

10:4–5

Bind Azâzêl hand and foot—On Azazel instead of Asael, see 1 Enoch 6:10; 8:1, 3. The binding language is the source of the same in New Testament passages about the "angels that sinned" (2 Peter 2:4; Jude 6). Second Peter 2:4 is especially noteworthy: "For if God did not spare angels when they sinned, but cast them into hell and committed them to chains of gloomy darkness to be kept until the judgment." The Greek verb rendered "cast into hell" is *tartaroō*, the verb found in the classical Greek story for the destination of the rebel Titans, a tale with clear relationships to the *apkallu* story that provides the original context for Genesis 6:1–4.[190] Bauckham writes in this regard:

> The verbs ταρταροῦν [*tartaroun*] and (rather more common) καταταρταροῦν [*katatartaroun*] mean "to cast into Tartarus," and were almost always used with reference to the early Greek theogonic myths, in which the ancient giants, the Cyclopes and Titans,

---

190. See Heiser, *Reversing Hermon*, chapter 3; Amar Annus, "On the Origin of the Watchers: A Comparative Study of the Antediluvian Wisdom in Mesopotamian and Jewish Traditions," *Journal for the Study of the Pseudepigrapha* 19.4 (2010): 277–320.

were imprisoned in Tartarus, the lowest part of the underworld, by Uranos, Kronos and Zeus…. They are not used in the Greek version of *1 Enoch*; though τάρταρος [*tartaros*] ("Tartarus") is used of the place of divine punishment in *1 Enoch* 20:2, as elsewhere in Jewish Greek literature (LXX Job 40:20; 41:24; Prov 30:16; *Sib. Or.* 4:186; Philo, *Mos.* 2.433; *praem* 152).[191]

Scholars have long noted that Azazel was a Satan figure in Second Temple Jewish thought (see the comments at 1 Enoch 9:6). Three conceptual threads found in 1 Enoch are important in this regard: (1) Azazel is conflated with Asael in 1 Enoch and other writings of the period; (2) Azazel/Asael is cast into darkness and bound in 1 Enoch 10; and (3) Azazel/Asael is called Satan in 1 Enoch 54:4–6. These items provide reference points as to how the New Testament writers thought of hell as a place for "the devil and his angels" (Matthew 25:41; cp.), an idea that is not articulated in the Old Testament. Though these connections are not made in the Old Testament, the data points of Old Testament demonology and supernatural rebellion are consistent with the theology of 1 Enoch and the New Testament on this point.[192]

an opening in the desert, which is in Dûdâêl…place upon him rough and jagged rocks, and cover him with darkness—Dûdâêl is a lifeless, threatening place. It is no coincidence that the description draws on Old Testament descriptions of the grave/underworld (Sheol).[193] Nickelsburg and

---

191. Richard J. Bauckham, *2 Peter, Jude* (vol. 50; *Word Biblical Commentary*; Dallas: Word, Incorporated, 1998), 249. In regard to Tartarus, Wright draws attention to the fact that the Titan Prometheus (who gave forbidden knowledge to humanity) was likewise case into Tartarus (Wright, *The Origin of Evil Spirits*, 116).

192. See Heiser, *Demons* (forthcoming).

193. See Job 17:13; 33:28; Psalm 49:19.

VanderKam note that the spelling of this place varies in the manuscripts, pointing readers to four associated readings: *dundāyn, dundayin, dunudāyn,* and *duydāyn*.[194] The place is certainly associated with the Azazel tradition of Second Temple Judaism. As I have written elsewhere:

> In his detailed study of the etymology of the name Azazel,[195] H. Tawil draws attention to ancient Near Eastern comparative evidence that make considering Azazel a demonic entity comprehensible. Specifically, Tawil explored Mesopotamian texts dealing with demons ("children of the netherworld") who were believed to exit the realm of the dead through holes and fissures in the earth. Once in the world of the living, "demons and other powers of hostility most common dwelling place is the 'steepe-land' (Sumerian *EDIN* = Akkadian *ṣēru*)…also to be understood as one of the symbolic designations of the netherworld." Tawil cites numerous examples of this terminology to make the telling observation that certain magical rituals and incantations bear striking similarities to both the vocabulary in Leviticus 16 and Azazel passages in the Semitic (Ethiopic) text of 1 Enoch. Further, he traces the Sumerian-Akkadian netherworld language to the domain of Mōt, the god of death at Ugarit. Tawil's research establishes that both biblical vocabulary and later Second Temple Jewish discussion of Azazel were firmly rooted in early Mesopotamian material about demonic powers of darkness.[196]

---

194. Nickelsburg and James C. VanderKam, *1 Enoch 2*, 233 (note a), 240. Black echoes this suspicion, that Dundayin and Doudael (=Duda el) are related. See Matthew Black, *The Book of Enoch or 1 Enoch* (In Veteris Testamenti Pseudepigrapha 7; ed. A. M. Denis and M. de Jonge; Leiden: E. J. Brill, 1985), 227.

195. Tawil, "'Azazel, the Prince of the Steepe," 48–49.

196. See Heiser, *Demons* (forthcoming).

The association of the desert wilderness as a place connected to the realm of the dead also lurks behind Leviticus 17:7: "So they shall no more sacrifice their sacrifices to goat demons, after whom they whore." This passage's immediate proximity to Leviticus 16 (and Azazel) is striking.

Azazel, the Satan figure of 1 Enoch, is thus consigned to the deep recesses of the earth. That the writer of 1 Enoch was tracking on the notion of Azazel's domain being the desert wilderness where the "goat demons" are is also evident from 1 Enoch 19:1, which links Deuteronomy 32:17 and Leviticus 17:7 in its explanation of where the Watchers are sent as punishment:

> And Uriel said to me, "There stand the angels who mingled with the women. And their spirits—having assumed many forms—bring destruction on men and lead them astray to sacrifice to demons as to gods until the day of the great judgment, in which they will be judged with finality."[197]

10:7

heal the earth which the angels have corrupted, and proclaim the healing of the earth—The archangel Raphael is commissioned with healing the earth. Nickelsburg comments:

> Verse 7 broadens the scope to include the perversion of the earth and the illegitimate revelations by all the watchers (8:3). Nonetheless, reference to the desolation of the earth corresponds to 8:2,

---

197. Nickelsburg, *1 Enoch: A Commentary on the Book of 1 Enoch*, vol. 1, 276. Deuteronomy 32:17 reads (LEB): "They sacrificed to the demons (*shēdîm*), not God, to gods whom they had not known" while Leviticus 17:7 has "So they shall no more sacrifice their sacrifices to goat demons, after whom they whore".

where Asael is blamed—as he is in 10:8, where the text returns to this chieftain and God's command that Raphael write an indictment or epitaph over the place of his interment.

The name Raphael (*rāpā'ēl*, "God has healed") implies this angel's healing activity (v 7), as it does in Tob 3:17; 12:14; and 1 Enoch 40:9.[198]

that all the children of men may not perish through all the secret things that the Watchers have disclosed—The wording conveys the author's conclusion that, had God not intervened with sentencing the Watchers and annihilating the giants (verse 8), all humanity would have been destroyed.

10:8

And the whole earth has been corrupted through the works that were taught by Azâzêl: to him ascribe all sin—This is a clear statement as to the notion that human depravity had its roots in the rebellion of the Watchers, not in the Fall of Adam and Eve. While not excusing Adam and Eve from guilt, Second Temple writers overwhelmingly do not view their deeds as the point of origin for an assessment such as Genesis 6:5.[199]

10:9

bastards—The term described the fact that the giants are the product of a forbidden union. The Dead Sea Scrolls use this language of the disem-

---

198. Nickelsburg, *1 Enoch: A Commentary on the Book of 1 Enoch*, vol. 1, 221.

199. See Miryam T. Brand, *Evil Within and Without: The Source of Sin and Its Nature as Portrayed in Second Temple Literature* (*Journal of Ancient Judaism Supplements* 9; Göttingen: Vandenhoeck & Rupprecht, 2013); Loren T. Stuckenbruck, Simon Gathercole, and Stuart Weeks, *Evil in Second Temple Judaism and Early Christianity* (Wissenschaftliche Untersuchungen Zum Neuen Testament 2. Reihe 417; Tübingen: Mohr Siebeck, 2016).

bodied spirits of the dead giants (i.e., demons).[200] As Wright notes, "The term 'bastard' is defined in the biblical texts as either a person of questionable birth (Deut 23:3) or a person whose lineage is pagan (Zech 9:6)."[201] Fröhlich observes, "The expression *rwḥwt mmzrym* ["bastard spirits"] in 4Q510–11 designates demons. Bastard spirits and ravaging angels probably originated in the Enochic tradition where the Watchers had illicit sexual relations with earthly women."[202]

destroy [the children of fornication and] the children of the Watchers from amongst men...send them one against the other that they may destroy each other in battle—Nickelsburg astutely observes:

> Different from Asael and Shemihazah and his companions, who are imprisoned until the final judgment (10:4–6, 11–13), the giants are to be immediately annihilated. For them there is no future judgment and punishment.... These verses together describe the first step toward the resolution of the crisis that arose

---

200. 4Q510 1 5; 4Q511 35 7; 4Q444 2 i 4.

201. Wright, *Origin of Evil Spirits*, 150. In another essay, Wright points readers to Greek material for 1 Enoch 10:15 that "identifies the spirits of the giants as 'bastards' (*ta pneumata tōn kibdēlōn*), while the Ethiopic refers to them as "souls of lust and sons of the Watchers." See Archie T. Wright, "The Demonology of 1 Enoch and the New Testament Gospels," in *Enoch and the Synoptic Gospels: Reminiscences, Allusions, Intertextuality* (ed. Loren T. Stuckenbruck and Gabriele Boccaccini; *Early Judaism and Its Literature* 44; SBL Press, 2016), 215–243 (esp. 226, note 43).

202. Fröhlich, "Theology and Demonology," 109. See also Giovanni Ibba, "The Evil Spirits in Jubilees and the Spirit of the Bastards in 4Q510 with Some Remarks on Other Qumran Manuscripts," *Henoch* 31 (2009): 111–16.

in the beginning of the narrative: the removal of the forces that have threatened to destroy the earth and its inhabitants.[203]

for length of days shall they not have—This probably reflects the writer's understanding of Genesis 6:3.

10:10

to live an eternal life, and that each one of them will live five hundred years— Black observes (and we concur) that the syntax of the Greek on which the Charles translation is based makes little sense. Black writes: "The reading of [Ethiopic] seems to me to give the only possible sense, [namely], that the giants, since, unlike their parents, are of the earth and flesh, not of spirit and heaven, should *not* be granted to live forever, but be given a life span of five hundred years."[204]

10:12

when their sons have slain one another, and they have seen the destruction of their beloved ones—The Watchers are forced to watch the destruction of their offspring, here called "beloved ones." Nickelsburg observes: "In v 12 'beloved' (*agapētos*) is a designation for the angels' sons, rather than their wives; cf. the parallelism in the interpretation of this verse in 12:6; cf. also 14:6. On the motif of the watchers' being forced to witness the destruction of their sons, cf. also 12:6 and 14:6. This cruelty was not unknown in the ancient world."[205]

---

203. Nickelsburg, *1 Enoch: A Commentary on the Book of 1 Enoch*, vol. 1, 223–224.

204. Black, *The Book of Enoch or 1 Enoch*, 136.

205. Nickelsburg, *1 Enoch: A Commentary on the Book of 1 Enoch*, vol. 1, 224. On this practice not being unknown, Nickelsburg cites Jeremiah 52:10 and Josephus, *J. W.* 1.4.6 §97; *Ant.* 13.14.2 §380.

seventy generations—The description here of the duration of the Watchers' punishment differs from the "forever" of verses 4 and 5. The difference is superficial, as "seventy generations" reflects a numerical typology that refers to "the rest of time" (the end of history). Additionally, the "forever" language appears at the end of the verse itself. The practice of dividing history into discrete periods—with multiples of seven being a common feature—is known from biblical books like Daniel (9:24–27) and other Second Temple Period sources. Milik was of the opinion that the genealogy of Luke (4:23–38) was intentionally structured so that seventy names occurred from Enoch to Jesus: "If one deducts the first six patriarchs, one finds again in the era of the patriarch Enoch the beginning of a computation of seventy generations—exactly the same, therefore, as *1 Enoch* 10:12."[206]

in the valleys of the earth—Nickelsburg opines that "these verses do not use the language of burial and underworld,"[207] but his reading is too literalistic. "Valleys" can speak of a "death destination" (i.e., Sheol or the Abyss; cf. Psalm 23:4). Some literal valleys also became associated with death or the realm of the dead.[208]

---

206. Milik, *The Books of Enoch,* 257. See also the studies of: Ron Haydon, "The 'Seventy Sevens' (Dan 9:24) in Light of Heptadic Themes in Qumran," *Journal of the Evangelical Study of the Old Testament* 3, no. 1 & 2 (2014–2015): 203–214; Roger T. Beckwith, "Daniel 9 and the Date of Messiah's Coming in Essene, Hellenistic, Pharisaic, Zealot and Early Christian Computation," *Revue de Qumran* 10.4 (40 (1981): 521–542.

207. Nickelsburg, *1 Enoch: A Commentary on the Book of 1 Enoch,* vol. 1, 225.

208. See K. Spronk, "Travellers," *Dictionary of Deities and Demons in the Bible* [ed. Karel van der Toorn, Bob Becking, and Pieter W. van der Horst; Leiden; Boston; Köln; Grand Rapids, MI; Cambridge: Brill; Eerdmans, 1999], 876–877; "Valley," in Leland Ryken et al., *Dictionary of Biblical Imagery* (Downers Grove, IL: InterVarsity Press, 2000).

10:13

to the abyss of fire…to the torment and the prison in which they shall be confined for ever—See comments at verses 4 and 5. Black (p. 138) notes that the idea of everlasting punishment is found in Josephus (*Ant* xviii 1.3.14).

10:14

*And whosoever shall be **condemned** and destroyed will from thenceforth be bound together with them to the end of all generations*—This is strikingly similar to the theology put forth in (taken collectively) Matthew 25:41 and Revelation 20:15; 21:8, where the wicked unrighteous suffer the same fate in the same place as the beast, the devil, his angels, and the false prophet. Nevertheless, 1 Enoch is not consistent in this regard:

> The two sentences of this verse correspond to vv. 12 and 13. According to the first sentence, the place of wicked humanity's confinement is the same as the watchers' temporary prison. This may suggest that both watchers and people will have the same place of final punishment, but this is by no means certain. Only such late texts as Matt 25:41 and Rev 20:10, 15 (cf. 19:20) speak of a single such place of final punishment. Both 1 Enoch 21:7–10 and 27:2–3 (parallel: 90:24–27) distinguish two places, identifying the place of humanity's punishment with the Valley of Hinnom. According to [1 Enoch] 103:7–8, wicked humanity will burn in Sheol.[209]

10:16

the plant of righteousness—The language is metaphorical. Since the context for the crimes and judgment of the Watchers is Noah's Flood, Nickels-

---

209. Nickelsburg, *1 Enoch: A Commentary on the Book of 1 Enoch*, vol. 1, 225.

burg (p. 226) associates this line with Noah's vineyard. The very next verse alludes to the escape of Noah and his family (verse 17: "And then shall all the righteous escape"). Charles sees things differently, apparently basing his view on Old Testament language about a plant ("branch") in association with the Messiah of Israel and other plant language in 1 Enoch (the references are all to 1 Enoch):

> Israel springs from a seed that "is sown" by God, 62:8: hence it is established as "a plant of the seed for ever," 84:6; is called "the plant of uprightness," 93:2; "the plant of righteousness," 93:5; "the eternal plant of righteousness," 93:10; and "the plant of righteous judgement," 93:5.[210]

Given the description that follows, it would appear that Charles' trajectory is the more coherent ("‹and it shall prove a blessing; the works of righteousness and truth› shall be planted in truth and joy for evermore").

10:17

And then shall all the righteous escape, And shall live till they beget thousands of children—The reference is to Noah and his family in terms of immediate context, and then their repopulation of the earth to the deliverance of humanity.

10:18–22

The vision of the post-Flood earth is Edenic and utopian. God is the speaker:

> And then shall the whole earth be tilled in righteousness, and shall all be planted with trees and be full of blessing. And all desirable

210. Charles, *Commentary on the Pseudepigrapha of the Old Testament*, vol. 2, 194.

trees shall be planted on it, and they shall plant vines on it: and the vine which they plant thereon shall yield wine in abundance, and as for all the seed which is sown thereon each measure (of it) shall bear a thousand, and each measure of olives shall yield ten presses of oil. And cleanse thou the earth from all oppression, and from all unrighteousness, and from all sin, and from all godlessness: and all the uncleanness that is wrought upon the earth destroy from off the earth. ‹And all the children of men shall become righteous›, and all nations shall offer adoration and shall praise Me, and all shall worship Me. And the earth shall be cleansed from all defilement, and from all sin and from all punishment, and from all torment, and I will never again send (them) upon it from generation to generation and for ever.

Nickelsburg comments in this regard:

The fertility of the earth, as an attendant circumstance of God's coming redemption, is a common motif in prophetic literature, sometimes with connotations of new creation,[44] as is the case here…. Although the numbers are stereotyped, the fantastic yields described in v 19 are of miraculous proportions, and are appropriate to the perfection of the eschaton…. [T]he obliteration of sin is followed by the appearance of the righteous, but now in an extended sense. To the number of "all the righteous" (v 17a) will be added "all the sons of men," that is, "all the peoples." Thus God's total sovereignty has not only a negative aspect (absence of sin) but a positive side.[211]

---

211. Nickelsburg, *1 Enoch: A Commentary on the Book of 1 Enoch*, vol. 1, 228. He adds a bit later: "For the continued emphasis on the conversion of the nations, cf. 1 Enoch 91:14; 90:37–38."

Translation: Chapter 11

11¹And in those days I will open the store chambers of blessing which are in the heaven, so as to send them down ‹upon the earth› over the work and labour of the children of men. ²And truth and peace shall be associated together throughout all the days of the world and throughout all the generations **of men**.

Commentary

10:22–11:2

The immediately preceding verse (10:22) has a textual corruption that becomes important when juxtaposed with the brief chapter 11. The textual addition is bracketed and boldfaced below. It is based on Ethiopic material.

10:22

"And the earth shall be cleansed from all defilement, and from all sin and from all punishment, and from all torment, and I will never again send [[a **Deluge**]] upon it from generation to generation and for ever." This is the reading adopted by Black.[212] When the promise to never again send a flood leads to 11:1–2, Nickelsburg's observation is noteworthy:

> The sequence of Gen 8:20–9:1 is reproduced in these verses. Verse 22a reiterates the theme of v 20 and thus recalls Noah's sacrifice (Gen 8:20). Verse 22b picks up God's promise not to curse the earth, employing language closer to the version of that promise in Gen 9:11. In the place of the curse will be the blessings of nature (1 Enoch 11:1; cf. Gen 8:22 and the specific mention of blessing in 9:1).[213]

212. Black, *The Book of Enoch or 1 Enoch*, 140.
213. Nickelsburg, *1 Enoch: A Commentary on the Book of 1 Enoch*, vol. 1, 228.

A Reader's Commentary on
1 Enoch 12–16

Section Summary

Scholars have noted, and close readers will discern, that 1 Enoch 12–16 is something of a commentary on 1 Enoch 6–11. The section develops the features and content of Enoch's heavenly journey, an idea based on Genesis 5:21–24. More specifically, 1 Enoch 12–16 "describes Enoch's ascent to the heavenly throne room as a prophetic commissioning in the tradition of Ezekiel 1–2."[214] The same source is quick to add that "the account also contains important characteristics of later Jewish accounts of mystical ascents."[215] By way of a succinct chapter-by-chapter content summary, Wright observes:

> In chapter 12, Enoch is commanded to go and warn the Watchers of their approaching destruction due to the sin they committed. Enoch first approaches Asa'el, informs him of his punishment, and then proceeds to convey the same message to the rest of the Watchers. As a result, the Watchers plead with him to intercede with God on their behalf (chap. 13). This is followed by Enoch's vision and God's response to the Watchers; they will be judged and will not have peace (chap. 14). A similar story line follows in

---

214. Nickelsburg, "Enoch, First Book of," *The Anchor Yale Bible Dictionary,* 510.
215. Ibid., 510.

chapters 15–16. The central theme of chapters 6–16 is the tale of the Watcher angels who rebelled against God by having sexual relations with women and the evil spirits that emerged from the bodies of the giants upon their death.[216]

Nickelsburg adds some important detail:

The figure of Enoch is central and crucial to these chapters, in distinction from chaps. 6–11, which do not mention him. His roles are analogous to those of the archangels in chaps. 6–11. He is an intercessor with access to God, albeit for the fallen watchers rather than for the giants' victims. Moreover, he is commissioned to go to the fallen watchers (cf. 10:4, 9, 11). While his commission is to announce the judgment rather than to effect it, the irrevocability of the decree makes him, in a real sense, an agent of judgment. Although Enoch's title in this section is "scribe" (12:3–4; 15:1), he functions as a spokesman for God. Indeed, he is the *first* prophet, and he is given unequalled access to the heavenly throne room. The description of this ascent is embodied in a narrative whose prototype appears in biblical accounts of prophetic commissionings.[217]

Translation: Chapter 12

12[1]Before these things Enoch was hidden, and no one of the children of men knew where he was hidden, and where he abode, and what had become of him. [2]And his activities had to do with the Watchers, and his days were with the holy ones.

[3]And I Enoch was blessing the Lord of **majesty** and the King of the ages, and lo! the Watchers called me—Enoch the scribe—and said to me:

---

216. Wright, *Early Jewish Literature: An Anthology*, vol. 2, 192.

217. Nickelsburg, *1 Enoch: A Commentary on the Book of 1 Enoch*, vol. 1, 229.

[4]"Enoch, thou scribe of righteousness, go, †declare† to the Watchers of the heaven who have left the high heaven, the holy eternal place, and have defiled themselves with women, and have done as the children of earth do, and have taken unto themselves wives: [5]"Ye have wrought great destruction on the earth: And ye shall have no peace nor forgiveness of sin: [6]and inasmuch as †they† delight themselves in† their† children, The murder of †their† beloved ones shall† they† see, and over the destruction of †their† children shall† they† lament, and shall make supplication unto eternity, but mercy and peace shall ye not attain.'"

Commentary

12:1

Was hidden (twice)—The translation of Charles is odd, but the same choice appears in Charlesworth. Nickelsburg has "was taken," which more clearly follows Genesis 5:24 (where the Hebrew verb is *laqaḥ*, which typically means "to take" and never "to hide"). The Ethiopic lemma concurs, offering no justification of "hidden" as a translation. The Greek verbal form is *elēmphthē*, the aorist passive of *lambanō* ("to take, receive"). Perhaps "receive" is what produces "hidden" (understanding "God took him" as "God received him [into heaven, which mortals cannot see]." This seems consistent with what follows in 1 Enoch 12:1 ("no one of the children of men knew where he was hidden, and where he abode, and what had become of him"). If this assumption about the wording is the case, the translation is too interpretive.

In his study comparing the reception of revelation in regard to Enoch (in the Book of the Watchers) and Jesus (in the New Testament), Gurtner observes that Enoch is portrayed as both passive and active modes as a recipient of divine revelation.[218] Passive examples include the fact that

---

218. The examples that follow are drawn from Daniel M. Gurtner, "The Revelatory Experiences of Enoch and Jesus: A Comparison between the Book of the Watchers and the Synoptic Tradition," in *Enoch and the Synoptic*

Enoch is not only "taken" in 12:1, but he is "brought" (14:25), "led away" (14:8), "hastened" (14:8), "sped along" (14:8), "raised up" (14:25), "made to stand" (14:25), and "made to fly" (14:8). In communicating, there are times when something is written down for him (33:4) and he is given words (14:3). His eyes are opened and he is shown visions (1:2; 22:1; 24:1). In terms of an active role, Enoch is at times in charge of his own movements ("comes" and "goes"; "arrives" and "travels"; 13:3, 7, 9; 14:9, 10, 13; 17:5–7; 18:6; 21:1; 26:1; 30:1; 32:2). He "speaks" (13:3, 10; 21:4; 22:2), "writes" (13:6; 14:4), and asks questions (22:6, 8; 23:3).

12:2

his activities had to do with the Watchers, and his days were with the holy ones—The Watchers in view in this statement are not fallen or in rebellion. "Watchers" and "holy ones" are in parallel. The statement means simply that Enoch spent time among the holy ones and makes the later choice of Enoch as intercessor comprehensible. While being in parallel, the wording nevertheless creates a distinction between Enoch's "activities" and "his days" with the holy ones, thus raising the question of whether the time being spent with the Watchers points to a circumstance before or after he was taken by God. Those familiar only with biblical content (Genesis 5:22–24) would presume the latter, but this is not the case with respect to Second Temple Jewish thought, which can indeed be justified in light of the biblical material. Nickelsburg explains:

> In the present context, this paraphrase of Gen 5:24 refers not to Enoch's disappearance at the end of his life, but to the beginning of a period of association with the angels (v 2), during which he is instructed in the secrets of the universe and, to some extent, of

Gospels: Reminiscences, Allusions, Intertextuality (ed. Loren T. Stuckenbruck and Gabriele Boccaccini; *Early Judaism and Its Literature* 44; SBL Press, 2016), 31–45 (esp. 38–40).

the end time. He receives this instruction in order to transmit it to his children before his final disappearance. We are not told the length of his sojourn with the angels, and later sources that are dependent on 1 Enoch differ. According to *Jub.* 4:21–23, whose language indicates familiarity with these chapters, after Enoch begat Methuselah at age 65, he spent six jubilees (294 years) with the angels. Thus he would have thereafter returned to earth a short time before he was taken to paradise (*Jub.* 5:23). *2 Enoch* 1:1 states that the patriarch's cosmic journey took place in the last year of his life. Both traditions are roughly consonant with 1 Enoch 81:5–10.[219]

This thinking is based on two interpretive decisions in Genesis 5:24. First, the line "Enoch walked with God" *precedes* his departure. Second, "God" in Genesis 5:24 is Hebrew *'elohim*, which can be semantically plural, though a singular semantic is the case in the overwhelming instances (more than two thousand occurrences) in the Hebrew Bible. Readers should note that *'elohim* occurs two times in Genesis 5:24 ("Enoch walked with God [*'elohim*], and he was not, for God [*'elohim*] took him"). The approach of 1 Enoch and other Second Temple Jewish literature presumes the *second* instance refers to God Himself, while the former points to a *group* of divine beings (the holy ones of the heavenly host).[220] This is

---

219. Nickelsburg, *1 Enoch: A Commentary on the Book of 1 Enoch*, vol. 1, 233.

220. For the meaning of plural *'elohim* as "divine beings" or "supernatural spiritual beings," see Heiser, *The Unseen Realm*, 21–37. For a more scholarly presentation of the same material, see Michael S. Heiser, "Monotheism, Polytheism, Monolatry, or Henotheism? Toward an Assessment of Divine Plurality in the Hebrew Bible," *Bulletin for Biblical Research* 18.1 (2008): 1–30; and Michael S. Heiser, "Does Divine Plurality in the Hebrew Bible Demonstrate an Evolution from Polytheism to Monotheism in Israelite Religion?" *Journal for the Evangelical Study of the Old Testament* 1.1 (2012): 1–24.

exegetically defensible and has precedent in Genesis 3 (comparing verses 5 and 22: "one of us").

12:3

I was blessing—A reference to prayer. Enoch is in prayer when he is commissioned by God to deliver a message to the imprisoned Watchers (13:7–8).

Lord of majesty—As Nickelsburg notes, this title "occurs with certainty only here in 1 Enoch but is probably to be read in 81:3…. God's majesty is mentioned in 5:4 and 101:3."[221]

King of the ages—Nickelsburg again notes that the title "occurs only here in 1 Enoch, although the singular, 'King of eternity (lit. "of the age")' appears in a blessing passage in 25:5."[222]

Enoch the scribe—This is expanded slightly in verse 4 to "righteous scribe." That wording occurs again in 1 Enoch 15:1. Black adds this interesting note:

> At 4Q EnGiants[b] 14 Enoch is further described as "distinguished scribe" and at [1 Enoch] 93:1 probably "skilled scribe." Ezek. 9:2ff. the man clad in white linen with an ink-horn by his side, clearly an angelic figure, is the only Biblical parallel to Enoch in his role as celestial scribe (cf. Jub 4:22–23). The idea of a celestial scribe is probably derived from Babylonian sources.[223]

---

221. Nickelsburg, *1 Enoch: A Commentary on the Book of 1 Enoch*, vol. 1, 235.
222. Ibid., 235.
223. Black, *The Book of Enoch or 1 Enoch*, 143.

This observation is correct in terms of the Mesopotamian ("Babylo-nian") antecedents.[224] The other note about the angelic scribe being the "only" biblical parallel is overstated. The Old Testament has a variety of passages that either state or presume members of the heavenly host are recording data about events on earth in service to God (Isaiah 4:3; 65:6–7; Jeremiah 17:13; Psalm 69:28; Daniel 7:9–10; 10:21; 12:1; Malachi 3:16).[225]

The characterization, not found in Genesis 5:22–24, as a heavenly scribe has deep Mesopotamian roots.[226] Later in 1 Enoch, we see Enoch the scribe reading heavenly tablets produced by the holy ones (1 Enoch 81:1–2; 93:1–3; 103:1–4; 104:1), a clear reference to learning presumed by 1 Enoch 12:3. For our purposes, the role of heavenly books in the final judgment (cp. Revelation 17:8; 20:12, 15; 21:27) is most significant, for the eschatological judgment is the context of the Book of the Watchers (see 1 Enoch 1 and the commentary notes above).

---

224. See Shalom M. Paul, "Heavenly Tablets and the Book of Life," *Journal of the Ancient Near Eastern Society"* 5:1 (1973):345–354; Andrew R. George, "Sennacherib and the Tablet of Destinies." *Iraq* 48 (1986): 133–146.

225. Compare passages that suggest God is the recorder: Exodus 32:32; Psalm 87:5–7.

226. See Andrei Orlov, "'The Learned Savant Who Guards the Secrets of the Great Gods': Evolution of the Roles and Titles of the Seventh Antediluvian Hero in Mesopotamian and Enochic Traditions: Part I: Mesopotamian Traditions," in *Scrinium I: Varia Ethiopica: In Memory of Sevir B. Chernetsov (1943–2005)* (ed. D. Nosnitsin, et.al; Gorgias Press, 2009), 248–264; Andrei Orlov, "'The Learned Savant Who Guards the Secrets of the Great Gods': Evolution of the Roles and Titles of the Seventh Antediluvian Hero in Mesopotamian and Enochic Traditions: Part II: Enochic Traditions," in *Scrinium II: Universum Hagiographicum: Memorial R. P. Michael van Esbroeck (1934–2003)* (ed. Basil Lourie and A. Mouraviev; Gorgias Press, 2009), 165–213.

Heavenly books…play a special role in beliefs about the final judgment, as these are articulated in all the major strata of 1 Enoch
except the Book of the Luminaries. They are a graphic way of
guaranteeing the reality and inevitability of that judgment. What
is already written down in the heavenly courtroom cannot be
expunged. In 1 Enoch heavenly books have three kinds of contents. They record: human deeds, notably those of the sinners who
oppress the righteous; the names of the righteous; and the rewards
of the righteous. These books are often explicitly associated with
the angels who are their scribes…. In 103:1–4, employing language reminiscent of 81:1–2, Enoch claims to have seen heavenly
tablets that contain a record of the rewards that have been prepared and thus must be given to the righteous who have died. The
similarity to 81:1–2 suggests that these books are the counterpart
to the books of human sins, containing not only the deeds of the
righteous but the rewards that result from these deeds.[227]

12:4

*who have left the high heaven, the holy eternal place, and have defiled them-
selves with women, and have done as the children of earth do, and have taken
unto themselves wives*—The focus is the Watchers' sin with human women,
though Shemihazah is not mentioned. Asael (Azazel) is mentioned in 1
Enoch 13:1 in conjunction with the condemnation here. The specifics
of the forbidden teaching of the Watchers is not mentioned in 1 Enoch
12–16, save (very obliquely) at the end of chapter 16 (but see 13:2 for a
general reference). The omission (or transparent imbalance) in relation to
1 Enoch 6–11 is an important factor as to why many scholars deem the
cohabitation crime and the forbidden knowledge crime to have derived
from two separate traditions. See the next verse.

---

227. Nickelsburg, *1 Enoch: A Commentary on the Book of 1 Enoch*, vol. 1, 478–
      479.

12:5

Ye have wrought great destruction on the earth—If the reader/interpreter takes this line about destruction to refer to the earthly destruction language found earlier in the book in connection with forbidden knowledge, the notion that 1 Enoch 12–16 focuses only on the cohabitation sin would not be accurate. However, the destruction may refer to the deeds of the giants (the language of destructive violence of the giants also occurs earlier), in which case the focus would still be the cohabitation.

ye shall have no peace nor forgiveness of sin—This is a clear statement that there is no opportunity for redemption for the fallen Watchers. It is this hope that prompts them to have Enoch intercede later on their behalf.

12:6

inasmuch as †they† delight themselves in† their† children—This line informs the reader that the Watchers were not repentant, at least until God responded in judgment. They rejoiced in the product of their sin (cf. 13:6).

The murder of †their† beloved ones shall †they† see—See the comments at 10:12. Nickelsburg notes, "As a result of the giants' destruction, which their fathers must witness, the fathers lament over them and make petition in their behalf. The destruction of the giants adds paternal grief to the watchers' punishment."[228]

Translation: Chapter 13

13[1]And Enoch went and said: "Azâzêl, thou shalt have no peace: a severe sentence has gone forth against thee to put thee in bonds: [2]And thou

---

228. Ibid., 236.

shalt not have toleration nor †request† granted to thee, because of the unrighteousness which thou hast taught, and because of all the works of godlessness and unrighteousness and sin which thou hast shown to men." ³Then I went and spoke to them all together, and they were all afraid, and fear and trembling seized them. ⁴And they besought me to draw up a petition for them that they might find forgiveness, and to read their petition in the presence of the Lord of heaven. ⁵For from thenceforward they could not speak (with Him) nor lift up their eyes to heaven for shame of their sins for which they had been condemned. ⁶Then I wrote out their petition, and the prayer †in regard to their spirits and their deeds individually and in regard to their requests that they should have forgiveness and length†. ⁷And I went off and sat down at the waters of Dan, in the land of Dan, to the south of the west of Hermon: I read their petition till I fell asleep. ⁸And behold a dream came to me, and visions fell down upon me, and I saw visions of chastisement, ‹and a voice came bidding (me)› to tell it to the sons of heaven, and reprimand them. ⁹And when I awaked, I came unto them, and they were all sitting gathered together, weeping in 'Abelsjâîl, which is between Lebanon and Sênêsêr, with their faces covered. ¹⁰And I recounted before them all the visions which I had seen in sleep, and I began to speak the words of righteousness, and to reprimand the heavenly Watchers.

Commentary

13:1

Azâzêl, thou shalt have no peace: a severe sentence has gone forth against thee to put thee in bonds—This is the only occurrence of the name Azazel (Asael) in 1 Enoch 12–16. Azazel is a Satan figure in 1 Enoch and other Second Temple literature (see comments on 1 Enoch 9–10). Since he (cf. spelling, Asael) is viewed as the leader of the Watchers who sinned with mortal women before the Flood, this verse loops the Satan figure into that sin. The same phrase ("ye shall have no peace") was used in 12:5 of the Watchers. But while the Satan figure is linked to the pre-Flood sin of the

Watchers here, 13:2 makes it evident that the sexual element of that sin is not in view. Azazel will be bound and cast into a pit (10:4).

The denial of peace is of interest. It suggests a relentless character to their incarceration, or perhaps the ongoing agitation the Watchers experience knowing they cannot be reconciled to their Lord.

13:2

the unrighteousness which thou hast taught, and because of all the works of godlessness and unrighteousness and sin which thou hast shown to men—This is a clear reference to what the Watchers taught humankind and its subsequent result, the acceleration and proliferation of depravity. As such, it is consistent with Azazel's sin described earlier in the book (8:1–2; 9:6). This is the more enduring catastrophe in the Second Temple Jewish mindset with respect to pre-Flood transgressions of the boundary between heaven and earth. The Nephilim giants are only the immediate threat.

13:4

And they besought me to draw up a petition for them that they might find forgiveness—This is the first of two requests the condemned Watchers make of Enoch. It obviously relates to Enoch's identity and role as a scribe. The goal of the petition is to seek God's forgiveness for what they have done. Note that there is no attempt to deny their crimes or make excuse. They know better. The Most High will not be deceived.

and to read their petition in the presence of the Lord of heaven—This is the second request. In the next chapter (14:24–15:1), Enoch makes a copy of the request he submitted to God and reads it to the Watchers. Nickelsburg reflects the opinion of some 1 Enoch commentators that, given the reading is to take place in God's presence, the "reading" may rightfully be understood as Enoch praying the words of the petition:

The watchers' second request, that he pray the petition, is based on their own unworthiness to approach God (v 5). It may also presume the theory that the prayer of a righteous man…is especially effective. Cf. Prov 15:29: 3 Macc 6:1–21; *2 Bar.* 2:2; Jas 5:16–18.[229]

This assessment seems to be correct given the wording of 13:6 (see below).

13:5

from thenceforward they could not speak (with Him)—In other words, with God.

nor lift up their eyes to heaven for shame of their sins—It is ironic that supernatural beings are asking a mere mortal to petition God, but they have no standing before their Maker.

13:6

Then I wrote out their petition, and the prayer—Here the petition is cast as a prayer. Though the author of the petition/prayer before God is Enoch, this sort of activity is part of the angelic job description in 1 Enoch elsewhere (and other ancient Near Eastern and Second Temple literature).[230] Nickelsburg observes in this regard:

> The "*memorandum* of petition"… is mentioned only in this section. Later references are simply to "your petition" (14:4, 7). In

229. Nickelsburg, *1 Enoch: A Commentary on the Book of 1 Enoch*, vol. 1, 237.
230. See the discussion and sources at 1 Enoch 9:1, along with Heiser, *Angels*, 107–111.

our literature a memorandum is a written or verbal communication, intended to call one's attention to certain facts. It may be simply a chronicle (Ezra 6:2). It may refer to a prayer (Tob 12:12) or even a book (Mal 3:16), set in the presence of God for the purpose of prodding God into action. The bringing of intercessory memoranda into God's presence is an angelic function according to 99:3 (cf. 104:1), although these reminders may be oral rather than written.... But the activities of angelic *scribe*-intercessors are depicted in 89:70–77.[231]

†*in regard to their spirits and their deeds individually and in regard to their requests that they should have forgiveness and length of days*†—As the cross ligatures in Charles' translation alerts us, there are textual issues here. Nickelsburg translates, "concerning themselves, with regard to their deeds individually, and concerning <their sons> for whom they were making request." The translation of Nickelsburg ("concerning themselves") is obviously self-referential on the part of the Watchers. They want Enoch to petition God for mercy upon themselves. "Their spirits" in Charles' translation might refer to the desire on the part of the Watchers that God be petitioned to spare the Watchers' spirit-offspring, the second-generation Watcher-giants. The Aramaic here is somewhat ambiguous (the noun *n-p-sh*, which can be rendered "spirit, soul, or self," plus the plural pronoun suffix). It is clear that Nickelsburg believes it is self-referential, as he adds (on the basis of 12:6 and the ending phrase "length of days," something denied to the giants in 10:9–10) the words "their sons" in brackets, presuming that "perhaps an explanatory 'their sons' has dropped from the text."[232] It seems best not to conjecture here without textual basis.

---

231. Nickelsburg, *1 Enoch: A Commentary on the Book of 1 Enoch*, vol. 1, 237.
232. Ibid., 238.

13:7

the waters of Dan, in the land of Dan, to the south of the west of Hermon—
See the note and resources on 6:7.

13:8

*behold a dream came to me, and visions fell down upon me—*Nickelsburg
notes that this occurs in the Old Testament and is something of a pattern
in Second Temple literature—that, while in prayer (12:3), the petitioner
receives a dream or vision in response to that prayer (Daniel 9:21; 4 Ezra;
2 Baruch; 3 Baruch 1).[233]

visions of chastisement…tell it to the sons of heaven, and reprimand them—
Nickelsburg has "visions of wrath." Aramaic reads "visions of reprimand."[234] God's response is thus summarized in one statement. Enoch
obeys and reads the determination of God and their sentence to them, the
content of which is found in 14:1–16:4.

13:9

*they were all sitting gathered together, weeping in 'Abelsjâîl, which is between
Lebanon and Sênêsêr—*Nickelsburg has Abel-Main in place of on the basis
of graphic confusion on the part of the translator(s); i.e., the misreading
of certain letters.[235] Greek has EBAΛΣATA (*ebalsata*), while Ethiopic reads

233. Ibid., 239.

234. Milik, *Enoch*, 193 (4QEnᶜ 1 6:5).

235. Nickelsburg (p. 248) explains: "On the basis of the parallel in *T. Levi*, Milik
     (*Enoch*, 196) makes an identification with Abel-Main, reading here Abel-
     Mayyâ. The original translator of 1 Enoch, Milik argues, wrote ABEΛΣAIA,
     reading the Aram. *mem* as a *samek*. In a Greek corruption, the *iota* was read

'ubelseyā'ēl. On Abel-Main, a known location in Upper Galilee, see the resources noted at 6:7. The general location of this collection of places is Upper Galilee toward Mount Hermon. Unlike many other scholars, Nickelsburg sees the connection between this location and its religious traditions (pagan and Second Temple Jewish Enochian material) to the "gates of hell" and transfiguration passages in the Gospels:

> The Matthean account of Simon's confession of Jesus' messiahship at Caesarea Philippi and Jesus' commissioning of Simon as "Peter" (Matt 16:13–19) is another revelatory tradition set in this geographical region that may be related to the stories of the commissioning of Enoch and Levi. Moreover, Mark's juxtaposition of this pericope and the story of Jesus' transfiguration "on a high mountain apart" (Mark 9:1–8) suggests a broader, post-resurrection revelatory tradition bound to the area of Hermon.[236]

With their faces covered—Even before the verdict is read, the Watchers assume the posture of shame and mourning (cp. Jeremiah 14:3–4).

---

as a *tau*. E indicates a confusion of a final *alpha* for a *lambda*. I have retained the form Abel-Main found in 4QLevi[b] ar frg. 2 line 13."

236. Nickelsburg, *1 Enoch: A Commentary on the Book of 1 Enoch*, vol. 1, 246. He adds in footnote 43: "The possible connection between *T. Levi* 2:3–5 and Matt 16:13–23 is noted briefly by Krister Stendahl, "Matthew," in Matthew Black, ed., *Peake's Commentary on the Bible* (London: Thomas Nelson & Sons, 1962) 787. Independently of this, it is placed in the broader context of other texts mentioned in this excursus by *Lipiński*, "El's Abode" 35; and Nickelsburg, "Enoch, Levi, and Peter," 590–99. This interpretation is set in a broader Christian context by Riesner, "Bethany Beyond the Jordan" and is developed by Tord Fornberg, "Peter—the High Priest of the New Covenant?" *East Asian Journal of Theology* 4 (1986) 113–21.

13:10

I recounted before them—Most scholars see this as a solemn assembly, not some casual follow-up encounter. Nickelsburg is representative:

> These verses describe a scene in which the assembled watchers hear Enoch's formal reading of the reprimand that has issued from the heavenly throne room.... In its broadest sense the expression ["read/recount before them"] denotes a situation in which a formal legal agreement or offer is made or in which a proclamation with the force of law is read (cf., e.g., Gen 23:10, 16; 2 Sam 3:19–20). That is, laws, covenants, legally binding agreements, and edicts must be spoken publicly in the hearing (or physical presence) of the parties involved.... Thus this section of Enoch describes a formal convocation, in which the sentence of the heavenly courtroom is read in the presence of those who have been sentenced.[237]

Translation: Chapter 14

14[1] The book of the words of righteousness, and of the reprimand of the eternal Watchers in accordance with the command of the Holy Great One in that vision. [2] I saw in my sleep what I will now say with a tongue of flesh and with the breath of my mouth: which the Great One has given to men to converse therewith and understand with the heart. [3] As He hath created and given to man the power of understanding the word of wisdom, so hath He created me also and given me the power of reprimanding the Watchers, the children of heaven. [4] I wrote out your petition, and in my vision it appeared thus, that your petition will not be granted unto you throughout all the days of eternity, and that judgement has been finally passed upon you: yea (your petition) will not be granted unto you. [5] And

---

237. Nickelsburg, *1 Enoch: A Commentary on the Book of 1 Enoch*, vol. 1, 250.

from henceforth you shall not ascend into heaven unto all eternity, and in bonds of the earth the decree has gone forth to bind you for all the days of the world. [6]And (that) previously you shall have seen the destruction of your beloved sons and you shall have no pleasure in them, but they shall fall before you by the sword. [7]And your petition on their behalf shall not be granted, nor yet on your own: even though you weep and pray and **speak all the words** contained in the writing which I have written. [8]And the vision was shown to me thus: Behold, in the vision clouds invited me and a mist summoned me, and the course of the stars and the lightnings sped and **hastened** me, and the winds in the vision caused me to fly and lifted me upward, and bore me into heaven. [9]And I went in till I drew nigh to a wall which is built of crystals and surrounded by tongues of fire: and it began to affright me. [10]And I went into the tongues of fire and drew nigh to a large house which was built of crystals: and the walls of the house were like a tesselated floor (made) of crystals, and its groundwork was of crystal. [11]Its ceiling was like the path of the stars and the lightnings, and between them were fiery cherubim, and their heaven was (clear as) water. [12]A flaming fire surrounded the walls, and its portals blazed with fire. [13]And I entered into that house, and it was hot as fire and cold as ice: there were no delights of life therein: fear covered me, and trembling gat hold upon me. [14]And as I quaked and trembled, I fell upon my face. And I beheld a vision, [15]And lo! there was a second house, greater than the former, and the entire portal stood open before me, and it was built of flames of fire. [16]And in every respect it so excelled in splendour and magnificence and extent that I cannot describe to you its splendour and its extent. [17]And its floor was of fire, and above it were lightnings and the path of the stars, and its ceiling also was flaming fire. [18]And I looked and saw therein a lofty throne: its appearance was as crystal, and the wheels thereof as the shining sun, and there was the **vision** of cherubim. [19]And from underneath the throne came streams of flaming fire so that I could not look thereon. [20]And the Great Glory sat thereon, and His raiment shone more brightly than the sun and was whiter than any snow. [21]None of the angels could enter and could behold His face by reason of the magnificence and glory, and no flesh could behold Him. [22]The flaming fire was round about Him, and a great fire stood before Him, and none around could draw nigh Him: ten thousand times ten thousand (stood) before Him, yet He needed no counsellor. [23]And the most holy ones who were nigh to Him did not leave by night nor depart from Him. [24]And until then I had been prostrate on my face, trembling: and the Lord called me with His own mouth, and said to me: "Come hither, Enoch, and hear my word." [25]And one of the holy ones came to me and waked me, and He made me rise up and approach the door: and I bowed my face downwards.

Commentary

14:1

The book of the words of righteousness, and of the reprimand of the eternal Watchers—The descriptive opening makes clear that chapter 14 is the content of God's answer to Enoch's petition on behalf of the fallen Watchers.

in accordance with the command of the Holy Great One—God Himself instructed Enoch to recite the sentence and its content.

in that vision—This wording follows the Greek. Nickelsburg has "in the dream that <I dreamt>," partially reconstructed on the basis of Milik's reconstruction of 4QEnc 1 6:10.[238] In either case, the reference is to the dream Enoch had in chapter 13 (see 14:2).

---

238. Nickelsburg, *1 Enoch: A Commentary on the Book of 1 Enoch*, vol. 1, 251.
       In a footnote on that page, Nickelsburg adds: "The length of the lines in
       4QEn[c] seems to require this reconstruction rather than the assumption
       that "in my dream" and "in this vision" have been transposed in G[a].
       The reconstruction presumes an omission of four words in the Aramaic
       archetype of G[a]."

14:2–3

with a tongue of flesh and with the breath of my mouth—A description befitting of a mere mortal. The point is a deliberate ironic contrast between him (the human messenger) and the divine origin of the message, as well as the fact that supernatural beings are the target of the reprimand. The ironic thought continues in verse 3: "As He hath created and given to man the power of understanding the word of wisdom, so hath He created me also and given me the power of reprimanding the Watchers, the children of heaven."

given to man the power of understanding the word of wisdom—Some scholars have seen a nod to gnostic thought here, but this is an overreach. There is no sense that understanding knowledge results in salvation. It is rather closer to the notion of understanding prophetic speech akin to 1 Corinthians 12–14.

the children of heaven—Points to their original creation as God's supernatural assistants. The description here will also serve the purpose of irony given their punishment.

14:4–6

your petition will not be granted unto you—Enoch gets right to the point, as commanded.

all the days of eternity...unto all eternity...all the days of the world—The length of the sentence is repeated three times in verses 4–6. The rejection of the petition of the Watchers and their sanction from ever returning to their original status are eternal. The finality and irreversibility of the decision is clear. Nickelsburg has some interesting observations in this regard:

Verse 4 refers to the heavenly judgment process itself.... Here the Ethiopic verb indicates a past tense, and the expression appears to refer to the completion of the heavenly decision-making process. It has resulted in a decree of damnation against the watchers. The use of גזירוא [*gzyrw'*] ("decree," 4QEn^c 1 6:14) here parallels Dan 4:14, 21 (17, 24 in English translations), where the noun גזרה [*g^ezērāh*] refers to the heavenly decree against Nebuchadnezzar.[239]

The parallel to Daniel 4:14, 21 is also ironic, as in Daniel the decree against Nebuchadnezzar is "by decree of the Watchers" and a "decree of the Most High." In other words, God's heavenly council has participatory governance that, by God's own design, includes the "holy ones" (the other description of the Watchers in Daniel 4:13). Here in 1 Enoch, it is the Watchers on the wrong side of that process.

in bonds of the earth—The Watchers committed their sin on the earth, and within the earth they will be bound. See 10:11–13; 18:11; 19:1; 21:7–10 for the same verdict and confinement.

And (that) previously you shall have seen the destruction of your beloved sons— The translation is awkward in part because of some textual corruption. Nickelsburg captures the gist of the text: "And that before these things, you will see the destruction of your sons, your beloved ones." Before the Watchers are punished (sent to the Abyss), they will be forced to witness the annihilation of the giants, their offspring.

14:8

the vision was shown to me thus—Beginning with this verse and continuing to 16:4, the end of the current section of the Book of the Watch-

---

239. Nickelsburg, *1 Enoch: A Commentary on the Book of 1 Enoch*, vol. 1, 253.

ers (chapters 12–16), Enoch's heavenly commissioning is detailed. This commissioning is consistent in pattern with that of other biblical figures who were "spokespersons for God."[240] Consequently, some of the earlier allusions put into Enoch's mouth receive elaboration here. Enoch will see God enthroned in His heavenly abode, and God speaks His judgment against the Watchers. Nickelsburg previews what the reader can expect:

> The flow of the narrative in vv 8–23 is climactic in several respects. First, there is a movement from the outside inward: from earth to heaven, then through the outer wall and court of the temple, into the main room, to the door of the holy of holies through which he can see the enthroned Deity. Corresponding to this Godward movement of his journey are the increasingly marvelous spectacles described at increasingly greater length: the outer wall, constructed of hailstones and fire, two mutually exclusive entities; the main room, in which the presence of snow and new fiery elements intensify the paradox; in the heart of the temple, the holy of holies, where the paradox of hot and cold give way to the unmitigated blazing fire that proceeds from the throne and envelops the Deity. Similarly climactic is the manner in which the successive components of the temple comprise a series of perilous barriers that threaten and impede the seer's progress inward: a belt of fire encircling the outer wall; a similar belt around the main room intensified by blazing flames in its doorways; a fiery furnace for a throne room. These increasingly perilous barriers have their respective effects on Enoch. At the sight of the first wall, he begins to fear, but he negotiates the fiery barrier. Similarly, he enters the main room. Here the effect is overwhelming. He quakes in terror and collapses. Beyond the door leading to the holy of holies he

---

240. For a summary, see Heiser, *Unseen Realm*, 232–239.

will not pass. The blazing fire of the divine presence constitutes a final barrier.[241]

in the vision clouds invited me and a mist summoned me—The wording is correct. Enoch reports being summoned by clouds and a mist. The language (for the clouds, at least) is likely describing divine messengers, since it is similar to that used in Scripture (Psalm 104:4). Verse 11 validates this approach, as its language is similar to Ezekiel 1. The full description in the verse makes it evident that Enoch is being transported, not just summoned, by these forces or figures.

The reference to a mist may reflect God's abode "upon the waters" above the firmament covering the world in ancient cosmology (Psalm 29:10). The wording of verse 11 perhaps substantiates this. However, it is possible that the Greek term, *homichlai*, on which the translation "mist" is based may better be rendered "dark cloud, gloom, gloomy darkness," which would be consistent with depictions of God's presence elsewhere (Exodus 20:21; Deuteronomy 4:11; Psalm 18:9; 97:2). Subsequent reference to lightning brings Old Testament storm-cloud theophanic descriptions to mind (Exodus 19:16; 20:18; Ezekiel 1:13–14).

---

241. Nickelsburg, *1 Enoch: A Commentary on the Book of 1 Enoch*, vol. 1, 258–260. Nickelsburg goes on to sketch the similarities and differences between Enoch's visionary journey and biblical commissioning texts and *merkabah* mystical texts, well known in the Second Temple period. *Merkabah* is a Hebrew term for God's throne-chariot. In 1 Chronicles 28:18, the cherubim throne of the Temple is specifically called Yahweh's "chariot" (*merkabah*). On *Merkabah* texts in the Second Temple Period, see James M. Scott, "Throne-Chariot Mysticism in Qumran and in Paul," in *Eschatology, Messianism, and the Dead Sea Scrolls* (1997): 101–119; Ira Chernus, "Visions of God in Merkabah Mysticism." *Journal for the Study of Judaism in the Persian, Hellenistic, and Roman Period,* 13.1/2 (1982): 123–146.

the course of the stars—Apparently, shooting or falling stars (cf. verses 12, 17). Rabbinic interpretation (*b. Ber.* 58b; *y. Ber.* 9:13c, *m. Ber.* 9:1) takes the terminology (Aramaic *ziyqiyn*) as referring "to a heavenly phenomenon passing through Orion, evidently a comet or shooting star."[242]

14:9–10

a wall which is built of crystals and surrounded by tongues of fire—Nickelsburg has "hailstones" instead of crystals, which makes good sense, given the preceding terms. The Greek term *chalaza* refers to hail.[243] Hail and snow (verse 10) are elements of the heavenly realms (Job 38:22). In addition to the pairing of hail and snow, the verse effectively pairs hail and fire, a combination that is also not unfamiliar to the Old Testament (Exodus 9:23; Psalm 18:13–14 [cf. 18:9's reference to gloomy darkness]; 148:8). In English Bibles, God's presence is described in crystalline terms (Ezekiel 1:22). The Hebrew word in that passage, *qerah*, elsewhere denotes ice or frost (Genesis 41:40; Job 6:16; 37:10). Consequently, the description of God's presence is a paradoxical one of "fire and ice," a combination made more explicit in 1 Enoch 71:5, where God's domain is "a structure built of crystals; and between those crystals tongues of living fire" (see also verse 13). The whole point is that God's presence is "unnatural" with respect to human experience.

I went into the tongues of fire—As with Acts 2:3, the "tongues" expression refers to the way a flame "licks" the air. The fact that Enoch penetrates this veil validates this interpretation of the "tongues" language of verses 9–10.

---

242. Nickelsburg, *1 Enoch: A Commentary on the Book of 1 Enoch*, vol. 1, 262.

243. William Arndt , Frederick W. Danker, and Walter Bauer, *A Greek-English Lexicon of the New Testament and Other Early Christian Literature* (Chicago: University of Chicago Press, 2000), 1075; Henry George Liddell, Robert Scott, Henry Stuart Jones, and Roderick McKenzie, *A Greek-English Lexicon* (Oxford: Clarendon Press, 1996), 1970.

a large house which was built of crystals: and the walls of the house were like a tesselated floor (made) of crystals, and its groundwork was of crystal—The divine abode is made of snow or frost (cf. the discussion of "crystal" above). Again, paradoxically, its walls and entryways were "surrounded by fire" (verse 12). Again, it is unlike the dwelling of men or anything in human experience.

14:11

Its ceiling was like the path of the stars and the lightnings and between them were fiery cherubim—This draws the vision more closely into the territory of Ezekiel 1, where God is seated in the starry sky on the cherubim throne. This connection will be reinforced in verse 18, where another reference to the cherubim is accompanied by other elements of Ezekiel 1 (see below).

The reference to the cherubim orients the reader's understanding of the vision. The four cherubim correspond to the cardinal points of the Babylonian zodiac.[244] That this is the case is evident from the rest of the language of Ezekiel, which provides context. The prophet's vision included

---

244. Daniel Isaac Block, *The Book of Ezekiel, Chapters 1–24* (*The New International Commentary on the Old Testament*; Grand Rapids, MI: Wm. B. Eerdmans Publishing Co., 1997), 324–325. On the difference between the four faces between Ezekiel 1 and 10, Block notes: "The description of the cherubim's faces differs significantly from the earlier account. Whereas 1:10 had ascribed four different faces to each of the cherubim, the plain reading of the Hebrew here points to four identical faces for each cherub, with each cherub having a different set. Whereas 1:10 had followed a human-lion-bull-eagle sequence, 10:14 lists them as cherub-human-lion-eagle. This reordering raises two questions. Why was the bull face displaced, and how is the cherubic face to be perceived?… While we cannot be sure how the ancients perceived true cherubic faces, some evidence suggests that they were not human. On the other hand, the contradiction at least in the order of faces is more apparent than real…. If the faces in 10:14 are also listed in clockwise order, the sequence is identical, and the cherub's is identified

"wheels within wheels" whose "rims" were "tall and awesome" and "full of eyes" (Ezekiel 1:17–18). In Ezekiel 10, we learn that these "eyes" were *within* the bodies of the cherubim, a detail that provides an important interpretive clue. Old Testament scholar Daniel Block notes that the word translated "eyes" (*'ayin*) in Ezekiel 1:17–18 "had been used earlier for 'sparkle, gleam' (vv. 4, 16), and this may point the way to its interpretation here."[245] "Sparkling" and "gleaming" are of course familiar descriptions for stars throughout ancient literature. As Pilch notes, this is one of the ways that the ancients described stars—specifically, *constellations*:

> The ancients called stars "eyes," and thought them to be living entities. Constellated stars, called "full of eyes," were perceived as animate beings like persons or animals. Since Ezekiel sees all four constellations moving at once, his vantage point was high above the entire cosmos (vv. 4–11).[246]

---

with the bull. Why the present enumeration commences with the cherub instead of the human face is unclear, but it may reflect the vantage from which the prophet observed the chariot. In order to witness the *k bôd* lifting from cherubim inside the temple, he must have been standing at the front of the building, perhaps at the eastern gate of the inner court." He adds in a footnote: "According to a 7th-century-B.C. Akkadian text, Namtartu (the concubine of Namtaru, vizier of the netherworld) had the head of a *kur bu* but human hands and feet (ANET, p. 109)." I would also add that since the bodies of cherubim were predominantly bovine, having the term *karub* here instead of ox/bull (Heb: *shor*) is a distinction without a difference.

245. Ibid., 100. Interestingly, an Akkadian cognate term (*nu*; "eye-stone") refers to a sparkling gem (see *HALOT,* 818).

246. John J. Pilch, *Flights of the Soul: Visions, Heavenly Journeys, and Peak Experiences in the Biblical World* (Grand Rapids, MI; Cambridge, U.K.: William B. Eerdmans Publishing Company, 2011), 37. See also Bruce J. Malina, *On the Genre and Message of Revelation: Star Visions and Sky Journeys* (Hendrickson Publishers, 1995), 97.

and their heaven was (clear as) water—Given that the context is the celestial heavens, this can only coherently refer to the "waters above" the firmament in Israelite cosmology (Psalm 29:10).

14:12

A flaming fire surrounded the walls, and its portals blazed with fire—Some commentators take the language here (given the celestial context) to fiery objects in the heavens, such as comets or meteors. See verse 8.

14:13

I entered into that house, and it was hot as fire and cold as ice—Again, the paradox is intentional (verses 8, 10).

14:14

And I beheld a vision—The prone prophet "sees the holy of holies of the heavenly temple, the throne room of God (vv 18–20)."[247]

14:15–17

there was a second house, greater than the former…in every respect it so excelled in splendour and magnificence…… its floor was of fire, and above it were lightnings and the path of the stars, and its ceiling also was flaming fire—Not only is this second dwelling larger than the first, but this one is characterized by fire—i.e., it is described as being made entirely of fiery material. Nickelsburg adds that "a fiery ceiling has displaced the shooting stars and lightning flashes."[248] Now the lightning and stars are distinguished from the elements of the divine home.

---

247. Nickelsburg, *1 Enoch: A Commentary on the Book of 1 Enoch*, vol. 1, 264.
248. Ibid., 264.

14:18–20

a lofty throne: its appearance was as crystal, and the wheels thereof as the shining sun, and there was the vision of cherubim…from underneath the throne came streams of flaming fire…the Great Glory sat thereon, and His raiment shone more brightly than the sun—The description here obviously borrows from Ezekiel 1 and 10:

> …in the midst of the <u>fire</u>, as it were <u>gleaming metal</u>. And from the midst of it came the likeness of four living creatures (<u>cherubim</u>, Ezek 10:1–2, 22)….
>
> As for the likeness of the living creatures, their appearance was like <u>burning coals of fire</u>, like the appearance of <u>torches</u> moving to and fro among the living creatures. And the <u>fire</u> was bright, and out of the <u>fire</u> went forth lightning….
>
> Now as I looked at the living creatures, I saw a <u>wheel</u> on the earth beside the living creatures, one for each of the four of them. As for the appearance of the <u>wheels</u> and their construction: their appearance was like the <u>gleaming of beryl</u>….
>
> Over the heads of the living creatures there was the likeness of <u>an expanse, shining like awe-inspiring crystal</u>, spread out above their heads….
>
> And above the expanse over their heads there was the likeness of <u>a throne</u>, in appearance like <u>sapphire</u>; and seated above the likeness of <u>a throne</u> was a likeness with <u>a human appearance</u>. And upward from what had the appearance of his waist I saw as it were <u>gleaming metal</u>, like the appearance of <u>fire</u> enclosed all around. And downward from what had the appearance of his waist I saw as it were the appearance of <u>fire</u>, and there was <u>brightness</u> around him. (Ezek 1:4–5, 13, 15–16, 22, 26–27)

Note that in 14:19, the "Great Glory" is a way of referring to God Himself.

and was whiter than any snow—The description above is also similar to
Daniel's vision (Daniel 7:9–10) of the Ancient of Days, whose clothing
"was white as snow" (Daniel 7:9). Goldingay opines, "White clothing (and
hair) could suggest purity (cf. 11:35; 12:10; Isa 1:18; Ps 51:9 [7]), but in
the context, with its description of the flaming throne, more likely…has
its more basic meaning of brightness and luminosity, thus nobility and
splendor."[249] John and Adela Collins note some similarities and differences
between Enoch's and Daniel's vision of the enthroned deity:

> This passage has some distinctive parallels to Daniel that do not
> appear in earlier biblical throne visions: the river of fire (plural in
> *Enoch*), clothing white as snow (whiter in *Enoch*), the entourage
> of "ten thousand times ten thousand." There are differences too:
> Enoch's vision is considerably more elaborate than Daniel's, and
> the latter is adapted to a court scene. Enoch ascends to a throne
> established in the heavens. In Daniel thrones (in the plural) are
> set up and the location is unclear. The specificity of the parallels,
> however, requires at the least a common tradition of speculation
> about the divine throne. Direct literary influence cannot be ruled
> out, even if it cannot be decisively proved.[250]

14:21

*None of the angels could enter and could behold His face by reason of the
magnificence and glory, and no flesh could behold Him*—The descrip-

---

249. John E. Goldingay, *Daniel* (vol. 30; *Word Biblical Commentary*; Dallas:
    Word, Incorporated, 1989), 165.

250. John Joseph Collins and Adela Yarbro Collins, *Daniel: A Commentary on
    the Book of Daniel* (ed. Frank Moore Cross; *Hermeneia—a Critical and
    Historical Commentary on the Bible*; Minneapolis, MN: Fortress Press,
    1993), 300.

tion appears to intentionally take readers to the idea that no one could behold the unveiled, unfiltered presence of God. In Exodus 33:20, this privilege was denied to Moses. In Isaiah 6, the seraphim cover their faces in God's presence (Isaiah 6:2). I say "unveiled, unfiltered" because God does appear to humans as a man in the Old Testament, most often as the Angel of Yahweh, where no indication is given that the conversations are not face to face (Genesis 18; 32:22–32; cp. Genesis 48:15–16).[251]

14:22

See the discussion of verses 15–20.

14:23

did not leave by night nor depart from Him—Interestingly, very similar wording is found in the Qumran Temple Scroll (11QT 62:1–11) of the king's bodyguard.[252]

14:25

one of the holy ones came to me and waked me, and He made me rise up and approach the door: and I bowed my face downwards—The posture and description are similar to the description of the prophet Daniel (Daniel 8:17–18; 10:8–9, 15). Though raised up by a holy one, he cannot look upon the enthroned God.

---

251. On the identification of the Angel of Yahweh with God Himself, see Heiser, *The Unseen Realm*, 127–148.

252. Nickelsburg, *1 Enoch: A Commentary on the Book of 1 Enoch*, vol. 1, 266.

Translation: Chapter 15

15 [1] And He answered and said to me, and I heard His voice: "Fear not, Enoch, thou righteous man and scribe of righteousness: approach hither and hear my voice. [2] And go, say to the Watchers of heaven, who have sent thee to intercede for them: 'You should intercede for men, and not men for you: [3] Wherefore have ye left the high, holy, and eternal heaven, and lain with women, and defiled yourselves with the daughters of men and taken to yourselves wives, and done like the children of earth, and begotten giants (as your) sons. [4] And though ye were holy, spiritual, living the eternal life, you have defiled yourselves with the blood of women, and have begotten (children) with the blood of flesh, and, **as the children** of men, have lusted after flesh and blood as those also do who die and perish. [5] Therefore have I given them wives also that they might impregnate them, and beget children by them, that thus nothing might be wanting to them on earth. [6] But you were formerly spiritual, living the eternal life, and immortal for all generations of the world. [7] And therefore I have not appointed wives for you; for as for the spiritual ones of the heaven, in heaven is their dwelling. [8] And now, the giants, who are produced from the spirits and flesh, shall be called evil spirits upon the earth, and on the earth shall be their dwelling. [9] Evil spirits have proceeded from their bodies; because they are born from **men**, and from the holy Watchers is their beginning and primal origin; they shall be evil spirits on earth, and evil spirits shall they be called. [[10] As for the spirits of heaven, in heaven shall be their dwelling, but as for the spirits of the earth which were born upon the earth, on the earth shall be their dwelling.] [11] And the spirits of the giants **afflict**, oppress, destroy, attack, do battle, and work destruction on the earth, and cause trouble: they take no food, but nevertheless hunger and thirst, and cause offences. [12] And these spirits shall rise up against the children of men and against the women, because they have proceeded from them.'"

Commentary

15:1

He answered and said to me—This is the holy one who had awakened Enoch in 14:25.

scribe of righteousness—Nickelsburg reads "scribe of truth," following G^a, which literally reads, "the true man, man of truth (*alētheias*), the scribe." The phrasing of Charles matches the wording of 12:4. The reading here may be drawn from that passage or the translation is an intentional alignment with LXX Genesis 6:9, cited by Black, who provides no Greek evidence for *dikaiosounē* ("righteousness").[253] The presumed original Aramaic word (not extant) was likely *qwšṭ'*, which "can mean either uprightness/ righteousness or truth."[254] Nickelsburg elsewhere adds:

> Enoch's righteousness is relevant here because by virtue of it he was permitted to enter the divine presence—as the vision describes. The second part of the title, however, appears to reflect 14:1: Enoch is the scribe who wrote "the Book of the Words of Truth." The precise connotations of the Aramaic original of 12:4 are uncertain. [Do they] anticipate 13:10–14:1? More likely, perhaps, the Greek translator at 12:4 saw correctly that the title there was a conflation of the double title here: Enoch the scribe was also an upright man.[255]

15:2

"You should intercede for men, and not men for you"—Intercession was, of course, a function of members of the heavenly host in the Old Testament

---

253. Black, *The Book of Enoch*, 152.

254. Nickelsburg, *1 Enoch: A Commentary on the Book of 1 Enoch*, vol. 1, 270.

255. Ibid., 270.

period. In Job 5:1, we see Eliphaz jousting with Job: "Call now; is there anyone who will answer you? To which of the holy ones will you turn?" This statement should be read in the context of Job 4:17–18 and 15:15, where Eliphaz mercilessly ridicules the suffering man, taunting him by essentially saying, "Who are you to think you're righteous? Are you better than the angels? Will any of them intercede for you? Go ahead; make an appeal to one of the holy ones." The reader is left with the impression that Job should expect no heavenly intercession on his behalf, since that is for the righteous. Clines adds:

> We have heard of such beings previously at 5:1, where Eliphaz warned Job that there was no point in calling out to such a heavenly being for deliverance from the web of sin and punishment in which he was now caught. There too the angel was envisaged as a mediator between humans and God who would seek mercy from God for the suffering human. The angel is an "interpreter" or "mediator" [*melits*], apparently meaning that its function is to... explain God's purpose in the infliction of suffering.[256]

The notion of intercession by heavenly advocates in God's employ, especially in regard to undeserved suffering, is very old. It can be found in the most ancient literature of the biblical world, such as Sumerian texts where the divine council of Sumer deliberated justice between both humans and gods.[257]

In the Second Temple Period, the motif of angelic intercession was common, especially in 1 Enoch. There are significant scholarly surveys

---

256. David J. A. Clines, *Job 21–37*, WBC 18A (Nashville: Thomas Nelson, 2006), 735.

257. See Thorkild Jacobsen, "Primitive Democracy in Ancient Mesopotamia," *JNES* 2 (1943): 159–72; Samuel Noah Kramer, "Sumerian Theology and Ethics," *Harvard Theological Review* 49 (1956): 45–62 (59).

in this regard.[258] First Enoch 20:6; 39:5; 40:6; and 47:1–2 are among the passages where archangels intercede and pray on behalf of humans.

15:3

giants—As elsewhere in Greek 1 Enoch, this is a form of the lemma *gigas*. The lemma occurs eight times in the Greek material.[259]

15:4

Holy ones and spirits—The Hebrew Bible uses the same terminology for members of the heavenly host (Hebrew: *qedoshîm, rûḥôt / rûchôt*).[260]

The blood of women...the blood of flesh... the children of men—In one regard, the meaning ("mortality, mortal beings") is made transparent in

---

258. Some of this research shows intersection with certain New Testament passages. See Nickelsburg, *1 Enoch: A Commentary on the Book of 1 Enoch*, vol. 1, 208–209; Daniel Johansson, "'Who Can Forgive Sins but God Alone?' Human and Angelic Agents, and Divine Forgiveness in Early Judaism," *Journal for the Study of the New Testament* 33.4 (2011): 351–374. The comment in 1 Timothy 2:5 against this backdrop brings Paul's statement into sharp focus. The risen Jesus subsumes the role of mediator.

259. Based on a search in the morphologically tagged Greek text 1 Enoch produced by Logos Bible Software: Ken Penner and Michael S. Heiser, "Old Testament Greek Pseudepigrapha with Morphology," Bellingham, WA: Lexham Press, 2008. The references are: 1 Enoch 7:2, 4; 8:3; 10:16; 15:3, 8, 11; 16:1.

260. "Holy ones" (Deuteronomy 33:2–3; Job 5:1; Zechariah 14:5; Daniel 4:17); "spirits" (1 Kings 22:19–23 [cp. 2 Chronicles 18:18–22]; Psalm 104:4). On these terms and the "evil spirit" terminology in the Hebrew Bible, see Heiser, *Angels*, 3–5, 10.

the phrase that follows, describing the Watchers as having "lusted after flesh and blood as those also do who die and perish." The phrase "blood of women" has another layer to it, one that has the Watchers violating their role as intercessors in a more nuanced way:

> Not only have the watchers polluted themselves through intercourse (v 3; cf. 7:1), they have slept with their wives during their menstrual period (v 4; cf. 10:11), which created a graver state of uncleanness according to Jewish ritual law (Lev 15:19–24). Holiness is a characteristic of God that belongs derivatively to those who serve him, especially his priests. The watchers have polluted that holy state that permitted them to draw near to him and serve him in his heavenly temple.[261]

15:5

Therefore have I given them wives—The referent is to human men, not the Watchers, as the ensuing explanation, as well as verse 7, makes clear.

that they might impregnate them, and beget children by them, that thus nothing might be wanting to them on earth—God gave Adam (and mankind) women for the purpose of having children to perpetuate the species on earth. Nickelsburg summarizes the violation of the Watchers in that context:

> Since humans are flesh and blood (i.e., mortal), they need progeny to perpetuate their name and line. God created women and sex as a means to this end. By contrast with flesh and blood, the watchers, being spiritual, are immortal and therefore have no

---

261. Nickelsburg, *1 Enoch: A Commentary on the Book of 1 Enoch*, vol. 1, 271–272.

need to procreate. Their sin in this case is that they have acted like human beings (thus the conclusion of v 4). They have begotten sons (cf. 6:2) where none were needed, mixing their seed with human blood (cf. Wis 7:2). Moreover, they have indulged in humanlike sexual desire (cf. 1 Enoch 6:2) inappropriate to their angelic state.[262]

15:7

I have not appointed wives for you—See comments at verses 4–5.

15:8–9

who are produced—The Greek verb lemma translated "produced" is *gennaō* ("to beget"; hence, here "begotten").

shall be called evil spirits—The Greek translated "evil spirits" is not the expected *daimonion* ("demons") or *pneumata ponēra* ("evil spirits"), but *pneumata ischura* "powerful spirits" (Greek lemma *ischuros*: "strong, mighty, powerful.")[263] *Pneumata ponēra* is found in the next verse twice. One would think that perhaps *ischura* reflects the Greek LXX at Genesis 6:4, translating Hebrew *gibborim* ("mighty ones"), but LXX of Genesis 6:4 does not render *gibborim* (assuming the translator's text read as much), but uses *gigas* twice, presumably for both *nephilim* and *gibborim* (but see 16:1). Nickelsburg observes that G^s and Ethiopic disagree with the *ischura* of G^a, reading *ponēra* and *'ekuyāna* respectively.[264] Perhaps the scribe of G^s chose the lemma to draw attention to the indestructability of these spirits. Nickelsburg writes that "because of their dual nature, the giants are both

---

262. Ibid., 272.
263. BDAG, 483; Liddell-Scott, 843.
264. Nickelsburg, *1 Enoch: A Commentary on the Book of 1 Enoch*, vol. 1, 267.

eradicable and immortal. On the one hand, the body of their flesh can die. On the other hand, their spirits have continued existence."[265]

15:10

As for the spirits of heaven, in heaven shall be their dwelling, but as for the spirits of the earth which were born upon the earth, on the earth shall be their dwelling—The point of the statement seems to be that the spirits born of the Watchers' transgression can never be part of God's heavenly realm. They have no hope of ever being included in God's heavenly host.

15:11

afflict—The verb is boldfaced because there is a textual corruption here. G^a inexplicably reads *nephelas* ("clouds"), which may be a bungled transliteration of *nephilim*.[266] Nickelsburg has "lead astray" instead, hypothesizing that the scribe responsible for G^s (which reads *nemomena*, "pasturing") was confused by a corrupted Aramaic text. The rendering of G^s translates Aramaic *r 'în*, which was a corruption of *t 'în* ("lead astray"). "Lead astray" fits the context well—the offspring of the Watchers who, aside from the cohabitation sin, led humanity astray into self-destruction and idolatry, would do as their fathers had done.

they take no food—This is not a contradiction to the earlier cannibalism of the giants, for this description is about their disembodied spirits.

hunger—Nickelsburg's translation has "abstain from food," which is more accurate.

---

265. Ibid., 272.
266. Elsewhere in Greek 1 Enoch, the form ναφηλειμ (*naphēleim*) occurs (G^s), which is almost certainly a transliteration of Hebrew *nephilim*. Nickelsburg comments on this form where it occurs in 1 Enoch 7:2; 16:1 (p. 185):

15:12

against the children of men and against the women—Charles' translation is
a bit awkward. Its point is that the evil spirits that have proceeded from
the giants will be the enemies of humanity generally and the women from
which they came (their mothers).

Translation: Chapter 16

16[1] From the days of the slaughter and destruction and death ‹of the
giants›, from the souls of whose flesh the spirits, having gone forth, shall
destroy without incurring judgement—thus shall they destroy until the
day of the consummation, the great ‹judgement› in which the age shall
be consummated, over the Watchers and the godless, yea, shall be wholly
consummated." [2]And now as to the watchers who have sent thee to intercede for them, who had been «aforetime in heaven», (say to them): [3]"You
have been in heaven, but ‹all› the mysteries had not yet been revealed to
you, and you knew worthless ones, and these in the hardness of your
hearts you have made known to the women, and through these mysteries
women and men work much evil on earth."
    [4]Say to them therefore: "You have no peace."

Commentary

16:1

the giants—G[s] adds both *naphēleim hoi ischurai tēs gēs hoi megaloi onomas-
toi* ("Nephilim, the strong ones of the earth, the ones of great renown"),
which is obviously drawn from Genesis 6:4.

"1 Enoch 7:2; 15:11; 16:1 - If Gk. ναφηλειμ with its Hebrew plural ending
does represent the original Semitic text, our author has taken over a word
from the biblical text as a technical term."

from the souls of whose flesh the spirits, having gone forth—In Second Temple Judaism, these spirits are evil because of the havoc they cause. They are known by various names (demons, unclean spirits, bastard spirits) in Second Temple writings.[267] In addition to the comments and sources at 7:1, Nickelsburg adds:

> There are several aspects of the watchers' sinful intercourse with women. Through this act the watchers have defiled themselves, partly because intercourse in itself causes ritual uncleanness, and more importantly because the watchers have polluted themselves with their wives' menstrual blood. Such uncleanness is, of course, remediable under Jewish ritual law. In the present case, however,

---

267. Stuckenbruck writes, "During the last twenty-five years an increasing number of publications have focused on the 'watchers' (often called 'fallen angels') and their 'giant' offspring (sometimes associated with 'demons') in Jewish literature of the second temple period. It has been recognized that a number of early Jewish traditions regarded these beings as essentially evil, representative of forces that are inimical to God's original purpose for creation." Elsewhere he adds: "This picture is, of course, most well-known through apocalyptic and wisdom literature composed prior to the Common Era, remains of some being attested among the Dead Sea Scrolls: the early Enoch traditions—so especially the Book of Watchers and Animal Apocalypse in 1 Enoch, and the Book of Giants—Ben Sira, the Book of Jubilees, Damascus Document, Wisdom of Solomon, 3 Maccabees, 3 Baruch, and several fragmentary texts from previously unknown works (e.g., 4QSongs of the Sage [4Q510-11]; 4QAges of Creation [4Q180-81]; 4QExhortation Based on the Floor [4Q370]; and 11QApocryphal Psalms (11Q11) col. 5). Loren T. Stuckenbruck, "The 'Angels' and 'Giants' of Genesis 6:1–4 in Second and Third Century BCE Jewish Interpretation: Reflections on the Posture of Early Apocalyptic Traditions," *Dead Sea Discoveries* 7.3 (2000): 354–77 (esp. 354–355).

there can be no atonement because the watchers' act was in itself
a violation of divine law. They have transgressed the created order
by confusing the heavenly and earthly realms.... The sin is com-
pounded by the fact that the watchers are priests in the heavenly
sanctuary. Thus their holiness is not simply a special pure state
that has been polluted. It is that state which allows them to draw
near to God and minister to him. Since they have contaminated
that state and violated God's order of creation, they are banished
from his presence in heaven and condemned to punishment on
the earth to which they descended in rebellion and with whose
populace they mingled.[268]

shall destroy without incurring judgement—thus shall they destroy until the
day of the consummation, the great ⟨judgement⟩ in which the age shall be
consummated—Some scholars have seen this as a contradiction to earlier
portions of 1 Enoch. Nickelsburg represents this view:

> The author's major reinterpretation of chaps. 6–11 is in his dis-
> cussion of the giants. According to 10:9–10, 12, the giants slaugh-
> ter one another in war, and that is the end of them. Different
> from their fathers and Asael (10:4b–6, 11, 12b–13), they are not
> bound in the underworld until a day of final judgment. The pres-
> ent author reverses this state of affairs. The giants' death is the pre-
> lude and presupposition for the continued violent and disastrous
> activity of their spirits, which goes on unpunished until the final
> judgment.[269]

Insisting on a contradiction here is unnecessary. In 16:1, the giants'
death is clearly mentioned. The commentary that follows is in relation

---

268. Nickelsburg, *1 Enoch: A Commentary on the Book of 1 Enoch*, vol. 1, 268–
      269.
269. Ibid., 268–270.

to the evil spirits that arise from them upon death. First Enoch 10:4b–6, 11, 12b–13 have the original Watchers (not the giants or the evil spirits that proceed from them) imprisoned. They will witness the destruction of their offspring, the giants. Nickelsburg apparently takes the absence of a comment about the spirits that proceed from the dead giants in 1 Enoch 10 as a contradiction to the present chapter (and other places) that mention them. This doesn't need to be construed as a "reinterpretation," because all the details between these portions of 1 Enoch that *are* mentioned align quite easily. Rather, it is more coherent to consider the comments about the evil spirits as an added detail. Additions do not necessarily create contradiction. This is easily understood by reading multiple newspaper accounts of any given event. Additional detail does not *require* that one account contradicts another.

shall destroy without incurring judgement—The comment about "not incurring judgement" sets the evil spirits of the giants apart from the original Watchers who are judged by God. The judgment of the evil spirits will not occur until the end of days.

16:2

aforetime in heaven—The description is bracketed. It is represented in the Ethiopic text, but could be a scribal addition, since it is absent in G^a and G^s.

16:3

but ‹all› the mysteries had not yet been revealed to you—"All" is bracketed to indicate another textual issue. It is not present in the Ethiopic. The Greek material also does not have "yet," while the Ethiopic does. Since Ethiopic is later, the scribe may have been confused by "all" in the Greek text (if we presume he was working from a Greek text, which seems reasonable). Charles is following Ethiopic here and including the Greek "all" in his translation. The result is "not all mysteries had yet been revealed" to the Watchers versus "no mysteries had yet been revealed" to the Watchers. The latter makes less sense, given the Watchers' pre-Fall proximity to God and their condemnation for teaching heavenly knowledge to humans.

you knew worthless ones—This is also garbled in the manuscript tradition. None of the manuscript traditions make sense. The options are "you knew worthless ones," "a stolen mystery you learned," or "a despised mystery you learned." The options can be retroverted to two hypothetical Aramaic lemmas: *bzz* ("[stolen] plunder") and *bz ʾ* ("despise"). Charles' translation reflects the latter ("you knew despised ones"), perhaps a reference to *forbidden* mysteries (despised in terms of their transmission to humans?), but this is mere conjecture. That said, what follows would make sense given that assumption: "these [despised mysteries] in the hardness of your hearts you have made known to the women, and through these mysteries women and men work much evil on earth."

A Reader's Commentary on
1 Enoch 17–36

Section Summary

Chapter 17 launches the final section of the Book of the Watchers (chapters 17—36). The section is dominated in focus by the heavenly journeys of Enoch. Wright observes that "the author details the various elements of the cosmos that play a part in his eschatological message: Sheol, the ends of the earth, places of punishment, paradise, God's throne, the tree of life, and Jerusalem."[270] Docherty suggests that the material "reassures the audience that the revelation he is passing on to them is authoritative and trustworthy."[271] Wright concurs: "While on these journeys, Enoch is given heavenly knowledge by an archangel that will be used to counter the teachings given to humanity in the instruction motif."[272]

Docherty further compares some of the prophet's experiences with Old Testament passages that feature the divine council and throne-room encounter with God:

> [Enoch] is also granted a vision of God's heavenly throne (14.8–25), which echoes several scriptural passages, especially those which describe the commissioning of the prophets (e.g. 1 Kings

---

270. Wright, *Early Jewish Literature: An Anthology*, vol. 2, 192.

271. Docherty, *The Jewish Pseudepigrapha*, 132.

22:19; Isa. 6:1–4; Ezek. 1:3–28; Hab. 3:3–15; cf. Dan. 7:9–14). The awesome nature of this experience and the utter transcendence of God is underlined, with the seer presented as trembling and unable to either look at God (14.20–4) or adequately describe God's house, which is, for example, both "hot as fire and cold as snow" (14.13).[273]

The final section of the Book of the Watchers breaks down as follows:

- Enoch's first journey, to the Northwest, where he sees the places where the rebel Watchers and "transgressing stars" are punished (17–19)
- Enoch's second journey, to the East (20–36)

Nickelsburg notes that scholars have observed a relationship between the content of Enoch's first journey and both the Mesopotamian Epic of Gilgamesh and Ezekiel 28:

It is possible that 1 Enoch reflects some rough secondhand knowledge of the ideas in the Gilgamesh Epic. Nonetheless, some of the corresponding elements function in very different ways, and a number of them could have derived directly from the Bible. The dark mountain guarded by the scorpion men, which bars Gilgamesh's approach to the garden of jewels, is on this side of the great sea, whereas the source of the waters, near Utnapishtim's island, is on the other side of that sea. In 1 Enoch the darkness and the great mountain are at a different place from the fiery beings. After that comes Oceanus and the great darkness, then more darkness and the abyss. After that is the bejeweled mountain range and then the mountain of God. These mountains appear to reflect Ezekiel 28 (which itself may or may not be dependent

---

272. Wright, *Early Jewish Literature: An Anthology*, vol. 2, 192

on Mesopotamian ideas). That the great waters rise at the foot of God's mountain throne is an idea documented in the Bible.[274]

Given the fact that, in the Book of Giants from Qumran, Gilgamesh is mentioned by name, the author of 1 Enoch may have had more than "rough secondhand knowledge" of this material.

Translation: Chapter 17

17[1]And they took ‹and brought› me to a place in which those who were there were like flaming fire, and, when they wished, they appeared as men. [2]And they brought me to the place of darkness, and to a mountain the point of whose summit reached to heaven. [3]And I saw the places of the luminaries ‹and the treasuries of the stars› and of the thunder, ‹and› in the **uttermost depths,** where were a fiery bow and arrows and their quiver, «and a fiery sword» and all the lightnings. [4]And they took me to the living waters, and to the fire of the west, which receives every setting of the sun. [5]And I came to a river of fire in which the fire flows like water and discharges itself into the great sea towards the west. [6]I saw the great rivers and came to the great ‹river and to the great› darkness, and went to the place where no flesh walks. [7]I saw the mountains of the darkness of winter and the place whence all the waters of the deep flow. [8]I saw the mouths of all the rivers of the earth and the mouth of the deep.

Commentary

17:1

they took ‹and brought› me—The first journey of Enoch (chapters 17—19) opens with an allusion to escorts. Enoch's guides are later identified as angels, including the archangel Uriel (18:14; 19:1). The wording sets the stage for what scholars have termed the "interpreting angel motif" in bib-

---

273. Docherty, *The Jewish Pseudepigrapha*, 132.

lical and other Jewish literature of the Second Temple Period. The episodes of the prophet Daniel in the book bearing his name (Daniel 8–10) are clear examples.[275] Ezekiel 8–11 is similar, as a heavenly figure takes the prophet into the Temple in a series of "visions of God" (Ezekiel 8:3). This phrase ("visions of God") therefore may suggest angelic escorts elsewhere, such as Ezekiel 40–48 (cf. Ezekiel 40:2, 32).[276] In his short excursus on this motif in his discussion of 1 Enoch 17–19, Nickelsburg writes:

> In this section of the Book of the Watchers, the combination of vision, question, and an answer by the interpreting angel is the sole vehicle of revelation…. Angelic interpretation of visions continues to play a major role in later Jewish and Christian apocalyptic literature. In *4 Ezra* the angel Uriel is Ezra's principal interlocutor, while *3 Baruch* is almost from start to finish the account of a seer's journey through the heavens in the company of an interpreting angel.[277]

---

274. Nickelsburg, *1 Enoch: A Commentary on the Book of 1 Enoch*, vol. 1, 279.

275. See David P. Melvin, "In Heaven as It Is on Earth: The Development of the Interpreting Angel Motif in Biblical Literature of the Neo-Babylonian, Persian, and Early Hellenistic Periods," PhD diss., Baylor University, 2012. Melvin writes (p. 3): "The interpreting angel appears in only a handful of biblical texts, all of them exilic or post-exilic (Ezek 40–48; Zech 1–6; Dan 7–8). In these passages, a human prophet sees a vision which is highly symbolic and complex and which, in many cases, draws on elaborate mythological imagery. The nature of the vision is such that the prophet is incapable of understanding its meaning apart from its interpretation by a heavenly being."

276. Is "he" in these verses God or some other supernatural figure? The latter is more likely given chapters 8–11.

277. Nickelsburg, *1 Enoch: A Commentary on the Book of 1 Enoch*, vol. 1, 294.

those who were there were like flaming fire, and when they wished, they appeared as men—The "they" are a group of entities at the place to which Enoch is brought. The description is similar to both the cherubim of Genesis 3:24 and (especially) Ezekiel 1:13–14.[278] Many scholars add the *seraphim* as an analogy, but that equivalence depends on whether the term is based on a verbal root that means "to burn" (*śaraph*). Equally viable, and in my judgment more coherent, is the possibility that *seraphim* is the plural of the Hebrew noun for "serpent" (*śaraph*).[279] Bautch postulates

---

278. On Genesis 3:24, see Ronald Hendel, "'The Flame of the Whirling Sword': A Note on Genesis 3:24," *Journal of Biblical Literature 104:4* (1985): 671–74.

279. See Philippe Provençal, "Regarding the Noun שרף [*śārāp̄*] in the Hebrew Bible." *Journal for the Study of the Old Testament* 29.3 (2005): 371–79. Wildberger agrees: "It is more likely correct to connect [*seraphim*] with the Egyptian *śfr*, 'fabulous winged creature,' as portrayed in a grave at Beni Hasan (*AOB* 392) (cf. the Demotic *serref* 'griffin'." See Hans Wildberger, *A Continental Commentary: Isaiah 1–12* (Minneapolis, MN: Fortress Press, 1991), 264. Certain portions of Isaiah (e.g., the name titulary in Isaiah 9:1–6) and the iconography of Hezekiah's royal seal (Hezekiah was one of the kings during Isaiah's ministry) are known for their Egyptian context. In addition to the discussion in Wildberger's commentary (pp. 399–406), the reader is directed to the following studies: Meir Lubetski, "King Hezekiah's Seal Revisited," *Biblical Archaeology Review* 27.4 (2001): 44–51; Máire Byrne, "The influence of Egyptian Throne names on Isaiah 9:5: A Reassessment of the Debate in Light of the Divine," in *A Land Like Your Own: Traditions of Israel and Their Reception* 2010): 87–100; Boyo Ockinga, "Hatshepsut's Appointment as Crown Prince and the Egyptian Background to Isaiah 9: 5," in *Egypt, Canaan and Israel: History, Imperialism, Ideology and Literature* (Leiden: E. J. Brill, 2011), 252–267. For a contrarian view of the names of Isaiah 6, see Paul D. Wegner, "A Re-examination of Isaiah IX 1–6," *Vetus Testamentum* 42:1 (1992): 103–112.

that associating the appearance of supernatural beings with fire may be a way of communicating the idea of shapeshifting.[280] This is far from clear (changing from what form into or after fire?), though if one associates fire with "light" in 2 Corinthians 11:14 ("for even Satan disguises himself as an angel of light"). This of course presumes the verse is about appearance, not something more abstract like truth.

17:2

to a mountain the point of whose summit reached to heaven—The passage repurposes the important Old Testament theme of the cosmic mountain—the divine abode.[281] The great height of the mountain allows Enoch to see celestial phenomena and parts of the divine abode.

---

280. Kelley Coblentz Bautch, "Heavenly Beings in Enoch Traditions and the Synoptic Gospels," in *Enoch and the Synoptic Gospels: Reminiscences, Allusions, Intertextuality* (ed. Loren T. Stuckenbruck and Gabriele Boccaccini; *Early Judaism and Its Literature* 44; SBL Press, 2016), 105–127 (esp. 112).

281. See Heiser, *Unseen Realm* (pp. 44–48, 221–231) for a condensed discussion. Major academic studies include Richard J. Clifford, *The Cosmic Mountain in Canaan and the Old Testament*, Harvard Semitic Monographs 4 (Cambridge: Harvard University Press, 1972; repr., Eugene, OR: Wipf & Stock, 2010); L. Michael Morales, *The Tabernacle Pre-Figured: Cosmic Mountain Ideology in Genesis and Exodus* (Biblical Tools and Studies 15; Leuven: Peeters, 2012); Daniel T. Lioy, "The Garden of Eden as a Primordial Temple or Sacred Space for Humankind," *Conspectus: The Journal of the South African Theological Seminary* 10 (2010): 25–57; Gordon Wenham, "Sanctuary Symbolism in the Garden of Eden Story," in *Cult and Cosmos: Tilting toward a Temple-Centered Biblical Theology* (ed. L. Michael Morales; Biblical Tools and Studies 18; Leuven: Peeters, 2014), 161–66. The major study on Enoch's cosmic visions in chapters 17–19 is Kelley Coblentz

17:3

places of the luminaries—i.e., the sun and moon.

and the treasuries of the stars and of the thunder—Nickelsburg notes, "Judging from the cosmology in 72:3; 75:6–8; 32:2–3; 36:3, the storehouses of the stars—and of the luminaries—must be located somewhere beyond the meeting point of the ends of the earth and the celestial vault, where the portals are located through which the luminaries and stars rise."[282] The Old Testament has similar language for the stars and meteorological activity originating from God's abode.[283]

Bautch, *A Study of the Geography of 1 Enoch 17-19: "No One Has Seen What I Have Seen,"* (*Supplements to the Journal for the Study of Judaism* 81; Leiden: E. J. Brill, 2003).

282. Nickelsburg, *1 Enoch: A Commentary on the Book of 1 Enoch*, vol. 1, 281. On ancient Israelite cosmology, see Michael S. Heiser, "The Old Testament and the Ancient Near Eastern Worldview." *Faithlife Study Bible*. Bellingham, WA: Lexham Press, 2012, 2016; Kyle Greenwood, Scripture and Cosmology: Reading the Bible Between the Ancient World and Modern Science (IVP Academic, 2015). More academic studies include Luis I. Stadelmann, *The Hebrew Conception of the World: A Philological and Literary Study* (Analecta Orientalia 39; Pontifical Institute Press, 1970); John H. Walton, *Genesis 1 as Ancient Cosmology* (Winona Lake, IN: Eisenbrauns, 2011).

283. Genesis 7:11; 8:2; Deuteronomy 28:12; Isaiah 24:18; Jeremiah 51:16; Malachi 3:10; Job 36:29; 38:22; Psalms 29:3; 33:7; 135:7. See comments under 1 Enoch 5:1 in the commentary and the resources in footnotes 77 through 79.

*the **uttermost depths***—Some Greek material has "depths of the ether (*aerobathē*)", which is likely an error (hence the boldfacing in Charles).[284] If it is authentic, Enoch is not looking down, but up into the vastness of the heavens.[285]

a fiery bow and arrows and their quiver and a fiery sword and all the lightnings—The language for lightning follows that of the Old Testament (Psalms 7:12–13; 18:15; 77:18–19; Lamentations 2:4; 3:12–13).

17:4

living waters—a common expression in the Old Testament for moving (flowing) waters (*mayim chayyim*; Song of Solomon 4:15; Zechariah 14:8). The waters in Eden, the cosmic mountain, were "living" (flowing; Genesis 2:10–14).

the fire of the west, which receives every setting of the sun—The reference is to the appearance of the sky at sunset. Black writes: "This is scarcely Gehenna, although the Talmud says that the sun is red in the evening because it passes the gate of Gehenna, and red in the morning when it passes the of the Garden of Eden (Baba Bathra 84a)."[286]

17:5

A river of fire—Nickelsburg wonders about a relationship to the language of 1 Enoch 14:19 and Daniel 7:10 before (reasonably) concluding:

---

284. According to the Liddell-Scott lexicon (p. 28), this word occurs only here in Greek literature.
285. Nickelsburg (p. 281, note 23) writes: "For this meaning of βάθος and βαθύς [*bathos, bathus*] see LSJ [Liddell-Scott], s.v. See esp. Euripides *Medea* 1297, αἰθέρος βάθος [*aitheros bathos*]."
286. Black, *The Book of Enoch*, 156.

In context, however, Enoch has just left the heavenly throne room and has not yet approached the mountain throne of God (18:16ff.). These verses are best understood in light of the Greek idea of the four great rivers.… The river of fire is Pyriphlegethon, often mentioned in Greek literature in connection with the underworld and journeys to it. A graphic description of this torrent in connection with the abyss (see vv 7–8), the realm of death, Belial, and eternal punishment occurs in 1QH 11(3):28–36. Cf. also the lake of fire in Rev 19:20; 20:14–15.[287]

into the great sea towards the west—The Mediterranean, not Oceanus, is in view.[288] The latter is referenced in the next verse.

17:6

the great rivers and came to the great river and to the great darkness—Nickelsburg notes that "The great rivers are the four, and the great river, Oceanus. Thus Enoch has arrived at earth's outer limits. Cf. *Testament of Abraham* 8 B, where Michael and Abraham arrive at the river Oceanus and the two gates leading to life and destruction. In the context of reference to the great rivers, the great darkness is perhaps best understood as Hades."[289]

---

287. Nickelsburg, *1 Enoch: A Commentary on the Book of 1 Enoch*, vol. 1, 283. Nickelsburg adds in a footnote that some scholars argue for an ancient Near Eastern source of the imagery since "the Greek derived their ideas from an oriental prototype," but argues that no ancient Near Eastern source "speaks of the great rivers of the west, nor of a river of fire." Black (*The Book of Enoch*, 156) agrees with the identification of the river of fire as Pyriphlegethon.

288. See William L. Reed, "Great Sea," *IDB* 2:472–73. Black again concurs (*The Book of Enoch*, 156).

289. Nickelsburg, *1 Enoch: A Commentary on the Book of 1 Enoch*, vol. 1, 283. Black (p. 156) notes that Dillmann and Milik agree with this assessment but doubts Milik's assertion that the origin of the imagery is a Babylonian source.

went to—Nickelsburg writes, "Having arrived at the river Oceanus, the western limits of the earth, Enoch turns northward, where his journey will culminate beyond the mountain throne of God in the far northwest."[290]

the place where no flesh walks—The realm of the dead (i.e., Hades, per the comments above).

17:8

I saw the mouths of all the rivers of the earth and the mouth of the deep—Cosmic mountain concepts are behind the language:

> Enoch is following the river Oceanus to its source, the subterranean *tehôm*, the primordial chaotic waters from which God created all things (Gen 1:2–3). Like the peoples of the ancient Near East, Plato also believed that the rivers of the earth issued from the waters of a great subterranean chasm, Tartarus. Different from them, he did not think of a single point of effluence.... Closely paralleling the present passage is the idea in Babylonian, Canaanite, and Israelite religious writings that God dwells on a mountain, from the foot of which issue great rivers of water. This parallel may argue for the close connection between 17:7–8 and 18:6–8, which describe the mountain range in the midst of which is God's mountain throne. Although that mountain and its waters are often thought to be in the north, here they have been transferred to the northwest, where the author believes God's throne to be located.[291]

290. Nickelsburg, *1 Enoch: A Commentary on the Book of 1 Enoch*, vol. 1, 283.
291. Ibid., 284.

Translation: Chapter 18

18[1]I saw the treasuries of all the winds: I saw how He had furnished with them the whole creation and the firm foundations of the earth. [2]And I saw the corner-stone of the earth: I saw the four winds which bear [the earth and] the firmament of the heaven. [3]«And I saw how the winds stretch out the vaults of heaven», and have their station between heaven and earth: «these are the pillars of the heaven». [4]I saw the winds of heaven which turn and bring the circumference of the sun and all the stars to their setting. [5]I saw the winds on the earth carrying the clouds: I saw «the paths of the angels. [6]I saw» at the end of the earth the firmament of the heaven above. And I proceeded and saw a place which burns day and night, where there are seven mountains of magnificent stones, three towards the east, and three towards the south. [7]And as for those towards the east, ⟨one⟩ was of coloured stone, and one of pearl, and one of **jacinth**, and those towards the south of red stone. [8]But the middle one reached to heaven like the throne of God, of alabaster, and the summit of the throne was of sapphire. [9]And I saw a flaming fire. [10]And beyond these mountains Is a region the end of the great earth: there the heavens were completed. [11]And I saw a deep abyss, with columns «of heavenly fire, and among them I saw columns» of fire fall, which were beyond measure alike towards the height and towards the depth. [12]And beyond that abyss I saw a place which had no firmament of the heaven above, and no firmly founded earth beneath it: there was no water upon it, and no birds, but it was a waste and horrible place. [13]I saw there seven stars like great burning mountains, and to me, when I inquired regarding them, The angel said: [14]"This place is the end of heaven and earth: this has become a prison for the stars and the host of heaven. [15]And the stars which roll over the fire are they which have transgressed the commandment of the Lord in the beginning of their rising, because they did not come forth at their appointed times. [16]And He was wroth with them, and bound them till the time when their guilt should be consummated (even) ⟨for ten thousand years⟩."

18:1

treasuries—See 17:3.

firm foundations of the earth—Refers to the ancient cosmological notion that the earth was placed atop foundations (or pillars; cf. verse 10).[292] In ancient Israelite cosmology, the "heavens and earth" are depicted as a building or temple.[293]

18:2

corner-stone of the earth—Job 38:6 uses the same terminology. Similar Hebrew terminology used elsewhere in the Hebrew Bible is often rendered "capstone" (Jeremiah 51:26; Zechariah 4:7). The vocabulary is, again, serving to depict the earth (and extended cosmos) as a building.

firmament of the heaven—More structural terminology for the cosmos. In Israelite cosmology (so here in 1 Enoch), the firmament is solid, covering the earth, with waters above it where God sits enthroned (Genesis 1:6; Job 22:13–14; 37:18; Psalm 29:10; Proverbs 8:27–28; Amos 9:6).

18:3

vaults of heaven»…«these are the pillars of the heaven—See 17:1–4; 18:1–2.

---

292. 1 Samuel 2:8; Job 9:6; 26:11; Psalms 18:15; 75:3; 82:5; Proverbs 8:29; Isaiah 24:18; Jeremiah 31:37; Micah 6:2.
293. For the temple aspect of this cosmology, see John H. Walton, *The Lost World of Genesis One: Ancient Cosmology and the Origins Debate* (InterVarsity Press, 2010). For the range of building terminology used in the Hebrew Bible for the heavens and earth (the cosmos), see Stadelmann, *The Hebrew Conception of the World: A Philological and Literary Study*.

18:4

the winds of heaven which turn and bring the circumference of the sun and all the stars to their setting—As is the case above, this language reflects a non-scientific cosmology in that it has the winds propelling the motion of the sun and stars (cp. 72:5; 73:2).

18:5

I saw the winds on the earth carrying the clouds: I saw «the paths of the angels—The verse may suggest the idea that winds were the means by which angels moved between heaven and earth. Some scholars cite Psalm 104:4 as a parallel biblical idea, but that verse doesn't suggest the same idea.

18:6

at the end of the earth the firmament of the heaven above—The idea is very similar to Proverbs 8:27–28 and Job 26:10, that the edge of the dome over the earth (the "firmament") meets the horizon, the boundary of light and darkness. Hence here in 18:5 the "end" of the earth (it's "edge") and the firmament meet (i.e., this is what Enoch sees).

which burns day and night—Are the mountains burning? The text isn't clear. The Greek text of 1 Enoch 24:1 has the mountains burning, but the Aramaic of that passage refers to the land between the mountains burning.[294] A similar scene of mountains of fire in the south of the earth is found elsewhere in material bearing a close relationship to 1 Enoch (Jubilees 8:22). It would seem from verses 9–10 that the location of the burning is not the mountains precisely, but some region beyond. Bautch,

---

294. Bautch, *1 Enoch 17–19*, 108.

along with other scholars, looks for a literal location in an arid, hot place, but concedes that no option has coherence.[295] Given the relationship of the cosmic geography of 1 Enoch to Babylonian and Greek cosmologies that have clear disconnections with the actual geography of the earth, it is best to assign such descriptions to the theological imagination.[296] That elements of the description (see the cosmological terminology above) also draw on Israelite cosmology,[297] this interpretive trajectory is the most fruitful. There need be no literal geographical place in mind; the description is the cosmic mountain, the abode of God.

seven mountains of magnificent stones, three towards the east, and three towards the south—The description of this place is not entirely consistent within the book. First Enoch 77:5 refers to seven mountains higher than any other mountains on earth, but doesn't describe it (or them) as burning. Nickelsburg adds that "according to chaps. 24–25 and 32, there are two ranges of seven mountains each, related to the two paradises in the northwest and the northeast."[298] Bautch comments:

> The mountains are oriented in a particular manner: three toward the east and three toward the south.... We learn in 1 Enoch 18:8 that the mountain between the three to the east and three to the south reaches to heaven. The mountain range depicted in 1 Enoch 18:6 is understood to form a right angle.... A tradition parallel to

---

295. Ibid., 108. Bautch laments, "While the exact nature of the mountains of fire eludes us, it becomes clear that one can isolate a tradition in which mountains burn incessantly suggesting a location subject to severe conditions."

296. Nickelsburg has a short excursus on these similarities (pp. 282–283).

297. See Michael Knibb, "The Use of Scripture in 1 Enoch 17–19," in *Essays on the Book of Enoch and Other Early Jewish Texts and Traditions* (Leiden: E. J. Brill, 2009).

298. Nickelsburg, *1 Enoch: A Commentary on the Book of 1 Enoch*, vol. 1, 285.

that of 1 Enoch 18:6 is to be found in 1 Enoch 24:1–3, in which seven mountains of precious stones are arranged similarly, three toward the east and three toward the south.[299]

The stones are described in verses 7–8 following next.

18:7

And as for those towards the east, <one> was of coloured stone, and one of pearl, and one of jacinth, and those towards the south of red stone.—Nickelsburg notes the transparent similarities to cosmic garden-mount (Edenic, Sinai) material in the Old Testament:

> The idea that God dwells on a mountain has a long and rich history in the ancient Near East. The description of God's throne is reminiscent of Exod 24:9–10, but the closest biblical parallel to the present passage is Ezek 28:13–19. As that text now stands, Eden, the garden of God (cf. 1 Enoch 24–25) is identified with "the mountain of God" (Ezek 28:13–14). It is replete with precious stones of many kinds. In the context of Ezek 28:2 and Isa 14:13–14.[300]

---

299. Bautch, *1 Enoch 17–19*, 110–111. She adds elsewhere (p. 114): "The tradition which most closely approximates that of 1 Enoch 18:6 is the description of the seven mountains in 1 Enoch 24, mountains of precious stones arranged similarly with three mountains to the east and three to the south. 1 Enoch 32 and 1 Enoch 77 do not shed light on the seven mountains of 1 Enoch 18:6 nor do they hint at their location."

300. Nickelsburg, *1 Enoch: A Commentary on the Book of 1 Enoch*, vol. 1, 285–286. See also Clifford, *The Cosmic Mountain*, 172. Scholars often attempt to use the gemstones in Ezekiel 28 to argue that the cherub in the chapter is Adam. The reasoning is that the gemstones are similar to those of the Israelite high priest, and so God's original high priest on earth was Adam.

The clear cosmic mountain imagery here, associated with Eden in Ezekiel 28, leads Nickelsburg and other scholars to note 1 Enoch 24's additional element of a special tree on the way to concluding that the divine abode in these chapters of 1 Enoch is supposed to denote a paradise.

> [3]And the seventh mountain was in the midst of these, and it excelled them in height, resembling the seat of a throne: and fragrant trees encircled the throne. [4]And amongst them was a tree such as I had never yet smelt, neither was any amongst them nor were others like it: it had a fragrance beyond all fragrance, and its leaves and blooms and wood wither not for ever: and its fruit is beautiful, and its fruit resembles the dates of a palm. (1 Enoch 24:3–4)

This conclusion overstates the data and the description (see commentary on 1 Enoch 24). Bautch concurs:

> The stones of Ezekiel 28 and the gems on the breastplate of the high priest, however, do not match. That the gemstones of Ezekiel do align with the description of the new Jerusalem in the book of Revelation informs us that they are mentioned to describe a *place,* not a person. For the relationship between the stones of Ezekiel 28 (and hence here in 1 Enoch) and those in Revelation, see Heiser, *The Unseen Realm*, 80, and the resources in footnote 7. The cosmic mountain or "garden of the gods" includes the element of being "bejeweled" in the Gilgamesh epic, with which the writer of 1 Enoch was familiar (see Annus, "On the Origin of the Watchers"). We have already noted that Mount Hermon, the place Enoch's Watchers descend to transgress with human women, was perceived as the dwelling place of the gods in Sumerian-Mesopotamian thought (Lipinski, "El's Abode"). On the bejeweled garden-mountain of Gilgamesh, see Keith Dickson, "The Jeweled Trees: Alterity in Gilgamesh," *Comparative Literature* 59 (2007): 193–208.

A tradition parallel to that of 1 Enoch 18:6 is to be found in
1 Enoch 24:1–3, in which seven mountains of precious stones
are arranged similarly, three toward the east and three toward the
south. Charles and apparently Nickelsburg take this mountain
range which features a tree with life-giving fruit to be a north-
western paradise. Perhaps they associate the scene with paradise
because the presence of a tree with life-giving fruit is reminiscent of the tree of life in Eden (Gen 3:9, 22, 24). Moving from
the assumption that 1 Enoch 24–25 describes a sort of paradise,
Charles points to 1 Enoch 70:3 where angels measure a location
in between the north and the west winds which serves as an abode
for the departed righteous. Charles connects this (heavenly?)
respite to a garden, specifically the garden described in 1 Enoch
24–25 with its seven mountains and "tree of life." But there is no
reference made to a garden or to a tree of life in 1 Enoch 70:3.
Neither is a garden mentioned in 1 Enoch 24 and 25.[301]

18:8

But the middle one—i.e., the seventh mountain between the two ranges of
three mountains alluded to earlier.

*reached to heaven like the throne of God, of alabaster, and the summit of
the throne was of sapphire*—See the comments above.[302] Citing Horowitz's

301. Bautch, *1 Enoch 17–19*, 111.
302. For a discussion of gemstone terminology in both the Hebrew Bible and
    the Septuagint (and so, the Greek of 1 Enoch), see James E. Harrell, "Old
    Testament Gemstones: A Philological, Geological, and Archaeological
    Assessment of the Septuagint," *Bulletin for Biblical Research* 21:2 (2011):141–
    172; James E. Harrell, James K. Hoffmeier, and Kenton F. Williams,
    "Hebrew Gemstones in the Old Testament: A Lexical, Geological, and
    Archaeological Analysis," *Bulletin for Biblical Research* 27:1 (2017): 1–52.

work, Bautch's comments reinforce the fact that the bejeweled description is common to the cosmic mountain motif:

> Horowitz explains that it is the floor of each of the heavens that is composed of the precious stones (luludanitustone, saggilmund-stone, and jasper). Each floor, then, would presumably be visible from below, comparable to the account in Exod 24:9–10 in which Moses and the elders of Israel see beneath God's feet "something like a pavement of sapphire stone, like the heavens for clearness."[303]

sapphire—lapis lazuli. This is the gemstone associated with God's throne in the Old Testament (Exodus 24:9–10; Ezekiel 1:26–28; 10:1).

18:9

And I saw a flaming fire—See verse 6. The fire (in correlation with the earlier gemstones, especially lapis lazuli/sapphire) takes readers once more back to Old Testament descriptions of theophany (Exodus 19:18; 24:17). If one reads 1 Enoch 18:6–9 along with 1 Enoch 24:1–25:7 one will

---

303. Bautch, 119. She cites Wayne Horowitz, *Mesopotamian Cosmic Geography* (Winona Lake, Indiana: Eisenbrauns, 1998), 4, 9, 101–102, 329. In a footnote on p. 119, Bautch alerts readers to the fact that Adela Y. Collins notes "correspondences between the gems which make up the seven mountains in 1 Enoch 18 and precious stones associated with the seven planets of antiquity." Bautch opines that the reason for the correspondence is unclear, but it seems to me that, given the association of celestial bodies with divine beings of the heavenly host or divine council, the correspondence reinforces the celestial nature of the place(s) Enoch is visiting. See Adela Y. Collins, *Cosmology and Eschatology in Jewish and Christian Apocalypticism* (Leiden: E. J. Brill, 1996), 21–23, 28–29, 53–54.

notice more affinities with Sinai scenes. However, it becomes evident in the ensuing verses that this burning place is where the Watchers are being punished.

18:10

the end of the great earth: there the heavens were completed—Enoch travels to the place where the heavens converge or meet the earth (the horizon; cf. Proverbs 8:27–28; Job 26:10) in ancient cosmology. This reading ("ends of the earth") follows the Greek material; Ethiopic reads "beyond the great earth." The "end of the great earth" is *peras tēs megalēs gēs* in Greek. Bautch notes that Black thinks the expression "the great earth" is unusual and therefore reflects a misreading of the Aramaic original.[304] Nickelsburg, however, sees a parallel to Hesiod's description of Tartarus, the place the Titans are sent for punishment (and which is referenced by 2 Peter 2:4). Hesiod describes Tartarus as *pelōrēs eschata gaiēs* ("at the ends of the huge earth").[305]

---

304. Bautch, *1 Enoch 17–19*, 128–129.

305. Ibid., 129, citing Nickelsburg, *1 Enoch: A Commentary on the Book of 1 Enoch*, vol. 1, 286. Nickelsburg writes: "Perhaps more than anywhere else in these chapters, this passage contains a complex of noteworthy verbal parallels with Hesiod, which may well indicate direct or indirect contact with the Greek tradition." The wording in 2 Peter 2:4 translated "cast into hell" is the Greek verb *tartaroo* ("cast into Tartarus"). See Bradley S. Billings, "'The Angels Who Sinned…He Cast into Tartarus' (2 Peter 2:4): Its Ancient Meaning and Present Relevance," *Expository Times* 119:11 (2008): 532–537; David M. Johnson, "Hesiod's Descriptions of Tartarus (Theogony 721–819)," *Phoenix* 53 (1999): 8–28. Billings applies a postmodern hermeneutic as to the relevance of the passage today, but the article is quite good at showing how 2 Peter directly dips into Hesiod.

18:11

a deep abyss—This description (*chasma mega*) is a word-for-word parallel to Hesiod's description of Tartarus.[306]

with columns «of heavenly fire, and among them I saw columns» of fire fall, which were beyond measure alike towards the height and towards the depth—"Falling" probably denotes the pillars or columns of fire descend into (or "spill into") the chasm. Bautch notes of this overall description:

> The imagery of the pillars of fire is especially unusual. We learn that they are gigantic, and in fact, beyond measure. It is hard to envision exactly their relationship to the chasm; they appear to be continually descending into the pit. It is possible, Nickelsburg suggests, that it is the chasm rather than the pillars that is of immeasurable height or depth. The chasm, then, would be a veritable bottomless pit, similar to the description of Tartarus in the *Theogony*, a chasm with the same dimensions as the distance between heaven and earth.... The expression "pillars of heavenly fire" calls to mind a display of divine might. For example, in Gen 19:24, Ps 11:6 and Ezek 38:22 God rains fire and sulfur from heaven on the wicked.[307]

[**Note:** At this point in 1 Enoch 18, modern scholars insert 1 Enoch 19:1–2. Chapter 19 of 1 Enoch constitutes only three verses and describes the chasm of 18:10–11. We will follow the order of Charles' translation, treating 1 Enoch 19:1–2 below after the completion of 1 Enoch 18.[308]]

---

306. Bautch, *1 Enoch*, 17–19, 130; Nickelsburg, *1 Enoch: A Commentary on the Book of 1 Enoch*, vol. 1, 286.

307. Bautch, *1 Enoch 17–19*, 130, citing Nickelsburg, *1 Enoch: A Commentary on the Book of 1 Enoch*, vol. 1, 286–287.

308. While 19:1–2 does offer an interpretation or explanation of 18:9–11,

18:12

And beyond that abyss I saw a place which had no firmament of the heaven above, and no firmly founded earth beneath it— The next place to which Enoch is led is "a place that lies outside not only the inhabited world, but also the bounds of the cosmos. Enoch is beyond the terrestrial disk, the atmosphere and the heavens. Enoch has eclipsed even the waters that surround the earth disk or make up the firmament."[309]

there was no water upon it, and no birds, but it was a waste and horrible place—See 1 Enoch 21:1–2. This place, beyond the cosmos as it were, is (also?) Hades or the underworld, the place where the Watchers are imprisoned (verses 13–14). The description is strange since, in Israelite cosmology, the underworld is situated amid "the waters under the earth" but here there is no water. Bautch notes a parallel that, nevertheless, seems to show that the writer has Hades in mind: "The claim that the place is absent of birds is reminiscent of the Latin synonym for Hades, Avernus, after the lake in Campania."[310] Elsewhere, the location of the Watchers' imprisonment (and the home of the devil) is associated with the arid, unforgiving desert wilderness. We should not look for consistency or literality in interpretation. The fact is that all of these descriptions are attempts to associate the realm of the dead, the prison of the Watchers, with a range of chaos elements in Old Testament thinking, places divorced from the presence of God and life that is hospitable to humankind. God originally created a world of abundance and glory (the

---

Nickelsburg admits, on the basis of Milik's work on the Aramaic material, that "4QEn^c 1 8:27–30 (Milik, *Enoch*, 200) almost certainly indicates that 18:12 followed immediately after 18:11 in that Aramaic text." See Nickelsburg, *1 Enoch: A Commentary on the Book of 1 Enoch*, vol. 1, 287.

309. Bautch, *1 Enoch 17–19*, 141.

310. Ibid., 141.

cosmic mountain) in which humanity was supposed to live as God's children. Their estrangement from God meant death and chaos, an "anti-Eden" existence and destiny. Biblical and later writers try to capture this state of affairs in the imagery used.

18:13

seven stars like great burning mountains—While "stars" is used in verse 15 is a term that points to the transgressing Watchers, the stars here are restricted to seven and are described as being "like burning mountains." The conclusion must be that the term can be used of both divine beings and objects. The conceptual overlap between celestial objects and divine beings in ancient cosmology is behind this seeming incongruity. The same sort of star-entity equation is witnessed in the Hebrew Bible (Job 38:7–8; Daniel 12:2–3; cp. the phrase "host of heaven" for heavenly beings; e.g., 1 Kings 22:19 and 1 Enoch 18:14).

18:14

This place is the end of heaven and earth: this has become a prison for the stars and the host of heaven—"This place" refers to the burning mountains and the earlier waterless (and so, lifeless) desert. The point of the imagery is that the fallen stars (Watchers) have been sent down to the underworld (or away from God's presence), and Enoch has now arrived at that place. Since these fallen beings are in that place, the location burns as falling stars (meteors, in our worldview) burn and smolder. The numbering at seven is likely a contrastive analogy to the seven mountains Enoch has just seen—three mountains on each side of the grand seventh, the divine abode. This place, these seven, is the anti-abode, displaced from God's presence. Again, this cosmic, spiritual separation and estrangement is the point being communicated, not a literal location with latitude and longitude.

18:15

And the stars which roll over the fire are they which have transgressed the com-mandment of the Lord—Essentially, the imagery is that the stars and their movement are restricted to this inferno—roasting over the fiery mountains, as it were. The imagery is both (counter) astronomical and theological. Bautch notes:

> Stars and other heavenly bodies were understood in antiquity to be sentient beings.... Isaiah 24:21 is quite reminiscent of 1 Enoch 18:13–14: at a time of universal judgment the Lord will punish both the host of heaven (here *tseba' hammārôm* ["host of the heights"]) and kings of the earth, throwing them into a pit where they will be shut up as in a prison and punished.... In the context of 1 Enoch 18:13–16, it is not clear what natural phenomena the author has in mind by stars that fail to come out at their appointed times. We know only that these stars are imprisoned at the end of heaven and earth (1 Enoch 18:14); according to the Greek gloss of 1 Enoch 18:15, that place is located outside of the heavens, best understood as a void.[311]

in the beginning of their rising, because they did not come forth at their appointed times—The language is clearly astronomical ("rising"; "coming forth"; "appointed times"). Bautch expresses uncertainty about its usage here: "In the context of 1 Enoch 18:13–16, it is not clear what natural phenomena the author has in mind by stars that fail to come out at their appointed times."[312]

---

311. Ibid., 144.
312. Ibid., 144.

Beckwith's major study of the Qumran (and Enochian) calendar system and chronology likely answers this question, at least insofar as its meaning to the ancient writer. The sect at Qumran, which had separated itself from the Jerusalem priesthood because of a disagreement over the calendar and the timing of various holy days, adhered to a 364-day mathematical year with perfectly symmetrical sabbaths, seasons, and priestly courses:

> In the biblical and intertestamental period, the solar year of 364 days (as distinct from 360, or indeed from 365) is only found, explicitly at least, in the Astronomical Book of Enoch (1 En. 72–82), the Book of Jubilees and the Qumran literature…. Although 1 Enoch does not lay stress on the fact, a 364-day calendar consists of precisely 52 weeks (364 being exactly divisible by seven), with the result that in every year dates would fall on the same day of the week…. [A] striking characteristic of the Essene calendar is its concern for numerical symmetry, precision and regularity. The Essenes were fascinated by numbers, as is shown also by their chronological texts, in which they try to date all important events from the creation onwards, and expect events to occur at regular intervals…. The same outlook is seen in their calendar, where the year consists of an exact number of days (1 Enoch 72:32) and an exact number of weeks (Jubilees 6:30), where each of the four seasons is of precisely equal length (1 Enoch 82:15, 18), and where the year will always agree with the sun and stars and never be a day out even unto eternity (1 Enoch 74:12).[313]

The Qumran priesthood believed the activities of the earthly priesthood were to be synchronized with heaven in accord with God's will and

---

313. Roger T. Beckwith, *Calendar and Chronology, Jewish and Christian: Biblical, Intertestamental and Patristic Studies* (Leiden: E. J. Brill, 2001), 94, 101, 106.

design. This was part of their doctrine of an *earthly* "angelic priesthood."[314] The rise of the Qumran community was due in no small part to the sharp disagreement over ritual calendar and sacred time. Those who held power in the Jerusalem priesthood did not follow what the Qumran sect insisted was the divine ordering of time and calendar described above. The Pharisees and Sadducees followed a lunar calendar, not the solar calendar conceived at Qumran. Beckwith summarizes the difference:

[The solar calendar] has twelve months of thirty days each (roughly a twelfth of the solar year), with a quarter[ly] day after the third, sixth, ninth and twelfth months, dividing the four seasons, and making those four months effectively 31 days long (1 Enoch 72:8–32; 75:1; 82:4–6, 11–20). The twelve lunar months, by contrast, are six of them reckoned as thirty days long and six of them as 29 days long, making twice 177 or 354 days in all, and falling short of the length of the solar year by ten days (1 Enoch 74:13–16; 78:15f; 79:4f).[315]

---

314. On the Qumran theology of angelic priesthood (human priests being angelic analogies on earth), see Carol A. Newsom, "He Has Established for Himself Priests: Human and Angelic Priesthood in the Qumran Sabbath Shirot," in *Archaeology and History in the Dead Sea Scrolls: The New York University Conference in Memory of Yigael Yadin* (*Journal for the Study of the Pseudepigrapha Supplement Series 8*; Sheffield: JSOT Press, 1990), 101–120; Devorah Dimant, "Men as Angels: The Self-Image of the Qumran Community," in *Religion and Politics in the Ancient Near East* (Bethesda, MD: University Press of Maryland, 1996), 93–103; E. G. Chazon, "Human and Angelic Prayer in Light of the Dead Sea Scrolls," in *Liturgical Perspectives: Prayer and Poetry in Light of the Dead Sea Scrolls* (*Studies on the Texts of the Desert of Judah 48*; Leiden: E. J. Brill, 2000), 35–48.

315. Beckwith, *Calendar and Chronology*, 94.

In a lunar calendar system, after several years, the calendar would slip thirty days, creating the need to add a thirteenth month of thirty days to even out the year. This no doubt seems quaint to us, but for the priests at Qumran, the Jerusalem priesthood's decision to follow a lunar calendar amounted to abandoning a mathematically symmetrical calendar revealed at Creation to one that required human tinkering. Whereas the Qumran system meant that every Sabbath, every sabbatical year, and every Passover would occur the same time as the one before in precise harmony, the lunar system was in need of perpetual adjustment.[316]

The Jerusalem system was therefore an imperfect human substitute for the precision God had instituted in the heavens at Creation. Why did the astronomy not align with the math? The Qumran sect believed this misalignment occurred because there had been disruption in the heavens—when the Watchers sinned. The cosmic malfunction was their fault. This is the point of the astronomically deviant description in 1 Enoch 18:15 (and elsewhere). While Black's connection of the seven stars in 1 Enoch 18:13–16 (cp. 21:3–6) to the seven planets (which have irregular orbits compared to "fixed stars") is interesting,[317] the priests at Qumran would simply default to their explanation that such irregularities were due to the transgression of the Watchers. They would presume that such

---

316. Beckwith elsewhere (p. 107) notes that in the Qumran/Essene calendar, "Every seventh day from the creation onwards had been sanctified in advance as a Sabbath; every 364th day from the world's first Nisan 14 and Siwan 5 had been sanctified in advance as a Passover and a Pentecost respectively, and so on." Nisan 14 was the day of the Passover (Exodus 12:6–8; cp. Esther 3:7). Siwan (Sivan) 5 is the first day of Pentecost (beginning the fifty-day count between the two on the initial evening of the sacrifice of the Passover lamb).

317. Black, *The Book of Enoch*, 160.

irregularities were related to calendrical irregularities related to the sun and moon.

Bautch, following the work of Albani, draws attention to the possibility that the language in 1 Enoch 18:15 may refer to the Pleiades. She writes:

> The "beginning of their rising" recalls the heliacal rising of the Pleiades, the first constellation to appear in the eastern morning sky shortly before the sun's ascent. The rising of the Pleiades was noteworthy in antiquity as it conveyed information about weather, the phases of the stars and the agricultural calendar. In Mesopotamia, for example, the rightly timed rising of the seven stars was a positive omen for the land; when the Pleiades did not rise at the expected time, an evil portent was given.
>
> In the ancient Near East, the Pleiades were associated with the binding of the Sibettu demons of which there are seven. The Sibettu-Pleiades were designated sons of the underworld god Enmešarra, who, when defeated by Marduk, were bound and placed in jail. Enmešarra and his sons remain under permanent guard, and at night the demon sons are the Pleiades in the eastern sky, seven stars bound. Job 38:31 may know of a similar tradition as it also refers to the chains or shackles of the Pleiades. The bound stars of 1 Enoch 18:13–16 and 21:3–6 greatly resemble Enmešarra's sons confined in the form of the constellation and the fettered Pleiades in Job.[318]

---

318. Bautch, *1 Enoch 17–19*, 147–148, referencing M. Albani, "'Der das Siebengestirn und den Orion macht' (Am 5,8) Zur Bedeutung der Plejaden in der israelitischen Religionsgeschichte,' in *Religionsgeschichte Israels: Formale und materiale Aspekte* (ed. Bernd Janowski and Matthias Köckert; Gütersloh: Chr. Kaiser/Gütersloher Verlagshaus, 1999), 139–207.

This trajectory may be worthwhile as it dovetails with Jewish thinking in regard to Genesis 6:1–4 and the presumed timing of the Flood in
concert with the Pleiades.[319] A conceptual connection with that passage of
course makes a connection to the Watchers all the more possible.

18:16

ten thousand years—More literally, "a myriad of years" (cf. 21:6). Consequently, the point is not a countable number.

Translation: Chapter 19

19[1]And Uriel said to me: "Here shall stand the angels who have connected
themselves with women, and their spirits assuming many different forms
are defiling mankind and shall lead them astray into sacrificing to demons
«as gods», (here shall they stand,) till «the day of» the great judgement in
which they shall be judged till they are made an end of. [2]And the women
also of the angels who went astray shall become sirens." [3]And I, Enoch,
alone saw the vision, the ends of all things: and no man shall see as I have
seen.

---

319. On this subject, see Ellen Robbins, "The Pleiades, the Flood, and the
    Jewish New Year," in *Ki Baruch Hu: Ancient Near Eastern, Biblical, and
    Judaic Studies in Honor of Baruch A. Levine* (ed. Robert Chazan, William W.
    Hallo, and Lawrence Schiffman; Winona Lake, Ind.: Eisenbrauns, 1999),
    329–344. Certain aspects of Robbins' work are summarized in Heiser,
    Reversing Hermon, chapter 4. A further connection (the Maqlû incantation
    texts of Mesopotamia) is also noted in passing by Bautch, but she apparently
    doesn't realize its potential significance. This series of incantations has
    clear connections to the *apkallu* of Mesopotamia. Annus has shown clear
    connections between the Watcher story and the *apkallu* rebellion (Annus,
    "On the Origin of the Watchers").

Commentary

19:1

Uriel—We now discover which angel is guiding Enoch, the archangel Uriel.

connected—The Greek verb is *migentes* ("mixing with").

their spirits—Does the phrase refer to the original fallen Watchers or to the evil spirits that harass humanity when their offspring, the giants, are killed? If the latter, the content of 1 Enoch is consistent in outlook. If not, then 19:1–2 creates a contradiction.

shall lead them astray—The future perspective of the verb tense would suggest that "these spirits" are the spirits of the dead giants. In addition, Enoch has journeyed to the place where the original Watchers are imprisoned. This would seemingly require us to see "these spirits" as the spirits of the dead giants. Nickelsburg opts for this perspective as well:

> Since the angels are themselves imprisoned, "their spirits" should be interpreted as functionally equivalent if not identical with "the evil spirits" that went forth from the bodies of the dead giants, according to 15:8–12.[320]

assuming many different forms—Spirit beings are not bound by physical form or flesh, so are perceived as being able to appear in various guises.

sacrificing to demons «as gods»—The wording is from Deuteronomy 32:17. As such, the demonology of the author of 1 Enoch is at odds with the Old

---

320. Nickelsburg, *1 Enoch: A Commentary on the Book of 1 Enoch*, vol. 1, 287.

Testament. The "demons" of Deuteronomy 32:17 are not the disembodied spirits of giants, but are rather territorial entities in rebellion against
Yahweh in the wake of the judgment at Babel (Deuteronomy 32:8, reading "sons of God" with the Dead Sea Scrolls in that verse).[321]

19:2

the women also of the angels who went astray shall become sirens—The Ethiopic text has the women becoming "peaceful." The Greek term translated
"siren" is *seirēn*, which is integral to explaining the difference between the
manuscript traditions. The difference is based on where to divide a string
of letters into two words:

> Many commentators note the use of the term "siren" (*seirēn*) for the
> wives of condemned watchers. In Greek mythology the term refers
> to deceitful, charming women, sometimes depicted as "half-women,
> half-birds," who lure and then slay men. The expression occurs only
> in the Greek of 1 Enoch 19:2. The Ethiopic states that the women
> shall become "peaceful" (salāmāwiyāt) and it appears that the Ethi-
> opic translator confused eis seirēnas for hōs eirēnaiai. Elsewhere in
> the Book of the Watchers, the women who have united with the
> angels are not referred to as sirens, nor are their fates disclosed.[322]

Given the uniqueness of the description alluded to by Bautch, it is
difficult to know which reading is correct. For sure the Greek text predates
the Ethiopic, but we do not have an extant Aramaic text for certainty.
Black proposes an interesting, though speculative, hypothesis:

---

321. See Heiser, *Unseen Realm*, 110–122; Michael S. Heiser, "Deuteronomy 32:8
     and the Sons of God," *Bibliotheca Sacra* 158 (January–March 2001): 52–74.
     Nickelsburg (p. 287) concurs: "Demons here are not evil spirits that lead
     humanity astray, but the spirit powers known as the gods of the nations."
322. Bautch, *1 Enoch 17–19*, 132.

In the LXX [Septuagint] *seirēn* usually renders *y 'nb* ("desert owl"), noted for its plaintive cry (Mic 1:8; Jer 27:39 [LXX 50:39]; Isa 13:21). (The word is also found in LXX, equivalent to *tn*, Isa 34:13 ("jackal", "wolf"), also associated with a wailing cry). Could the original have been *bnt n 'myyn* ([Aramaic] Targum Isa 13:21), lit. "daughters of loveliness", a term apparently applied to these "desert owls" on account of their attractive looks.[323]

Nickelsburg suggests (without telling his readers why) that, since Sirens in Greek mythology lured men to their doom, "they are fitting companions for the spirits of the angels."[324] The description earlier in 1 Enoch, that the disembodied spirits of the giants are to harass humans and possess them, isn't quite the same as sending them to their doom. To date, no coherent explanation for the "sirens" reference has been put forth that has garnered consensus support.[325]

---

323. Black, *The Book of Enoch*, 161.

324. Nickelsburg, *1 Enoch: A Commentary on the Book of 1 Enoch*, vol. 1, 287.

325. In a subsequent technical journal article on the textual criticism of 1 Enoch 19:2, Bautch attempts to reconstruct the original Aramaic on the basis of Ethiopic and Qumran material behind some Isaiah passages related to desert creatures. Instead of a noun that would support Greek "siren," she proposes a verb form (*sh-l-m*) that means "to bring to and end utterly." The effect of this proposal is that "the women are merely terminated and removed from the exposition.... Rather than offering an excessively positive or negative evaluation of the wives, this proposed reading of 19:2 makes a statement about the relative unimportance of the wives in the account." In other words, 1 Enoch 19:2 removes the wives from the Watcher story, considering them unimportant. See Kelley Coblentz Bautch, "What Becomes of the Angels' 'Wives'? A Text-Critical Study of 1 Enoch 19:2," *Journal of Biblical Literature* 125:4 (2006): 766-780 (esp. 779–780).

Translation: Chapter 20

20¹And these are the names of the holy angels who watch. ²Uriel, one of the holy angels, who is over the world and over Tartarus. ³Raphael, ⁴one of the holy angels, who is over the spirits of men. Raguel, one of the holy angels who †takes vengeance on† the world of the luminaries. ⁵Michael, one of the holy angels, to wit, he that is set over the best part of mankind «and» over chaos. ⁶Saraqâêl, one of the holy angels, who is set over the spirits, who sin in the spirit. ⁷Gabriel, one of the holy angels, who is over Paradise and the serpents and the Cherubim. ⁸Remiel, one of the holy angels, whom God set over those who rise.

Commentary

As noted earlier, 1 Enoch 20 begins the last subsection of the Book of the Watchers, chapters 20–36, Enoch's second journey. Nickelsburg writes:

> With its superscription and subscript, this list is a kind of counter-
> part to the list of rebel angels in 6:7–8. It serves two literary func-
> tions. It separates the two accounts of Enoch's visits to the places of
> punishment (18:6–19:2 | 21:1–10), and it introduces the angels
> who serve as Enoch's guides in chaps. 21–33. The names of the
> first six angels (allowing for two emendations later) and the func-
> tions ascribed to them correspond to the order of these chapters
> (21:5, 9; 22:3, 6; 23:4; 24:6; 27:2; 32:6).³²⁶

20:1

The holy angels who watch—Gᵃ reads "angels of the powers" (*angeloi tōn dunameōn*). The phrase "holy angels who watch" occurs only here in Charles' translation, so Nickelsburg suspects it is not original, preferring

---

326. Nickelsburg, *1 Enoch: A Commentary on the Book of 1 Enoch*, vol. 1, 294.

(as elsewhere), "watchers and holy ones" in its place.[327] In 9:1, four arch-angels are listed. Here there are seven, and the remainder of the Book of the Watchers (1 Enoch 20–36) will presume these seven. First Enoch 81 also has seven archangels. Rabbinic tradition identifies four archangels (Michael, Gabriel, Uriel, and Raphael).[328] It is uncertain why the book moves from four to seven. Black thinks the increase to seven reflects the "localized angelology" of the writer.[329] Nickelsburg notes that the book of Revelation appears to reflect both traditions in its descriptions of "the seven spirits who are before his throne" (1:4; 4:5) and "the four living creatures that stand on the four sides of the throne" (4:6–8).[330]

As with ancient earthly kings, God is served by elite courtiers who have specific tasks.

20:2

Uriel—See comments at 9:1.

who is over the world and over Tartarus—Having Uriel over Tartarus makes sense, as he turns out to be Enoch's guide to that place (21:5, 9; 19:1). Ethiopic has "for (he is) of the world and of trembling," which Black and Nickelsburg agree reflects an errant, corrupted text.[331] "Over the world" does not mean that Uriel has authority over the earth, but rather over the celestial sphere (which is "over" the earth), through which he guided Enoch on his journey.

First Enoch 20 introduces us to the notion in Second Temple literature that angels are tasked by God with governing various realms. As Bautch

---

327. Ibid., 294.
328. Ibid., 207.
329. Black, *The Book of Enoch*, 162.
330. Nickelsburg, *1 Enoch: A Commentary on the Book of 1 Enoch*, vol. 1, 207.
331. Ibid., 207; Black, *The Book of Enoch*, 162.

notes, "Enochic literature gives angels oversight of inaccessible places like the realm of the dead, places of punishment, and paradise.... [A]ngels play a role in attending to the deceased or the places affiliated with the afterlife."[332] In another part of her discussion, Bautch draws attention to the fact that descriptions of these realms and their oversight are not consistent in 1 Enoch:

> Because Enochic texts are themselves of varied backgrounds, views of liminal places are not homogenous. For example the Book of the Watchers (fourth or third century BCE) understands the dead to await final judgment in an inaccessible place at the ends of the earth. In 1 Enoch 22, the realm of the dead is conceived as a mountain with pits that holds the spirits of the deceased (22:1–3); the realm is likely presented also as a place of darkness near infernal rivers (17:6), comparable to Sheol or Greco-Roman views of the netherworld. The Parables [of Enoch] of the first century BCE or CE, present the righteous dead dwelling in heaven (39:4–5). Thus these writings evince various views of the realm of the dead and of afterlife.[333]

20:3

Raphael—See comments at 9:1.

20:4

over the spirits of men—See 22:3, 6. In 10:7, we noted that Raphael was commissioned with healing the earth. That suggests that the name "Rapha-el" is in part derived from Hebrew *r-p-ʾ* ("to heal"). Nickelsburg

---

332. Bautch, "Heavenly Beings in Enoch," 119.
333. Ibid., 119–120.

wants to connect this to *rephaim* and suggest that Raphael had jurisdiction over the shades of the dead, but that is far from clear either in the present passage or earlier. Can we really say the dead are in view in these passages?

Having noted this uncertainty, Jewish tradition does exist for angels guiding the souls of the righteous to the Lord's presence:

> In Luke 16:19–31, the parable of the rich man and Lazarus, we read this line: "The poor man died and was carried by the angels to Abraham's side" (Luke 16:22). Abraham's "side" (or "bosom") was figurative language referring to the blessed afterlife.
>
> Bock notes that "an angelic escort [to heaven] is a common Jewish image. In the Christian apocrypha, such imagery took on great detail, with pictures of angels doing battle over the souls of people who had passed away."[334]

There are two clear examples of this idea: The Testament of Job 47:10–11; 52:1–12 and the Testament of Abraham 20:10–12 (Recension A).[335] Raphael is not mentioned in any of these passages. Unlike Enochic

---

334. Heiser, *Angels*, 173. The Bock citation comes from Darrell L. Bock, *Luke: 9:51–24:53* (vol. 2) (*Baker Exegetical Commentary on the New Testament*; Grand Rapids, MI: Baker Academic, 1996), 1368. In a footnote on the same page, Bock adds: "For the reprobate, a satanic escort to hell is also a possibility, T. Asher 6.4–6 (Marshall 1978: 636 notes that this text is textually disputed); SB 2:223–27; Tg. Song 4.12)."

335. Unlike 1 Enoch, in the *Testament of Job* angelology is constrained to the role of angels taking the human deceased to heaven, the function known to scholars as that of the "psychopomp," the one who conducts souls to the afterlife. On the *Testament of Abraham*, See Anitra B. Kolenkow, "The Angelology of the Testament of Abraham," in *Studies in the Testament of Abraham* (ed. George W. E. Nickelsburg; Septuagint and Cognate Studies 6; Missoula, MT: Scholars Press, 1976), 153–162.

material, in Luke 16 we have no conversations on the part of the angels or descriptions of realm supervision. Likewise, in New Testament scenes of angels at the tomb of Jesus (Matthew 28:2–7; Luke 24:23 [cf. 24:4]), we have no parallel to 1 Enoch 20. Bautch notes, "The angels in the empty tomb scenes are not explicitly angels associated with the realm of the dead, angels who have guided the deceased from the tomb to the afterlife, or angels who have liberated Jesus from the realm of the dead."[336]

Raguel—Nickelsburg has *Reuel*. There is no contradiction. *Raguel* is a transliteration that renders the *'ayin* in *re'u - 'el* as a *g* (cp. *Gomorrah*, whose first letter is not *gimel*, Hebrew *g*, but *'ayin*, which is pronounced in the back of the throat like hard *g*). *Reuel* means "friend of God."

one of the holy angels who †takes vengeance on† the world of the luminaries—The † symbol indicates the text is problematic. Black concurs with Milik, who argues that the Aramaic verb corresponding to the Greek was *radaph* ("to pursue"). The semantic can be positive or negative—pursue with the intent of persecution (hence the "take vengeance" idea from Charles) or, in Milik's thinking, "simply of pursuit, as when a shepherd follows his flock."[337] The imagery then points us to Reuel as the shepherd of the luminaries, whatever that might mean—perhaps keeping them in motion or maintaining their light? The latter may be suggested by 23:4.

20:5

Michael—See comments at 9:1.

---

336. Bautch, "Heavenly Beings in Enoch," 123. Mark 16:5 could be added to the list, though Mark does not specifically call the young man an angel.
337. Milik, *The Books of Enoch*, 219.

the best part of mankind—Charles appears to be following Ethiopic here, though in abbreviated form ("for he has been put in charge of the good ones of humanity, in charge of the people"). The "best part of mankind" may be a circumlocution for Israel as God's chosen portion. This would make sense, since Daniel 10:13, 21; 12:1 have Michael as the prince of Israel.

«and» over chaos—Nickelsburg writes, "Since the later chapters give no indication that Michael is in charge of chaos, we may assume that, whatever the cause of the confusion, the reading 'chaos' was not original."[338] He omits the phrase accordingly, as does Black.

20:6

Saraqâêl—Black considers this spelling an erroneous transliteration from a corrupt Ethiopic manuscript since it is "otherwise unknown."[339] He opts for Sariel, as does Nickelsburg.

who is set over the spirits, who sin in the spirit—In 1 Enoch 10:1–3, Sariel was sent to Noah by God, which has no resemblance to this duty. Black notes that the text "manifestly corrupt" here, which contributes to the uncertainty of Sariel's task. "Sin in the spirit" may be somewhat clarified by the comments on Sariel in 27:2.

20:7

Gabriel—See comments at 9:1.

---

338. Nickelsburg, *1 Enoch: A Commentary on the Book of 1 Enoch*, vol. 1, 294, note a.

339. Black, *The Book of Enoch*, 163.

who is over Paradise and the serpents and the Cherubim—Unlike Sariel, this charge is clear enough, though in 10:9–10 Gabriel is tasked with the elimination of the giants. In 32:6, Gabriel is the speaker and relates events as though he had firsthand knowledge of Adam and Eve's failure and exile from the Garden of Eden.

20:8

This entire verse is not found in the Ethiopic text of 1 Enoch, though the numbering of seven archangels argues for its genuineness.

Remiel, whom God set over those who rise—The name Remiel is a combination of the verb *rûm* ("to lift up, exalt, to be high") + the divine name El ("El/God lifts up"). The name suggests "God raises" (as in resurrection). Ramael would be an alternate vocalization. A possible wordplay on the language of Isaiah 52:13 may be in view: "Behold, my servant shall act wisely; he shall be high (*rûm*) and lifted up, and shall be exalted" (ESV).

Translation: Chapter 21

21[1]And I proceeded to where things were chaotic. And I saw there something horrible: [2]I saw neither a heaven above nor a firmly founded earth, but a place chaotic and horrible. [3]And there I saw seven stars of the heaven bound together in it, like great mountains and burning with fire. [4]Then I said: [5]"For what sin are they bound, and on what account have they been cast in hither?" Then said Uriel, one of the holy angels, who was with me, and was chief over them, and said: "Enoch, why dost thou ask, and why art thou eager for the truth? [6]These are of the number of the stars ‹of heaven›, which have transgressed the commandment of the Lord, and are bound here till ten thousand years, the time entailed by their sins, are consummated." [7]And from thence I went to another place, which was still more horrible than the former, and I saw a horrible thing: a great fire there which burnt and blazed, and the place was cleft as far as the abyss, being full of great descending columns of fire: neither its extent or magnitude could I see, nor could I conjecture. [8] Then I said: "How fearful is the place and how terrible to look upon!" [9] Then Uriel answered me, one of the holy angels who was with me, and said unto me: "Enoch, why hast thou such fear and affright?" And I answered: "Because of this fearful place, and because of the spectacle of the pain." [10] And he said «unto me»: "This place is the prison of the angels, and here they will be imprisoned for ever."

Commentary

21:1–2

I proceeded—The verb (*ephodeuō*; "to make rounds") is infrequent in 1 Enoch. It launches Enoch's journey eastward, which includes the places he'd already been in reverse order. For that reason, the material here is very similar to (parallel to) chapters 18 and 19. Many scholars would assign the overlaps to different sources.

I saw there something horrible…a place chaotic and horrible—See 18:12. This is the place where the stars (the Watchers) are being punished (verses 3, 6). It is noteworthy that the Greek word translated "chaotic" is *akataskeuastos*, which the Septuagint uses to translate *bōhû* of Genesis 1:2 ("formless"). Given this fact, along with the parallel in 18:12, Nickelsburg suggests whether "desolate" of 18:12 (Greek *erēmos*) might render the phrasal partner of *bōhû* in Genesis 1:2, *tōhû* ("empty"). At any rate, the word choice (terms associated with conditions prior to God's creative work that begins in Genesis 1:3) is apparently intended to make the reader think of a place or set of conditions devoid of God's interest. This place—and so the Watchers' prison—is separate from God's ordered world.

21:3

like great mountains and burning with fire—See comments on 18:12–16.

21:4

For what sin are they bound—The question makes little sense, as the Watchers' earlier petition and God's response through Enoch to that petition make this obvious. The incoherence of the question suggests (again) a different source text that was reconciled to other material by an editor.

21:5

was chief over them—It is not clear how Uriel is over other angels. Nickelsburg and Black note that the same expression is found elsewhere and applied to Michael (24:6).[340] Black opines that "all that is probably meant is that Michael or Uriel was an *archangelos,* i.e., 'a leader among them' rather than 'the leader of all angels.'"[341] In the Ethiopic text of 72:1; 74:2, the expression "designates Uriel's authority over the heavenly luminaries."[342]

21:6

bound here till ten thousand years—See 18:16.

the time entailed by their sins—Ethiopic reads "the number" of their sins. The wording is interesting, for it suggests that, just as the time of the imprisonment ("myriad of years"—i.e., an uncountable number) is beyond numbering, so is the extent of the Watchers' sins (i.e., that its magnitude cannot be calculated).

---

340. Nickelsburg, *1 Enoch: A Commentary on the Book of 1 Enoch,* vol. 1, 298; Black, *The Book of Enoch,* 164.

341. Black, *The Book of Enoch,* 164.

342. Nickelsburg, *1 Enoch: A Commentary on the Book of 1 Enoch,* vol. 1, 298.

21:7–10

See comments at 18:6–19:2, though there are differences:

> If we may judge from chaps. 17–19, especially the juxtaposition of
> 18:6–8 and 18:9–11 + 19:1–2, the pit of the angels' punishment
> runs past God's throne (see chaps. 24–25) to the great abyss....
> Reference to size here could apply to the columns of fire or to the
> chasm.... A parallelism of expression occurs in each of the mem-
> bers of this section: terrible, fearful; frightened, shaken; terrible,
> fearful; prison, confined. Different from vv 5–6, Enoch responds
> to the angelic counter-question. The reference to this place as a
> prison (*desmōtērion*, v 10) links this vision with the one that fol-
> lows (22:1–4).[343]

Translation: Chapter 22

In this chapter, Charles periodically (i.e., for some verses) translates both
his Greek and Ethiopic text for the reader, setting them side by side:

22[1]And thence I went to another place, and he showed me in the west
‹another› great and high mountain [and] of hard rock.

Ethiopic	Greek (G^a)
[2]And there was in it †four† **hollow** places, deep and wide and very smooth. †How† smooth are **the hollow places** and deep and dark to look at.	[2]And there were †four† hollow places in it, deep and very smooth: †three† of them were dark and one bright and there was a fountain of water in its midst. And I said: "†How† smooth are these hollow places, and deep and dark to view."

343. Ibid., 298–299.

[3]Then Raphael answered, one of the holy angels who was with me, and said unto me: "These hollow places have been created for this very purpose, that the spirits of the souls of the dead should assemble therein, yea that all the souls of the children of men should assemble here. [4]And these places **have been made** to receive them till the day of their judgement and till their appointed period [till the period appointed], till the great judgement (comes) upon them."

Ethiopic	Greek (G[a])
[5]I saw the spirits of the children of men who were dead, and their voice went forth to heaven and made suit.	[5]I saw ⟨the spirit of⟩ a dead man making suit, and his voice went forth to heaven and made suit.
[6]Then I asked Raphael the angel who was with me, and I said unto him: "This spirit—whose is it, whose voice goeth forth and maketh suit?"	[6]And I asked Raphael the angel who was with me, and I said unto him: "This spirit which maketh suit, whose is it, whose voice goeth forth and maketh suit to heaven?"

[7]And he answered me saying: "This is the spirit which went forth from Abel, whom his brother Cain slew, and he makes his suit against him till his seed is destroyed from the face of the earth, and his seed is annihilated from amongst the seed of men."

Ethiopic	Greek (G[a])
[8]Then I asked regarding it, and regarding all the **hollow places:** "Why is one separated from the other?"	[8]Then I asked regarding all the **hollow places:** "Why is one separated from the other?"
[9]And he answered me and said unto me: "These three have been	[9]And he answered me saying: "These three have been made that

Ethiopic

made that the spirits of the dead might be separated. And such a division has been made ⟨for⟩ the spirits of the righteous, in which there is the **bright** spring of water.

[10]**And** such has been made for sinners when they die and are buried in the earth and judgement has not been executed on them in their lifetime.

[11]Here their spirits shall be set apart in this great pain till the great day of judgement and punishment and torment of those who curse for ever and retribution for their spirits. There He shall bind them for ever.

[12]And such a division has been made for the spirits of those who make their suit, who make disclosures concerning their destruction, when they were slain in the days of the sinners.

[13]Such has been made for the spirits of men who were not righteous but sinners, who were complete in transgression, and of the transgressors they shall be companions: but

Greek (G^a)

the spirits of the dead might be separated. And **this** division has been made for the spirits of the righteous, in which there is the bright spring of water.

[10]And **this** has been made for sinners when they die and are buried in the earth and judgement has not been executed upon them in their lifetime.

[11]Here their spirits shall be set apart in this great pain, till the great day of judgement, scourgings, and torments of the accursed for ever, **so that** (there may be) retribution for their spirits. There He shall bind them for ever.

[12]And **this** division has been made for the spirits of those who make their suit, who make disclosures concerning their destruction, when they were slain in the days of the sinners.

[13]And this has been made for the spirits of men who shall not be righteous but sinners, who are godless, and of the lawless they shall be companions: but their

Ethiopic	Greek (Gᵃ)
their spirits shall not be slain in the day of judgement nor shall they be raised from thence."	spirits shall not be punished in the day of judgement nor shall they be raised from thence."
¹⁴Then I blessed the Lord of glory and said: "Blessed be my Lord, the Lord of righteousness, who ruleth for ever."	¹⁴Then I blessed the Lord of glory and said: "Blessed art Thou, Lord of righteousness, who ruleth over the world."

Commentary

22:1

thence I went to another place—Nickelsburg orients us:

> From the places of punishment for the transgressing stars and rebel angels (chap. 21), Enoch proceeds to a great mountain with huge pits that serve as repositories for the souls of the dead—both good and evil.... In its form and idiom, this vision parallels others in this journey (see the analysis in the Introduction to chaps. 20–36.... In its emphasis on the eschatological fate of human beings, it is one of several sections that distinguish this second journey from the one described in chaps. 17–19.[344]

he showed me—Given what has preceded the reader expects "he" to be Uriel. However, in verse 3, it is Raphael who is guiding Enoch. Nickelsburg notes that the language here ought to influence what is found in other

---

344. Nickelsburg, *1 Enoch: A Commentary on the Book of 1 Enoch*, vol. 1, 301–302.

passages in 1 Enoch where we read in translation "I saw." Enoch is being shown specific sights, and so the passive translation better reflects this.[345]

22:2

there was in it †four† hollow places, deep and wide and very smooth—"In it" situates the hollow places in the mountain. Consequently, the imagery seems to be that of caves in the mountain. This is no surprise, as caves were used as burial places (cf. verse 3) in antiquity (in mountains or otherwise; Genesis 23:9–20).

24:3

Then Raphael answered—The angel guide has changed from Uriel. Scholars note that the change appears appropriate because the place Enoch is being shown is where the dead (the "shades"/*rephaim*) reside. The name "Raphael" shares several consonants with that term.

These hollow places have been created for this very purpose, that the spirits of the souls of the dead should assemble therein—The hollow places are clearly for the dead. Nickelsburg notes the relationship of some of the ensuing imagery and the Old Testament:

> In their descriptions of the place of the dead, both major stages of the tradition in chap. 22 depend on biblical teaching and transcend it, using ideas current elsewhere in antiquity. That the disembodied shades of all the dead were taken to the gloomy regions of Sheol is a widespread idea in the Hebrew Bible, and in this

---

345. Ibid., 300. See 1 Enoch 21:1, 7; 23:2; 24:2; 26:1, 2, 3; 28:1; 29:1; 30:1, 3; 32:1, 3; 33:1, 2, 3; 34:1, 2; 35:1; 36:1, 2, 4.

respect the dark pits originally described in vv 1–4 are consonant with biblical imagery.

In at least two respects, however, the original description in vv 1–4 differed from most biblical portrayals of Sheol. First, Sheol was thought to be in the underworld and not a mountain in the west. For the latter idea Babylonian religion and cosmography provide the best analogies, although aspects of these are common in Greece and the ancient Near East. Second, almost without exception, the biblical texts portray Sheol as the final residence for the shades of the dead. The exceptions are Isa 26:14–19, which may posit a resurrection of the righteous, and Dan 12:2, which speaks of the fate of "many" of the righteous and wicked.[346]

The phrase "the spirits of the souls of the dead" is defined by the ensuing line, "the souls of the children of men"—i.e., the human dead. The terminology and context therefore inform us that the Raphael is not showing Enoch where spirit beings, angels, Watchers, or the spirits of the dead giants are kept. That place was earlier in the journey. In verses 5–7, the righteous dead are in view. Later (verses 10, 13) the unrighteous ("sinners") will be the focus.

22:4

*these places **have been made** to receive them till the day of their judgement—* This new place is the abode of the unrighteous dead until their final judgment. Language similar to that in 22:4 is found in 1 Enoch 10:12; 22:11; 84:4 ("great day of judgment"); and 16:1; 19:1; 25:4; 94:9; 98:10; 99:15; 104:5 ("day of great judgment").[347]

---

346. Ibid., 303–304.
347. Ibid., 305.

22:5–7

I saw the spirits of the children of men who were dead—The Ethiopic has a singular individual/entity in view (cp. Luke 16 and see verses 8–9). Black notes that there is some Greek manuscript evidence for an original singular and takes the ensuing reference to Abel (a sole individual) as proof of the same.[348]

their voice went forth to heaven and made suit—The idea does not seem to be (see comments at 9:1) that the human dead are desiring angelic mediation with God to resolve their suffering—they're already dead. Rather, the context points to the notion of the dead wanting justice. Hence the text (verse 7) uses righteous Abel as a foil. Perhaps this tradition operates in concert with the "blood of righteous Abel" in the Gospels (Matthew 23:35; Luke 11:51; Hebrews 12:24). Nickelsburg notes in this regard:

> The terminology in vv 5–6 is especially close to 1 Enoch 9:2, 10, where the narrative of Genesis 6–9 has been interpolated with the extraneous motif of the dead pleading for vengeance. Both here and in 1 Enoch 6–11, the cry of the dead (and of the earth that has soaked up the blood of the dead, 7:6; 9:2, 9; cf. Gen 4:11) continues to bring accusation until divine judgment is executed against the murderer(s).... Here "the spirit" of Abel brings suit against his murderer and his seed.[349]

---

348. Black, *The Book of Enoch*, 166.
349. Nickelsburg, *1 Enoch: A Commentary on the Book of 1 Enoch*, vol. 1, 305–306.

22:8–9

These three have been made that the spirits of the dead might be separated— The hollows (caves) are from this point numbered and distinguished: "The originally unspecified number of pits, which Raphael interpreted as receptacles to *gather* the multitude of human souls (vv 3–4), are now interpreted as four repositories that *separate* the dead according to the individual's ethical quality and lot in life."[350]

*the spirits of the righteous, in which there is the **bright** spring of water—*Here the righteous dead are put into a separate category from the three divisions of the unrighteous dead. The bright spring of water is an image apparently drawn from classical Greek material about Hades. Black observes that "in the Greek Hades there was a spring of forgetfulness on the left, while on the right was the spring of memory…by the drinking of which consciousness and memory were quickened, the first condition of the full and blessed life."[351] Nickelsburg concurs: "This author's debt to Greek ideas (esp. those of the Pythagorean and Orphic provenance preserved in Plato) is especially evident in his divisions between the various kinds of sinners and in the imagery of the fountain."[352]

22:10–13

There are parallels to Luke 16 in the descriptive phrases found in these verses:

The parable of Dives[353] and Lazarus (Luke 16:19–31) is an interesting example of the early Christian use of the kind of cosmology pre-

---

350. Ibid., 306.

351. Black, *The Book of Enoch*, 167.

352. Nickelsburg, *1 Enoch: A Commentary on the Book of 1 Enoch*, vol. 1, 307.

353. "Dives" is the Latin proper name for the rich man: "The Latin adjective

sumed here and its function in a context concerned with theodicy.
The parable contrasts poor, oppressed Lazarus with the rich man,
who does not obey the Law and the Prophets and unjustly enjoys
good things in his life and honor in his burial. Their situations are
reversed after death. In Abraham's bosom, Lazarus is refreshed with
water, while Dives suffers torments in Hades. The cosmology of
the parable differs somewhat from the present chapter in its details,
but not in its function. In the place of pits that separate the righteous from the sinners, there is a single great chasm that separates
the two groups. In both cases mythic cosmology undergirds an
assertion about the execution of divine justice.[354]

judgement has not been executed on them in their lifetime—The dead in this
hollow are those "whose unspecified sins went unpunished during their
lifetimes [who] now undergo bitter and tortuous punishment."[355]

*the spirits of men who were not righteous but sinners...their spirits shall not
be slain in the day of judgement nor shall they be raised from thence*—From
verse 13; this group of sinners is of course distinct from the earlier groups,
but scholars are unsure as to how. The best guess seems to be that those
in this group were judged in their own lifetime, perhaps by means of the
way they died.

---

dives simply means "rich" or "wealthy." The addition of a proper name to
the rich man, which is not present in Luke's version of the parable, was
likely added by medieval scribes who translated the Greek text into Latin."
See Eric P. Costanzo, "Lazarus and Dives," ed. John D. Barry et al., *The
Lexham Bible Dictionary* (Bellingham, WA: Lexham Press, 2016); Henry
Joel Cadbury, "A Proper Name for Dives," *Journal of Biblical Literature* 81:4
(1962): 399–402.

354. Nickelsburg, *1 Enoch: A Commentary on the Book of 1 Enoch*, vol. 1, 307.
355. Ibid., 307.

22:14

The Lord of glory—See 14:19.

Translation: Chapter 23

23¹From thence I went to another place to the west of the ends of the earth. ²And I saw a burning fire which ran without resting, and paused not from its course day or night but (ran) regularly. ³And I asked saying: "What is this which rests not?" ⁴Then Raguel, one of the holy angels who was with me, answered me «and said unto me»: "This course ‹of fire› «which thou hast seen» is the fire in the west which †persecutes† all the luminaries of heaven."

Commentary

23:1

I went—Aramaic reads ʾwblt (4QEnᵈ 1 11:3), which means "I was transported."[356] Other language of Enoch being "transported" is found in 1 Enoch 14:8; 32:2; 36:1.

23:2

ran without resting, and paused not from its course—Nickelsburg points out that the primary texts contain "terminological similarities" between verses 2, 4 and 17:4–5, where the referent was a combination of fire and "living waters." This suggests to him "that this is the equivalent of the fiery waters described in the first journey. The four-times repeated image of motion and restlessness (v 2) suggests that the author has a river in mind."[357] In

---

356. Milik, *The Books of Enoch*, 218.
357. Nickelsburg, *1 Enoch: A Commentary on the Book of 1 Enoch*, vol. 1, 310.

other words, Nickelsburg thinks the point is a river of fire. First Enoch 14:19–23 has streams of fire issuing from God's throne, so the imagery isn't unprecedented. Daniel 7:9–10 has "a stream of fire" issuing forth from (before?) the Ancient of Days.

23:4

Raguel.... This course ‹of fire›...†persecutes† *all the luminaries of heaven.*— The diacritical marks in the translation point to the fact that there are several textual difficulties in the verse. On Raguel, see comments at 20:4, where Reuel should be the reading. The verbal †persecutes† is a translation of *ekdiōkō* ("pursue, persecute"). In 20:4, the verb was *ekdikeō* ("to take revenge"). In 20:4, we read "the world of luminaries" instead of "all the luminaries" here. The meaning is uncertain. If, however, we take *ekdiōkō* as "pursue" the imagery may refer to an unceasing fire that propels (as opposed to trailing from) the luminaries. That imagery may refer to an endless source of fire that follows the luminaries—maybe a comet trail or meteoric trail. But this is mere speculation, and it begs the question as to what is endless about meteor showers or intermittent comets. Perhaps the point is an enduring source of the light of celestial objects. The point in any event is that Enoch has been transported to another section of the heavens—in effect, another neighborhood of the cosmos that is, for the ancient mind, the realm of spiritual beings. See 18:13–15.

Translation: Chapter 24

24^{1} «And from thence I went to another place of the earth», and he showed me a mountain range of fire which burnt «day and» night. ^{2}And I went beyond it and saw seven magnificent mountains all differing each from the other, and the stones (thereof) were magnificent and beautiful, magnificent as a whole, of glorious appearance and fair exterior: «three towards» the east, «one» founded on the other, and three towards the south, «one» upon the other, and deep rough ravines, no one of which joined with any other. [3]And the seventh mountain was in the midst of these, and it excelled them in height, resembling the seat of a throne: and fragrant trees encircled the throne. [4]And amongst them was a tree such as I had never yet smelt, neither was any amongst them nor were others like it: it had a fragrance beyond all fragrance, and its leaves and blooms and wood wither not for ever: and its fruit «is beautiful, and its fruit» resembles the dates of a palm. [5]Then I said: "‹How› beautiful is this tree, and fragrant, and its leaves are fair, and its blooms «very» delightful in appearance." [6] Then answered Michael, one of the holy «and honoured» angels who was with me, and was their leader.

Commentary

First Enoch 24 in fact is something of a conceptual turning point in Enoch's second journey (chapters 20–36):

> In chapters 24–25 the seer is once again at the mountain throne of God. The description of 18:6–9 has been augmented by reference to God's final visitation of the earth, mention of the tree of life, and a description of the blessings that the righteous will experience in the new Jerusalem. Enoch's vision of the Holy City in chapters 26–27 has a similar emphasis. Chapters 25–27 take up eschatological predictions in Isaiah 65–66 and set them in the revelatory form that is typical of these chapters of 1 Enoch. Chapters 28:1–32:2 modify this vision form. Paralleling 17:1–5 they rapidly recount landmarks that document the seer's journey along the eastern spice routes, which culminates in his arrival at paradise (again the vision form in 32:3–6) and beyond it at the ends of the earth (33:1).[358]

358. George W. E. Nickelsburg, *Jewish Literature between the Bible and the Mishnah : A Literary and Historical Introduction* (2nd ed.; Minneapolis, MN: Fortress Press, 2005), 52.

24:1

a mountain range of fire—Chapters 24–25 describe a seven-mountain range that parallels that of 1 Enoch 18. With respect to 1 Enoch 18, Nickelsburg observed about the range that "its apex, to the northwest, is the throne of God, and its two sides, comprising three mountains each, lie on west-east and north-south axes."[359] In her study on the cosmic geography of 1 Enoch 17–19, Bautch comments about the similar tradition of 1 Enoch 24–25:

> There is nothing about the arrangement that indicates, ipso facto, that the mountain range is located in the northwest. It is made clear by the text that the apex of the arrangement is toward the northwest, but there is no indication in 1 Enoch 18:6 where the range itself is located…. A tradition parallel to that of 1 Enoch 18:6 is to be found in 1 Enoch 24:1–3, in which seven mountains of precious stones are arranged similarly, three toward the east and three toward the south.[360]

The ensuing details will use Edenic terminology. However, this is the heavenly Eden, not the original home of Adam and Eve. "Eden language" is applied in the book to a cosmic abode, a glorified Jerusalem, and the "old" (original) Eden situated in Enoch's vision east of Jerusalem (see chapters 28–32; cf. 32:6).

24:2

the stones (thereof) were magnificent and beautiful—The ensuing elaboration of verse 2 ("magnificent as a whole, of glorious appearance and fair

---

359. Nickelsburg, *1 Enoch: A Commentary on the Book of 1 Enoch*, vol. 1, 285.
360. Bautch, *1 Enoch 17–19*, 110–111.

exterior: «three towards» the east, «one» founded on the other, and three towards the south, «one» upon the other, and deep rough ravines, no one of which joined with any other") indicates that the magnificent stones are the mountains. These fiery mountains (see verse 1), which are spectacular, glimmering gemstones, are drawn from ancient Near Eastern conceptions of the abode of the God/the gods and His/their council. On the bejeweled cosmic mountain abode of the gods/God, see comments and footnoted sources at 18:7. This is the point of the language of Ezekiel 28:11–14. When the prophet describes the anointed cherub as "walking among the stones of fire," his point is that the cherub was in the divine abode, the place of the divine council.

24:3–4

the seventh mountain was in the midst of these, and it excelled them in height, resembling the seat of a throne: and fragrant trees encircled the throne—The description of the seventh mountain will be described more explicitly as God's throne in 25:3. This identification solidifies that the point of the "fiery bejeweled mountains" is the place of the divine assembly, God, and His heavenly host. First Enoch 18:8 makes the same identification.

And amongst them was a tree such as I had never yet smelt—The tree imagery that begins in verses 3–4 has also drawn the attention of scholars in regard to the divine abode of the God of the Bible:

> Charles and apparently Nickelsburg take this mountain range which features a tree with life-giving fruit to be a northwestern paradise. Perhaps they associate the scene with paradise because the presence of a tree with life-giving fruit is reminiscent of the tree of life in Eden (Gen 3:9, 22, 24).[361]

---

361. Ibid., 111.

Lest the reader think this language is too unlike the description of Eden with its Tree of Life and the Tree of the Knowledge of Good and Evil, trees (plural) are part of the Old Testament's cosmic imagery of Eden:

> [15]Thus says the Lord GOD: On the day the cedar went down to Sheol I caused mourning; I closed the deep over it, and restrained its rivers, and many waters were stopped. I clothed Lebanon in gloom for it, and all the trees of the field fainted because of it. [16]I made the nations quake at the sound of its fall, when I cast it down to Sheol with those who go down to the pit. And all the trees of Eden, the choice and best of Lebanon, all that drink water, were comforted in the world below. [17]They also went down to Sheol with it, to those who are slain by the sword; yes, those who were its arm, who lived under its shadow among the nations. [18]Whom are you thus like in glory and in greatness among the trees of Eden? You shall be brought down with the trees of Eden to the world below. You shall lie among the uncircumcised, with those who are slain by the sword. (Ezekiel 30:15–18; cf. Ezekiel 30:7–9)

Readers should note that the idea here in 1 Enoch 24 is that Enoch sees the Tree of Life planted in Jerusalem, signifying that Jerusalem is the cosmic mountain abode of God. The "old" Eden will be described in chapters 28–32 (cf. 32:6) as being situated east of Jerusalem.

its leaves and blooms and wood wither not for ever—This detail suggests that this tree is the Tree of Life. The description in 25:3–5 ("no mortal is permitted to touch it till the great judgement.... Its fruit **shall be** for food to the elect: it shall be transplanted to the holy place, to the temple of the Lord, the Eternal King") also suggests that this is the case, mainly on the basis of Revelation 2:7 ("To the one who conquers I will grant to eat of the tree of life, which is in the paradise of God"). Nickelsburg concurs and adds some Second Temple literary correlation: "The inaccessibility of the tree until the eschaton is an important structural feature of the later Adam literature (*Apocalypse of Moses* and *Adam and Eve*), and the theme is explicit in *T. Levi* 18:10–11 and is alluded to in Rev 2:7."[362]

Translation: Chapter 25

25[1]And he said unto me: "Enoch, why dost thou ask me regarding the fragrance of the tree, and ‹why› dost thou wish to learn the truth?" [2]Then I answered him «saying»: "I wish to know about everything, but especially about this tree." [3]And he answered saying: "This high mountain «which thou hast seen», whose summit is like the throne of God, is His throne, where the Holy Great One, the Lord of Glory, the Eternal King, will sit, when He shall come down to visit the earth with goodness. [4]And as for this fragrant tree no mortal is permitted to touch it till the great judgement, when He shall take vengeance on all and bring (everything) to its consummation for ever. [5]It shall then be given to the righteous and holy. Its fruit **shall be** for food to the elect: it shall be transplanted to the holy place, to the temple of the Lord, the Eternal King.

[6]Then shall they rejoice with joy and be glad,
And into the holy place shall they enter;
And its fragrance shall be in their bones,
And they shall live a long life on earth,
Such as thy fathers lived:
And in their days shall no «sorrow» or plague
Or torment or calamity touch them."

[7]Then blessed I the God of Glory, the Eternal King, who hath prepared such things for the righteous, and hath created them and promised to give to them.

---

362. Nickelsburg, *1 Enoch: A Commentary on the Book of 1 Enoch*, vol. 1, 314.

Commentary

25:2

especially about this tree—See comments on 24:3–4.

25:3

This high mountain «which thou hast seen», whose summit is like the throne of God, is His throne—See comments on 24:3–4.

The Holy Great One, the Lord of Glory—G^a reads (more literally), "the great Lord, the Holy One of Glory."[363] See 1:3, where (as in this verse) the epithet occurs along with "eternal God." See also 14:19.

the Eternal King—Similar to "eternal God" in 1:3, where it is accompanied by "Great Holy One," very similar to the epithet in the current verse. "Eternal king" also occurs in verses 5 and 7. The Greek translated "eternal king" reads *ho basileus tou aiōnos*, which is similar to 9:4 *kuriōn tōn aiōnōn* (G^s—"Lord of ages"). Other Greek material has "God of ages" (*theon tōn aiōnōn*). The title "lord of eternity/ages" is attested in Aramaic in the Genesis Apocryphon among the Dead Sea Scrolls (*mrh 'lmy*).[364] Black suggests that these titles "seem to be elaborating on the original expression…from Dt. 10:17 LXX *theos tōn theōn, kurios tōn kuriōn* ["God of gods, Lord of lords"]. For "king of kings" [see] Ezek 26.7 (but for the king of Babylon), Dan 2.37, Ezr 7.12."[365]

to visit the earth with goodness—In other words, with blessing.

---

363. Ibid., 312, footnote c.
364. Black, *The Book of Enoch*, 130.
365. Ibid., 130.

25:4

as for this fragrant tree—See comments on 24:3–4.

Till the great judgement, when He shall take vengeance on all and bring (everything) to its consummation for ever—This refers to the Day of the Lord, the time in biblical eschatology when the wicked are punished and the righteous are vindicated. See comments on 10:12–17. By way of a succinct definition:

> The Day of the Lord is a significant recurring theme in the prophetic literature of the OT. At its essence, it refers to a time of Yahweh's unmistakable and powerful intervention. It appears in a variety of contexts in prophetic literature and draws together a wide array of images…. The Day of the Lord resonates across the canon and is picked up in the NT in the context of the work of Jesus Christ and the inauguration of the church. It continues to employ powerful and evocative images of cosmic upheaval and divine judgment to emphasize the overwhelming importance of this day.[366]

25:5

It shall then be given to the righteous and holy—"It" refers to the Tree of Life (i.e., life in the *new* Eden, Jerusalem, after God's judgment).

*Its fruit **shall be** for food to the elect: it shall be transplanted to the holy place, to the temple of the Lord, the Eternal King*—See comments at 24:3–4; 25:3. "Elect" (i.e., the chosen) is used in parallel with "the righteous" in 1:8–9; 5:4–9.

---

366. J. D. Barker, "Day of the Lord," *Dictionary of the Old Testament: Prophets* (ed. Mark J. Boda and Gordon J. McConville; Downers Grove, IL; Nottingham, England: IVP Academic; Inter-Varsity Press, 2012), 132, 142.

25:6

The content of 25:6 apparently draws on the new earth vision of Isaiah 65–66:

1 Enoch 25:6	Isaiah 65–66
⁶Then shall they rejoice with joy and be glad,	(65:19) I will rejoice in Jerusalem and be glad in my people…
And into the holy place shall they enter;	(66:23) all flesh shall come to worship before me, declares the LORD…
And its [the tree of life]³⁶⁷ fragrance shall be in their bones,³⁶⁸	(65:20) No more shall there be in it an infant who lives but a few days, or an old man who does not fill out his days…
And they shall live a long life on earth, Such as thy fathers lived:	(66:14) your heart shall rejoice; your bones shall flourish like the grass…
And in their days shall no «sorrow» or plague	(65:19) no more shall be heard in it the sound of weeping and the cry of distress…
Or torment or calamity touch them.'	(65:8) so I will do for my servants' sake, and not destroy them all…

367. See 24:3–4 (cp. 10:17). Nickelsburg (p. 315) notes: "The fruit of the tree of life and its fragrance bring long life, not simply in the sense of Exod 20:12, but a life whose length is compared to that of Enoch's forebears, that is, more than nine hundred years."

368. Nickelsburg points out that the Aramaic term that presumably underlies "bones" here "may refer to the seat of sensation" or the self (p. 315, quoting

the eternal King—See comments on 25:3. Nickelsburg adds, "The title 'Lord (or 'God' or 'King') of glory,' which appears also in 22:14; 25:3, 7; 27:3, 5; 36:4; 63:2; 81:3; 83:8, alludes to the effulgent splendor that envelops the enthroned deity...and complements other terms that define the transcendent God."[369]

25:7

God of Glory—See 14:19. Of this title (and others in this section), Nickelsburg notes, "The title 'Lord (or 'God' or 'King') of glory,' which appears also in 22:14; 25:3, 7; 27:3, 5; 36:4; 63:2; 81:3; 83:8, alludes to the effulgent splendor that envelops the enthroned deity."[370]

Translation: Chapter 26

26[1] And I went from thence to the middle of the earth, and I saw a blessed place ‹in which there were trees› with branches abiding and blooming [of a dismembered tree]. [2] And there I saw a holy mountain, «and» underneath the mountain to the east there was a stream and it flowed towards the south. [3] And I saw towards the east another mountain higher than this, and between them a deep and narrow ravine: in it also ran a stream ‹underneath› the mountain. [4] And to the west thereof there was another mountain, lower than the former and of small elevation, and a ravine ‹deep and dry› between them: and another deep and dry ravine was at the extremities of the three ‹mountains›. [5] And all the ravines were deep «and narrow», (being formed) of hard rock, and trees were not planted upon

---

Marcus Jastrow, *A Dictionary of the Targumim, the Talmud Babli and Yerushalmi, and the Midrashic Literature* (repr. 2 vols.; New York: Pardes Publishing House, 1950), vol. 1, 270.

369. Nickelsburg, *1 Enoch: A Commentary on the Book of 1 Enoch*, vol. 1, 316.
370. Ibid., 316.

them. [6]And marveled «at the rocks, and I marveled» at the ravine, yea, marveled very much.

Commentary

26:1

to the middle of the earth—In other words, the geographical center of the earth, not inside the earth. Enoch is still being transported from above the earth (see 1 Enoch 14:8; 23:1; 32:2; 36:1) and so is taken to what the writer conceived as the geographical center of the earth's land mass.

In biblical thought, the geographical "center of the earth" was Jerusalem (Ezekiel 5:5; 38:12). In modern cartographic terms, this is not a literal geographical possibility. The idea is best understood as cosmic-geographical theological conception. That is, Jerusalem was conceived of as the center of God's interest, attention, and plans on earth because it was the place He chose to establish His name (presence).[371] Nickelsburg adds that "the idea is explicit in *Jub.* 8:12, 19. The phrase expresses in geographical terms Israel's self-understanding as God's special, chosen people."[372]

Blessed—The Ethiopic word here means "fertile," which the ensuing description ("there were trees with branches abiding and blooming") confirms is in view. For the tree imagery, see 1 Enoch 10:18–19; 25:4–6.

[of a dismembered tree]—This bracketed information is found in Ethiopic and G[a]. The brackets inform us that it is suspect. Of the phrase, Nickelsburg writes, "The reference to the felled tree (see n. b) is most likely a

---

371. For the name as God Himself and establishment of His name as dwelling, see for example, Deuteronomy 12:11; 2 Samuel 6:1–2; 1 Chronicles 22:19; Psalm 20:1, 7; Isaiah 30:27–28; 60:9, along with Michael S. Heiser, "The Name Theology of the Old Testament," *Faithlife Study Bible*. Bellingham, WA: Lexham Press, 2012, 2016.

372. Nickelsburg, *1 Enoch: A Commentary on the Book of 1 Enoch*, vol. 1, 318.

later gloss, alluding to the idea of a remnant sprouting from Israel's fallen tree."[373] Charles sees allusion to Daniel 11:16, 41, 45 and John 15:5 (the Messiah representing Jerusalem and the cosmic center of God's plan).[374]

26:2

there I saw a holy mountain—Given the identification of the "center of the earth" as Jerusalem, this reference to a holy mountain at this center must refer to Mount Zion. Jerusalem as a holy mountain, Mount Zion, is of course an Old Testament description (Isaiah 27:13; 56:7; 57:13; 65:11, 25; 66:20; Daniel 9:16, 20; Joel 2:1; Obadiah16; Zechariah 8:3). Atop this mountain or hill was the Temple. This raises an obvious question: Why is the Temple not mentioned? Nickelsburg makes his opinion clear: "That the author makes no reference to the temple reflects his fictional antediluvian setting rather than a value judgment on the situation in Jerusalem during his own time."[375] This makes good sense in terms of the chronology of the events of the Book of the Watchers.

Elsewhere Nickelsburg enters more speculative turf when he informs readers that he suspects the absence of the mention of the Temple, coupled with the geography of Enoch's supernatural dream (north in Dan, Abel-Main), reflects a negative view of the Jerusalem priesthood (which is located in the south of the country) on the part of the author:

> 1 Enoch 12–16 is a tradition that appears to have emanated from circles in Upper Galilee who viewed the Jerusalem priesthood as defiled and therefore under the irrevocable judgment of God. These people regarded the area around Dan and Hermon as sacred territory that was catalytic of revelation.[376]

---

373. Ibid., 318.
374. Charles, *Commentary on the Pseudepigrapha of the Old Testament*, vol. 2, 205.
375. Nickelsburg, *1 Enoch: A Commentary on the Book of 1 Enoch*, vol. 1, 318.

Underneath the mountain to the east there was a stream and it flowed towards the south—This part of the author's description aligns well with the geography of Jerusalem. This stream would be the Gihon Spring. Other details in verses 3–4 are more difficult.

26:3–4

towards the east another mountain higher than this, and between them a deep and narrow ravine: in it also ran a stream ‹underneath› the mountain. And to the west thereof there was another mountain, lower than the former and of small elevation, and a ravine ‹deep and dry› between them: and another deep and dry ravine was at the extremities of the three ‹mountains›—Nickelsburg notes some congruities and inconsistencies with Jerusalem:

> From the east side of its southern extension, Mount Ophel, the spring of Gihon flows out into the Kidron Valley and then southward. To the east of Zion-Ophel is the towering Mount of Olives. Between them is the next-mentioned deep valley, the Kidron. In the text of Eth, the western mountain (v 4) is er-Ras, the lower slope of *Ğebel* Abû-Tôr, "the Hill of Evil Counsel," which lies west of the Mount of Offense, the southern lobe of the Mount of Olives. The barren, dry Valley of Hinnom runs easterly at the foot of them. The last of the valleys is the slopes of Silwan. If the text of G^a is correct with its omission of "beneath it," the western hill could be Ophel, which is lower than the Temple Mount, the valley in v 4b is the Tyropoeon Valley, which was situated between Zion-Ophel and the main western Hill of Jerusalem (Christian Zion). The last valley would then be the Valley of Hinnom, which issues at the foot of the Mount of Olives, Ophel, and the Hill of Evil Counsel. Verse 5 with its reference to barrenness contrasts with v 1.[377]

---

376. Ibid., 230.
377. Ibid., 318.

Translation: Chapter 27

As was the case in chapter 22, Charles presents two versions of this short chapter.

27[1] Then said I: "For what object is this blessed land, which is entirely filled with trees, and this accursed valley «between»?" [2] «Then Uriel, one of the holy angels who was with me, answered and said: "This» accursed valley is for those who are accursed for ever: here shall all ‹the accursed› be gathered together who utter with their lips against the Lord unseemly words and of His glory speak hard things.

Ethiopic	Greek (G^a)
Here shall they be gathered together, and here shall be their place of judgement. [3] In the last days there shall be upon them the spectacle of righteous judgement in the presence of the righteous for ever: here shall the merciful bless the Lord of glory, the Eternal King.	Here shall they be gathered together, and here shall be the place of their habitation. [3] In the last times, in the days of the true judgement in the presence of the righteous for ever: here shall the **godly** bless the Lord of glory, the Eternal King.

[4] In the days of judgement over the former, they shall bless Him for the mercy in accordance with which He has assigned them (their lot). [5] Then I blessed the Lord of Glory and set forth His ‹glory› and lauded Him gloriously.

Commentary

27:1

"For what object is this blessed land, which is entirely filled with trees, and this accursed valley «between»?"—"Blessed" (as earlier in 26:1) means "fertile," which matches the description of being filled with trees. There is an

obvious contrast intended, one that sets up the ensuing description of the occupants of Jerusalem with those forbidden entrance into the city (and the presence of God).

27:2

«*Then Uriel, one of the holy angels who was with me, answered and said: "This*»—This material in double brackets reflects the Ethiopic text. It is missing in G[a]. Given the textual corruption, some scholars have marshaled arguments that we should read Sariel here, not Uriel:

> Three factors indicate…that we should read "Sariel." Uriel has already been mentioned in chap. 21, in accordance with his place and function in 20:2. The sequence in chap. 20 leads us to Sariel in 20:6, whose function mentioned there fits the present chapter. Elsewhere in 1 Enoch, Sariel and Uriel are confused.[378]

Black does not argue for Sariel here, but notes the inconsistency of Uriel: "At 24:6 it is Michael who accompanies Enoch. There has been no indication of any change in Enoch's accompanying angel, from Michael to Uriel or Raphael since 24:6."[379] See below under 27:3.

Accursed valley—The Greek reads *gē kataratos*. While *gē* is used in places in LXX to translate Hebrew *'erets* ("land, earth"), this may be a transliteration of Hebrew *gay'/gēy'* ("valley"), suggesting an identification (both in light of the description "accursed" and the Jerusalem proximity) with Hebrew *gēy 'hinnôm* ("Valley of Hinnom") or Aramaic *gēhinnām* (Gehenna), "a valley located on the south slope of Jerusalem (Josh 15:8;

---

378. Ibid., 319.
379. Black, *The Book of Enoch*, 173–174.

18:16)."[380] This valley was the site of pagan worship in the late preexilic era, one that involved taking children and "passing them through the fire" (2 Kings 23:10; 2 Chronicles 28:3; 33:6; Jeremiah 7:31; 32:35).

For those who are accursed for ever: here shall all ‹the accursed› be gathered together…. Here shall they be gathered together, and here shall be their place of judgement—The reference is obviously to the judgment of the wicked unrighteous (the opposite of the occupants of the holy mountain). Nickelsburg notes why the possible reference to the Valley of Hinnom here would fit the context: "Without specifically naming the valley, Isa 66:24 alludes to it as a place of fiery punishment after the judgment, to be executed eternally in the sight of the righteous…. In 1 Enoch 90:26 the apostates are cast into the Valley of Hinnom and not the abyss in which the rebel angels and the seventy shepherds are cast."[381]

27:3

In the last days there shall be upon them the spectacle of righteous judgement in the presence of the righteous—The righteous see the wicked punished. Noting that in 1 Enoch 24:6, it is Michael accompanying Enoch, Daniel 12:1–2 is of interest in this regard:

> [1]At that time shall arise Michael, the great prince who has charge of your people. And there shall be a time of trouble, such as never has been since there was a nation till that time. But at that time your people shall be delivered, everyone whose name shall be found written in the book. [2]And many of those who sleep in the dust of the earth shall awake, some to everlasting life, and some to shame and everlasting contempt.

---

380. J. Lunde, "Heaven and Hell," *Dictionary of Jesus and the Gospels* (ed. Joel B. Green and Scot McKnight; Downers Grove, IL: InterVarsity Press, 1992), 310.

381. Nickelsburg, *1 Enoch: A Commentary on the Book of 1 Enoch*, vol. 1, 319.

Do the righteous of Daniel 12:2 see the punishment of the wicked? Nickelsburg provides evidence that the LXX and Latin Vulgate translators seem to have believed so:

> Both the LXX and V of Dan 12:2 render this noun with a reference to sight (*eis horasin; ut videant semper*), suggesting a derivation from Heb. *r'h* ("to see"), and indicating knowledge of this motif in Isa 66:24. The motif of the righteous seeing the punishment of their enemies becomes traditional in the literature.[382]

merciful (vs. godly in alternate translation)—"Merciful" is an odd way to describe the righteous. The text is uncertain, but "godly" makes more sense, especially give their blessing toward God (why would "the merciful" be blessing God?).

Eternal king—See 1 Enoch 25:3, 5, 7.

27:4

Lord of glory—See 14:19.

Translation: Chapter 28

28[1]And thence I went «towards the east», into the midst «of the mountain range» of the desert, and I saw a wilderness and it was solitary, full of trees **and plants.** [2]«And» water gushed forth from above. [3]Rushing like a copious watercourse [which flowed] towards the north-west it caused clouds and dew to ascend on every side.

---

382. Ibid., 319. Isaiah 66:24 says, "And they shall go out and look on the dead bodies of the men who have rebelled against me. For their worm shall not die, their fire shall not be quenched, and they shall be an abhorrence to all flesh." See also 1 Enoch 48:9.

Commentary

28:1

«towards the east»—This is absent in the Greek text. The directional orientation of Enoch's movement is indicated only in the Ethiopic material. It is likely original because the ensuing description in chapters 29–32 reflects a knowledge of regions east of Jerusalem (cf. 26:1–2), namely Petra.[383] Other scholars divorce the details of the description to follow from literal geography. Nickelsburg (disapprovingly) notes the idea that the spices mentioned in Chapter 29 "were actually common to Palestine and its vicinity. They were important for their connection with funereal matters, and the purpose of this section is to trace Enoch's journey to the land of eternal life."[384]

«of the mountain range»—As with the earlier phrase, textual evidence is divided. The phrase is likely original in light of 29:1 ("this mountain range").

a wilderness and it was solitary, full of trees and plants—The imagery is lush, but this is not the Jerusalem-paradise dwelling of God noted earlier. Enoch has moved east of Jerusalem, and will keep moving east. The reader will soon learn that the place now in view is the old Eden, original home of Adam and Eve (32:6).

Translation: Chapter 29

29[1]And thence I went to another place in the desert, and approached to the east of this mountain range. [2]And «there» I saw **aromatic** trees exhal-

---

383. Milik in particular makes this argument. See Milik, *The Books of Enoch*, 26. Nickelsburg tentatively agrees: "The northwest orientation of the watercourse indicates, in his view, familiarity with the aqueduct in es-Sîq, the narrow gorge that leads into [Petra]." See Nickelsburg, *1 Enoch: A Commentary on the Book of 1 Enoch*, vol. 1, 324.

384. Ibid., 323.

ing the fragrance of frankincense and myrrh, and the trees also were simi-lar to the almond tree.

Commentary

29:2

another place in the desert, and approached to the east of this mountain range—This is the first time that the Greek text includes the eastern ori-entation found in other chapters in this section.

frankincense—This spice is known in the Bible not only in association with the birth of Jesus, but also with the Old Testament. The geographical details of 29:1–2 are consistent with this material:

> Frankincense [is] a fragrant gum resin exuded in large, light yellow-ish-brown tears from Boswellia trees *(Boswellia Carterii, Boswellia Papyrifera, Boswellia Thurifera)* which grow in South Arabia, Ethiopia, Somaliland, and India. Frankincense was imported into Judah by camel caravan from Sheba (Isa. 60:6; Jer. 6:20), a trade connection that originated with the queen of Sheba's visit to Jeru-salem in the reign of Solomon (1 Kings 10:10; 2 Chron. 9:9).... Exod. 30:34–38 contains the recipe for a frankincense-based incense dedicated for ritual use. No other incense was permitted on the altar (Exod. 30:9) and secular use of the sacred recipe was absolutely forbidden (Exod. 30:38).[385]

myrrh—This spice is "an aromatic gum that grows in Arabia, Abyssinia, and India. Highly prized from earliest times (Gen. 37:25), it was used in

---

385. Paul J. Achtemeier, *Harper's Bible Dictionary* (San Francisco: Harper & Row and Society of Biblical Literature, 1985), 322. See also J. Innes Miller, *The Spice Trade of the Roman Empire* (Oxford: Clarendon, 1969) 102–4, and map 5, opposite p. 144.

incense (Exod. 30:23)…[and was] also used in embalming (Mark 15:23; John 19:39)."[386] Myrrh was native to several areas in Africa and Arabia.[387]

Translation: Chapter 30

30[1]And beyond these, I went afar to the east, and I saw another place, a valley (full) of water. [2]And therein there was a tree, the colour (?) of fragrant trees such as the mastic. [3]And on the sides of those valleys I saw fragrant cinnamon. And beyond these I proceeded to the east.

Commentary

30:1

I saw—More accurately from the original text, "I was shown"; i.e., Enoch is being escorted and shown specific sights. See note at 22:1–5.

beyond these—In other words, Enoch has moved still more eastward, beyond the earlier locations.

a valley—Ethiopic has "valleys."

30:2

a tree, the colour (?) of fragrant trees such as the mastic—The description is imprecise and prevents a secure identification. The phrasing is present in Aramaic as *qny' ṭby'*, which is closely parallel to *qnh ḥṭwb* in Jeremiah 6:20, where an imported spice ("sweet cane" in ESV) is mentioned in tandem with frankincense (cf. 29:2). Exodus 30:23 also mentions *qnh bshm* as one of the ingredients of the anointing oil. Milik notes that these ingredients

---

386. Achtemeier, *Harper's Bible Dictionary*, 672.
387. Miller, *The Spice Trade*, 4.

are known to grow in Lebanon,[388] but Nickelsburg thinks India itself may be in view by virtue of the ingredients and the ongoing eastward orientation of Enoch: "It is widely supposed, however, that the aromatic grasses were imported from India and its environs, and this would fit with the text, which tracks Enoch's journey to the east (29:1) and then far to the east (30:1).[389] See verse 3.

30:3

fragrant cinnamon—This spice supports a geographical identification of the place to which Enoch journeys as India: "The 'fragrant cinnamon' (v. 3, *kinnamōmon aramatōn* [in] G[a], *qwnm bśm'* [in] 4QEn[c] 1 12:25) is the species *Cinnamomum zeylanicum* Nees, which was native to Ceylon and the coast of India."[390]

And beyond these I proceeded to the east—How much farther east can Enoch journey after India? The prophet will ultimately wind up at the "ends of the earth."

Translation: Chapter 31

31[1]And I saw other mountains, and amongst them were ‹groves of› trees, and there flowed forth from them nectar, which is named sarara and galbanum. [2]And beyond these mountains I saw another mountain ‹to the east of the ends of the earth›, «whereon were aloe-trees», and all the trees were full **of stacte**, being like almond-trees. [3]And when one **burnt** it, it smelt sweeter than any fragrant odour.

---

388. Milik, *The Books of Enoch*, 28.
389. Nickelsburg, *1 Enoch: A Commentary on the Book of 1 Enoch*, vol. 1, 325.
390. Ibid., 325.

Commentary

31:1

nectar, which is named sarara and galbanum—The spice terminology here is associated with Persia, which is not east of India (by our knowledge of geography). One of these spices (galbanum) was native to Persia.[391] In regard to sarara and galbanum, Nickelsburg notes:

> This tree exudes a resin of medicinal value, which could be accurately referred to in this text as "nectar" (*nectar*).... Galbanum (*chalbanē* G[a]) was a resin exuded from the lower stem and rootstock of the species *Ferula gummosa* Boiss. (fennel), a tall herbaceous plant of the carrot family.[392]

31:2

«*whereon were aloe-trees*»—The reference to aloe trees is based on the Ethiopic text. In general, "aloe" is a transliteration of the Greek term *aloē*, of which one type was *aloe vera*, used for medical purposes and embalming.[393] Nickelsburg believes the present passage refers to a different type of aloe due to the geographical orientation of the passage: "The second type of *Aloe*, the so-called lignaloes, was the dark, fragrant heartwood taken from the decaying eaglewood tree (*Aquillaria agallocha* Roxb.), which was native to India and Ceylon."[394]

---

391. Miller, *The Spice Trade*, 99.

392. Nickelsburg, *1 Enoch: A Commentary on the Book of 1 Enoch*, vol. 1, 325.

393. Miller, *The Spice Trade*, 36.

394. Nickelsburg, *1 Enoch: A Commentary on the Book of 1 Enoch*, vol. 1, 325.

Translation: Chapter 32

As in earlier chapters (22, 27), Charles presents two versions of this short chapter.

Ethiopic	Greek (Gᵃ)
32 [1] And after these fragrant odours, as I looked towards the north over the mountains I saw seven mountains full of choice nard and fragrant trees and cinnamon and pepper.	32 [1] To the north-east I beheld seven mountains full of choice nard and mastic and cinnamon and pepper.

[2] And thence I went over the summits of ‹all› these mountains, far towards the east ‹of the earth›, and passed above the Erythraean sea and went far from it, and passed over «the angel» Zotîêl.

E	Gg
[3] And I came to the Garden of Righteousness, and saw beyond those trees many large trees growing there and of goodly fragrance, large, very beautiful and glorious, and the tree of wisdom whereof they eat and know great wisdom.	[3] And I came to the Garden of Righteousness, and from afar off trees more numerous than these trees and great—†two† trees there, very great, beautiful, and glorious, and magnificent, and the tree of knowledge, whose holy fruit they eat and know great wisdom.

[4] ‹That tree is in height like the fir, and its leaves are› like (those of) the Carob tree: and its fruit is like the clusters of the vine, very beautiful: and the fragrance of the tree penetrates afar. [5] Then I said: "‹How› beautiful is the tree, and how attractive is its look!" [6] Then Raphael the holy angel, who was with me, answered me «and said»: "This is the tree of wisdom,

of which thy father old (in years) and thy aged mother, who were before thee, have eaten, and they learnt wisdom and their eyes were opened, and they knew that they were naked and they were driven out of the garden."

Commentary

32:1

And after these fragrant odours (Eth)…vs. [omission in Greek]—Milik's reconstruction of the Aramaic fragments available at this location produces "Beyond these mountains."[395] This reading is accepted by both Nickelsburg and Black and is based on Milik's argument for an accidental omission.

north over the mountains (Eth)… vs. north-east (Greek)—The difference here again derives from textual discrepancies. For some reason, Enoch's journey does not continue east, but diverts north. This diversion may explain a scribal addition of "east" in the Greek text.

seven mountains—Another set of seven mountains—perhaps. The Aramaic fragment does not have the number "seven" here, only the Aramaic word for "(an)other."

nard and fragrant trees and cinnamon and pepper (Eth)…vs. nard and mastic and cinnamon and pepper (Greek)—The difference in word choice derives again from the textual situation. The Aramaic fragment reads an uncertain (and so, untranslated by Nickelsburg) *ṣpr* within the listing. Spikenard is native to the Himalayas, which certainly reflects a northern (!) turn (and, one could argue, east). For cinnamon, see above. Pepper is native to India.[396] The Aramaic term *ṣpr* is uncertain, as noted.

---

395. Milik, *The Books of Enoch*, 201, 232.
396. Miller, *The Spice Trade*, 88–92.

32:2

far towards the east ‹of the earth›—Apparently having been transported far enough north (32:1), Enoch's journey veers east again.

the Erythraean sea—The Red Sea. The Greek word for "red" is *eruthros.*[397] The geography requires some comment:

> [Red Sea] referred in antiquity variously (depending on the authors) not only to the Arabian Gulf but also to the Persian Gulf and the Indian Ocean. The term occurs twice in 77:6–7, where it includes at least the Persian Gulf. For the present author, it extends far to the east and must include at least part of the Indian Ocean. Beyond it lies the darkness.[398]

passed over «the angel» Zotîêl—The wording is very odd. Milik, working from the Aramaic material, has "passed over the darkness," which is followed by Nickelsburg.[399] In place of the Aramaic word for "darkness," the Greek reads *zōtiēl*. Ethiopic has *lamal'ak zut'ēl* ("the angel *zut'el*"). Since none of those options makes sense over "darkness," Milik theorizes that the Greek text (G^a) and Ethiopic both "reflect a corruption of Gk. *zophros* or *zophōdēs* (*topos*) ("darkness"/"dark [place]").[400] This is quite plausible given the data.

---

397. BDAG, 393.

398. Nickelsburg, *1 Enoch: A Commentary on the Book of 1 Enoch*, vol. 1, 326.

399. Milik, *The Books of Enoch*, 232.

400. J. T. Milik, "Hénoch au pays des aromates (ch. XXVI à XXXII): Fragments araméens de la grotte 4 de Qumran (pl. 1)," *RB* 65 (1958) 76, note 2. Translated and quoted in Nickelsburg, *1 Enoch: A Commentary on the Book of 1 Enoch*, vol. 1, 320, note f.

32:3

the Garden of Righteousnes—Old Testament Eden, as will become clear in 32:6.

many large trees growing there and of goodly fragrance, large, very beautiful and glorious—See Ezekiel 31:7–9, 15–18 for the great trees in Eden and earlier comments on 1 Enoch 24:3–4. Nickelsburg, who thinks there are two distinct and somewhat contradictory Eden stories in Genesis 2–3 and Ezekiel 28, 31, writes:

> The description of the paradise of righteousness and its tree is also a counterpart to the description of God's mountain paradise and its tree in 24:2–7. Both describe a garden of trees dominated by a single tree that is one of the two trees central to the narrative in Genesis 2–3. In both 1 Enoch 24:2–25:6 and 32:3–6, the respective tree and its significance is of prime importance, and the details of the two descriptions closely parallel one another: one tree is singled out among many; its various elements are mentioned and compared to those of other trees…. The Hebrew Bible itself provides two descriptions of the Garden of Eden…. [In Ezekiel 31] the garden of trees…is equated with the mountain of God (perhaps hinted at in Gen 2:10, which could reflect the idea of the waters that flow from the base of the cosmic mountain)…. 1 Enoch 20–36 reflects both biblical versions of the Eden story. In 24:2–25:7 the mountain of God, which stands at the apex of a range of bejeweled mountains, is a garden of trees, in whose midst stands the tree of life. In 32:3–6, at the easternmost edges of the earth, Enoch visits the garden of trees mentioned in Genesis 2–3, which is dominated by the tree of wisdom, whose fruit was eaten by the first parents.[401]

---

401. Nickelsburg, *1 Enoch: A Commentary on the Book of 1 Enoch*, vol. 1, 326-327.

Nickelsburg's approach to these passages is in part driven by his view that the anointed cherub in Ezekiel 28 is Adam. Readers of my book *The Unseen Realm* will recognize that I reject that identification. Consequently, for that and other reasons, I disagree with Nickelsburg's perspective on these passages.[402]

whereof they eat—Who are the ones eating of this tree? The Greek text followed by Charles more literally reads "from whose holy fruit they eat" (with *hagiou* as genitive singular and functioning adjectivally). However, other Greek manuscripts read *hagioi* ("holy ones") and have the holy ones eating the fruit. Many scholars consider the latter more coherent. Black accepts "holy ones" (*hagioi*) and remarks that the word order makes the alternative improbable.[403]

Second Temple Judaism did indeed have a tradition of angels' food, though textual references are sparse.[404] The idea is a fanciful one. The discussion begins with Psalm 78:23–25 and its reference to manna:

> [23]Yet he commanded the skies above
>   and opened the doors of heaven,
> [24]and he rained down on them manna to eat
>   and gave them the grain of heaven.
> [25]Man ate of the bread of the angels;
>   he sent them food in abundance.

---

402. See Heiser, *The Unseen Realm*, 74–91 and chapter 3 in Michael S. Heiser, *Demons: What the Bible Really Says about the Powers of Darkness* (forthcoming, Lexham Press, 2020).

403. Black, *The Book of Enoch*, 179.

404. Some readers might also think of Genesis 18, where Yahweh and two angels (Genesis 19:1) have a meal with Abraham. That episode of course occurs on earth—and that is where 1 Enoch 32 still has Old Testament Eden! One early Jewish textual example is the early second century AD pseudepigraphical work *Joseph and Aseneth* (chapters 16–18). For discussion

The phrase "bread of angels" merely describes the manna's place of origin. Manna fell from the sky—the heavens, where angels dwell. But some Jewish writers took this passage and added the statement of Exodus 16:31 to derive the idea of angelic food: "Now the house of Israel called its name manna. It was like coriander seed, white, and the taste of it was like wafers made with honey." Further, the tandem of these passages gave rise to the belief that angels fed on honeycombs.

With respect to 1 Enoch 32:3, given that the context has the Tree of Wisdom as the food source, those scholars who prefer *hagioi* consider the description to be consistent with the tradition that knowledge was transmitted to humans by holy ones. The holy ones in this location (Old Testament Eden) fed on the tree that made them wise so they could in turn impart wisdom to humans. In this respect, the idea is the positive side of the dark wisdom given to humanity by the Watchers.

32:6

This is the tree of wisdom, of which thy father old (in years) and thy aged mother, who were before thee, have eaten, and they learnt wisdom and their eyes were opened, and they knew that they were naked and they were driven out of the garden.—The description obviously refers to Adam and Eve and their fall in Eden. Nickelsburg's observations are of interest:

---

of some of the ancient Jewish texts and traditions about the "food of angels," see George J. Brooke, "Men and Women as Angels in Joseph and Aseneth," *Journal for the Study of the Pseudepigrapha* 14.2 (2005): 159–177 (esp. 168–169); Tobias Nicklas, "'Food of Angels' (Wis 16: 20)," in *Studies in the Book of Wisdom* (Leiden: E. J. Brill, 2010), 83–100; Kevin Sullivan, "Jesus, Angels, and the Honeycomb in Luke 24:42," in *The Open Mind: Essays in Honour of Christopher Rowland* (Bloomsbury, 2015), 240–255 (esp.); D. Goodman, "Do Angels Eat?" *Journal of Jewish Studies* 37 (1986): 160–75.

In the present passage, the eastern location of paradise corresponds to the description in Gen 2:8. Different from many Jewish texts, including 1 Enoch 60:8; 61:12; and 70:3, it is described here not as the dwelling place of the righteous dead (they are in the mountain in the west; cf. chap. 22), but as the location of the tree with which the first parents' sin is associated. According to [the Aramaic], Enoch himself does not enter the garden, but draws up alongside it (4QEnᶜ 1 26:21) and views it from the outside. Also different from other Jewish writers, this author does not anticipate that the righteous will ever again have access to this paradise. They will eat the fruit of the tree of life in Jerusalem (25:3–6).[405]

Translation: Chapter 33

33[1]And from thence I went to the ends of the earth and saw there great beasts, and each differed from the other; and (I saw) birds also differing in appearance and beauty and voice, the one differing from the other. And to the east of those beasts I saw the ends of the earth whereon the heaven rests, and the portals of the heaven open. [2]And I saw how the stars of heaven come forth, and I counted the portals out of which they proceed, [3]and wrote down all their outlets, of each individual star by itself, according to their number and their names, their courses and their positions, and their times and their months, as Uriel the holy angel who was with me showed me. [4]He showed all things to me and wrote them down for me: also their names he wrote for me, and their laws and their companies.

---

405. Nickelsburg, *1 Enoch: A Commentary on the Book of 1 Enoch*, vol. 1, 327.

Commentary

33:1

from thence I went to the ends of the earth…to the east of…the ends of the earth whereon the heaven rests—Enoch has now journeyed from the *western* "ends of the earth" (23:1) and, after being transported ever eastward (see text and comments on 26:3; 29:1; 30:1; 31:1; 32:1–2), has reached the opposite side of the "ends of the earth." The phrase "whereon the heaven rests" reflects the nonscientific, ancient cosmology of the writer's time and of the earlier biblical period (see comments and sources at 17:3; 18:1–3). Nickelsburg observes:

> Enoch travels to a place, where he sees certain things that are interpreted by an angel. The form differs here because the author is alluding to the lengthy tradition now partly preserved in the Book of the Luminaries…. At the eastern edge of the earth's disk, where the heavenly canopy rests like an inverted cup on a saucer of the same diameter, Enoch views the gates from which the stars begin their celestial journey (chaps. 72–82).[406]

great beasts, and each differed from the other; and (I saw) birds also differing in appearance and beauty and voice, the one differing from the other—Some scholars take the references to the beasts and birds as the natural fauna counterparts to the various references to flora—the trees and spices. However, no specific species are mentioned. Nickelsburg is among those who take this content absence as an indication that the beasts, unlike the plants that get attention in chapters 28–32, are not natural, but mythical. He writes:

> This suggests that whatever the origin of the author's knowledge of these animals, they are envisioned primarily in mythic terms.

---

406. Ibid., 329.

Evidence for such a mythic tradition appears at a number of points in the cartology of the ancient world. In the Babylonian *Mappa Mundi* of the fifth century B.C.E., the sixth island that lies east of the Bitter River is said to be the place where "a horned bull dwells and attacks the newcomer." Much later maps from the Common Era depict sea monsters and other beasts lurking in the farthest recesses of land and sea. Doubtless these reflect a tradition much older than the charts on which they are found. This evidence is geographically and chronologically much too disparate to serve as specific evidence for the interpretation of the present text, but it does indicate a widespread tendency to associate mythical beasts with the ends of the earth. Whether the present text refers to demonic beings banished to the outer reaches of the world is uncertain.[407]

---

407. Ibid., 329–330. In regard to this interpretive option, Nickelsburg refers his readers in reference to Jonathan Z. Smith, "Towards Interpreting Demonic Powers in Hellenistic and Roman Antiquity," *Aufstieg und Niedergang der römischen Welt* (Berlin: DeGruyter) 2.16.1:427. See also J. H. Rogers, "Origins of the Ancient Constellations: I. The Mesopotamian Traditions," *Journal of the British Astronomical Association* 108:1 (1998): 9–28; J. H. Rogers, "Origins of the Ancient Constellations: II. The Mediterranean Traditions," *Journal of the British Astronomical Association* 108:2 (1998): 79–89; José Lull and Juan Antonio Belmonte, "The Constellations of Ancient Egypt," *Search of Cosmic Order: Selected Essays on Egyptian Archaeoastronomy* (American University in Cairo Press, 2009): 157–161; Lorenzo Verderame, "The Primeval Zodiac: Its Social, Religious, and Mythological Background," *Cosmology Across Cultures* 409 (Astronomical Society of the Pacific Conference Series, 2009); Francesca Rochberg-Halton, "Elements of the Babylonian Contribution to Hellenistic astrology," *Journal of the American Oriental Society* (1988): 51–62.

33:2—4

I saw how the stars of heaven come forth, and I counted the portals out of which they proceed...wrote down all their outlets, of each individual star by itself, according to their number and their names, their courses and their positions, and their times and their months—While the idea (verse 1) that the beasts and birds may refer to mythical monsters has merit, it must also be acknowledged, in light of the passage's connections to the Book of the Luminaries (1 Enoch 72–82), that the references to these beasts and birds might be rooted in ancient astronomical/astrological symbols and constellations. The reference to the beasts and birds is made in connection with the place "the portals of the heaven open," (and subsequent "the portals out of which [the stars] proceed" in verse 2), which may also lend credence to a celestial interpretation. Nickelsburg doesn't entertain this possibility, but goes on to say, "The author of chap. 33 appears to be saying that Enoch's astronomical instruction, recorded in detail in chaps. 72–82, took place at this point in his journey."[408]

Uriel the holy angel who was with me—The instructing angel is now Uriel, whose name ("light/light-bearer of God") makes him the ideal knowledge keeper for the subject matter. The text omits any instruction from Uriel about the sun and moon, but instead focuses on the stars. In this regard, it is noteworthy that Uriel and Enoch count the stars (verses 2–3: "counted the portals" and "wrote down all their outlets, of each individual star by itself, according to their number"). The numbering of the stars brings to mind Genesis 15:5. Scholarly research has shown that, in Second Temple Judaism, this verse was interpreted not only quantitatively (how many stars) but qualitatively (the stars were considered divine). The language of Genesis 15:5 of course correlates the "star language" with the earthly fam-

---

408. Nickelsburg, *1 Enoch: A Commentary on the Book of 1 Enoch*, vol. 1, 331.

ily of Yahweh—believers, as it were. This language and its implications spill into the New Testament to speak of the glorification of believers in Christ.[409]

Translation: Chapter 34

34[1] And from thence I went towards the north to the ends of the earth, and there I saw a great and glorious device at the ends of the whole earth. [2] And here I saw three portals of heaven open in the heaven: through each of them proceed north winds: when they blow there is cold, hail, frost, snow, dew, and rain. [3] And out of one portal they blow for good: but when they blow through the other two portals, †it is with violence and affliction on the earth, and they blow with violence.†

Commentary

34:1

from thence I went towards the north to the ends of the earth—Enoch has been to the western and eastern "ends of the earth" and is now taken to the third (of four) "quadrants" of the circular, flat, domed earth of ancient cosmology.[410]

there I saw—Better, "I was shown." See comments on 22:1 about this language.

409. See David Anthony Burnett, "Abraham's Star-Like Seed: Neglected Functional Elements in the Patriarchal Promise of Genesis 15," M. A. Thesis, Criswell College, 2015; David A. Burnett, "A Neglected Deuteronomic Scriptural Matrix for the Nature of the Resurrection Body in 1 Corinthians 15:39–42?" in *Scripture, Texts, and Tracings in 1 Corinthians* (Scripture and Paul Series; ed. Linda L. Belleville and B. J. Oropeza; New York: Fortress Academic, 2019), 187–212.

410. See comments and sources at 17:3; 18:1–3; 33:1.

great and glorious device—The translation "device" is based on Charles' reading of the Ethiopic *mekra*. Aramaic 4QEnᵉ 1 27:21 reads "a great and glorious wonder" (*mankera 'abiya wasebuḥa*).[411] Black adopts this Qumran reading for his interpretation of the Ethiopic.[412] The translation of the singular here ("great and glorious *wonder*"—not a device) makes good sense in light of 36:4 ("great and glorious *wonders*"—not devices, for which there is no Ethiopic evidence).[413] First Enoch 34 does not exist in Greek.

34:2–3

I saw three portals of heaven open in the heaven: through each of them proceed north winds: when they blow there is cold, hail, frost, snow, dew, and rain. And out of one portal they blow for good: but when they blow through the other two portals, †it is with violence and affliction on the earth, and they blow with violence—Both Black and Nickelsburg direct readers to 1 Enoch 76:1–4 with respect to the content of these verses. Milik and Nickelsburg think that 34:36:2 are a summary of 76:1–14.[414] On the present two verses, Nickelsburg writes:

> Verses 2–3 are a summary of 76:10–11, applying to the three northern gates the principle that 76:4 enunciates about all twelve gates of the winds: the wind blowing through the center gate is for good; those blowing through the two gates flanking it are for evil. (For "violence" and "affliction" [*ḥāyl, ṣā 'er*] 76:4 has "calamities"

411. Milik, *The Books of Enoch*, 235, in agreement with Knibb, *The Ethiopic Book of Enoch*, 123.
412. Black, *The Book of Enoch*, 180. Black in part justifies this decision by observing that the Septuagint at times uses a plural of *thaumasios* ("wonder, marvel") when Ethiopic translations read *manker* in the same passages.
413. See Knibb, *The Ethiopic Book of Enoch*, 124.
414. Black, *The Book of Enoch*, 180; Milik, *The Books of Enoch*, 284–288.

and "destroy" [*maqšaft* and *damsasa*].) Of the elements in 34:2, hoarfrost, snow, dew, and rain are mentioned in 76:10–11. Cold occurs in 76:6 in connection with the gate in the east-northeast. Hail is not mentioned in chap. 76.[415]

Translation: Chapter 35

35[1]And from thence I went towards the west to the ends of the earth, and saw there three portals of the heaven open such as I had seen in the †east†, the same number of portals, and the same number of outlets.

Commentary

35:1

from thence I went towards the west to the ends of the earth—Enoch was at the "ends of the earth" to the north and is now escorted westward along the rim ("ends") of the earth toward the last quadrant of the "ends of the earth," the south (36:1).

three portals—Earlier this term ("portal") was used in connection with stars. Nickelsburg comments on the interpretive implication: "omission of any reference here to the winds suggest that the author is thinking here of outlets for the stars, thus paralleling the description of the east in 36:2–3."[416]

Translation: Chapter 36

36[1]And from thence I went to the south to the ends of the earth, and saw there three open portals of the heaven: and thence there come dew, rain, †and wind†. [2]And from thence I went to the east to the ends of the

---

415. Nickelsburg, *1 Enoch: A Commentary on the Book of 1 Enoch*, vol. 1, 332.
416. Ibid., 332.

heaven, and saw here the three eastern portals of heaven open and small portals above them. ³Through each of these small portals pass the stars of heaven and run their course to the west on the path which is shown to them. ⁴And as often as I saw I blessed always the Lord of Glory, and I continued to bless the Lord of Glory who has wrought great and glorious wonders, to show the greatness of His work to the angels and to **spirits** and to men, that they might praise His work and all His creation: that they might see the work of His might and praise the great work of His hands and bless Him for ever.

Commentary

36:1

from thence I went to the south to the ends of the earth—Enoch is transported to the south, the last "ends of the earth" quadrant of the round earth. He has now seen "the ends of the earth" at the four cardinal directions. Resuming the opinion noted above that chapters 34–36 summarize 1 Enoch 76:1–4, Nickelsburg writes, "Compared to its counterpart in 34:1–3, this summary of 76:7–9 is very brief. According to the latter passage, dew and rain are brought by the winds blowing through the south and south-southwest gates."[417]

36:2

from thence I went to the east to the ends of the heaven—Enoch is returned to the place he started his "ends of the earth" tour. The itinerary of course makes sense if one is following the "rim" of the place where the sky meets the horizon on the round, flat earth.[418]

---

417. Ibid., 332.

418. See comments and sources at 17:3; 18:1–3; 33:1; 34:1.

36:3

through each of these small portals pass the stars of heaven and run their course—See earlier comments on similar language in chapters 32–35.

Lord of glory—See 14:19.

36:4

I blessed—The verse is essentially a doxology.

Lord of Glory—See comments at 25:3, 5, 7; cp. 14:19.

great and glorious wonders—See the earlier comments at 34:1.

*the angels and to **spirits** and to men, that they might praise His work and all His creation*—Nickelsburg takes "spirits and men" as "spirits of men," but this is by no means necessary. He writes that the language of this verse "is reminiscent of chap. 22, where, however, there is no mention of the human spirits praising God."[419] That said, see 27:3, which might be read as such.

Subscript

At the close of Nickelsburg's commentary in 1 Enoch 36, the end of the Book of the Watchers, he transitions into 1 Enoch 81–82. Readers should recall that the first volume of his two-volume scholarly work on 1 Enoch covers chapters 1–36 and 81–108. He comments on some of the language of 36:4 as follows:

---

419. Nickelsburg, *1 Enoch: A Commentary on the Book of 1 Enoch*, vol. 1, 332.

Perhaps more important, the cluster, "I praised the Lord of glory…
his deeds" parallels 81:3, "I blessed the great Lord, the King of
glory because he made all the deeds of eternity." The similarity
supports the notion that 81:1–4 was originally located near or
at the end of the Book of the Watchers (see comm. on chaps.
81–82).[420]

First Enoch 81:5 says, "And those seven holy ones brought me and
placed me on the earth before the door of my house, and said to me:
"Declare everything to thy son Methuselah, and show to all thy children
that no flesh is righteous in the sight of the Lord, for He is their Creator."
First Enoch 81–82 is the account of the end of Enoch's heavenly journey,
so the assumption of Nickelsburg (and others) makes good sense.

The next volume of this commentary, however, will follow the numerical order of the chapters in Charles' translation.

---

420. Ibid., 332.

Select Key Resources Cited

Annus, Amar. "On the Origin of the Watchers: A Comparative Study of the Antediluvian Wisdom in Mesopotamian and Jewish Traditions," *Journal for the Study of the Pseudepigrapha* 19.4 (2010): 277–320.

Bautch, Kelley Coblentz. *A Study of the Geography of 1 Enoch 17–19: "No One Has Seen What I Have Seen,"* (Supplements to the Journal for the Study of Judaism 81; Leiden: E. J. Brill, 2003).

Black, Matthew. *The Book of Enoch or 1 Enoch: A New English Edition with Commentary and Textual Notes in Consultation with James C. VanderKam* (SVTP 7; Leiden: Brill, 1985).

Brand, Miryam T. *Evil Within and Without: The Source of Sin and Its Nature as Portrayed in Second Temple Literature* (Journal of Ancient Judaism Supplements 9; Göttingen: Vandenhoeck & Rupprecht, 2013.

Charles, R. H., and W. O. E. Oesterley. *The Book of Enoch* (London: Society for Promoting Christian Knowledge, 1917).

Charles, R. H. *Commentary on the Pseudepigrapha of the Old Testament* (Oxford: Clarendon Press, 1913).

Dimant, Devorah. "1 Enoch 6–11: A Methodological Perspective," in *Society of Biblical Literature Seminar Papers* 1978 (Missoula: Scholars, 1978), pp. 323–39

Docherty, Susan. *The Jewish Pseudepigrapha: An Introduction to the Literature of the Second Temple Period* (London: SPCK, 2014)

Drawnel, Henryk. "The Mesopotamian Background of the Enochic Giants and Evil Spirits," *Dead Sea Discoveries* 21:1 (2014): 14–38.

Esler, Philip F. *God's Court and Courtiers in the Book of the Watchers: Re-interpreting Heaven in 1 Enoch 1–36* (Wipf and Stock Publishers, 2017).

Fröhlich, Ida. "Mesopotamian Elements and the Watchers Traditions," in *The Watchers in Jewish and Christian Traditions* (ed. Angela Kim Hawkins, Kelley Coblentz Bautch, and John C. Endres, S. J.; Fortress Press, 2014), 11–24.

Hawkins, Angela Kim, Kelley Coblentz Bautch, and John C. Endres, S. J. *The Watchers in Jewish and Christian Traditions* (Fortress Press, 2014).

Heiser, Michael S. *Reversing Hermon: Enoch, the Watchers, and the Forgotten Mission of Jesus Christ* (Defender, 2017).

Heiser, Michael S. *Angels: What the Bible Really Says About God's Heavenly Host* (Lexham Press, 2018).

Heiser, Michael S. *Demons: What the Bible Really Says About the Powers of Darkness* (Lexham Press, 2020).

Isaac, Ephraim. "1 (Ethiopic Apocalypse of) Enoch," in *Old Testament Pseudepigrapha*, vol. 1 (ed. James H. Charlesworth; Garden City, NY: Doubleday, 1983–85), 5–89.

Knibb, Michael A. *The Ethiopic Book of Enoch: A New Edition in the Light of the Aramaic Dead Sea Fragments* (Oxford University Press, 1978).

Kvanvig, Helge. *Primeval History: Babylonian, Biblical, and Enochic: An Intertextual Reading* (Journal for the Study of Judaism Supplement 149; Leiden: E. J. Brill, 2011)

Melvin David. "The Gilgamesh Traditions and the Pre-History of Genesis 6:1–4," *Perspectives in Religious Studies* 38:1 (2011): 23–32.

Milik, J. T. *The Books of Enoch: Aramaic Fragments of Qumran Cave 4* (Oxford: Clarendon, 1976).

Nickelsburg, George W. E. "Enoch, Levi, and Peter: Recipients of Revelation in Upper Galilee," *Journal of Biblical Literature* 100 (1981): 575–600.

Nickelsburg, George W. E. *1 Enoch: A Commentary on the Book of 1 Enoch* (Hermeneia—a Critical and Historical Commentary on the Bible; ed. Klaus Baltzer; Minneapolis, MN: Fortress, 2001).

Nickelsburg, George W. E. and James C. VanderKam. *1 Enoch 2: A Commentary on the Book of 1 Enoch, Chapters 37–82* (Hermeneia—a Critical and Historical Commentary on the Bible; ed. Klaus Baltzer; Minneapolis, MN: Fortress, 2012)

Stuckenbruck, Loren T. "Introduction to the Apocalypse of Weeks," in *Early Jewish Literature: An Anthology* (ed. Brad Embry, Ronald Herms, and Archie T. Wright; vol. 2; Grand Rapids, MI: William B. Eerdmans Publishing Company, 2018).

Stuckenbruck, Loren T. "The Book of Enoch: Its Reception in Second Temple Jewish and Christian Tradition," *Early Christianity* 4 (2013): 7–40

Wright, Archie T. *The Origin of Evil Spirits: The Reception of Genesis 6:1–4 in Early Jewish Literature* (*Wissenschaftliche Untersuchungen zum Neuen Testament* 198, second series; Tübingen: Mohr Siebeck, 2013).

Wright, Archie T. "Introduction to the Book of Watchers," in *Early Jewish Literature: An Anthology* (ed. Brad Embry, Ronald Herms, and Archie T. Wright; vol. 2; Grand Rapids, MI: William B. Eerdmans Publishing Company, 2018).

VanderKam, James C. "1 Enoch, Enochic Motifs, and Enoch in Early Christian Literature," *The Jewish Apocalyptic Heritage in Early Christianity* (ed. James C. VanderKam and William Adler; *Compendia rerum iudaicarum ad Novum Testamentum* 3/4; Minneapolis: Fortress Press, 1996).